PR

UNDERSTANDING THE HILLBILLY THOMIST

"Fr. Damian Ference has provided a substantive look into the philosophical underpinnings of the homespun fictional stories published by the fervently Catholic and intensely intelligent Flannery O'Connor. He adeptly systematizes the core influence of Thomistic philosophy and theology in O'Connor's down-to-earth wisdom as she presents it within her narrative art. His scholarly work is a great contribution to the understanding of one of America's most influential authors, who used the incarnate human experience to expand the soul's ability to receive the mystery of transformative grace."

—**Bishop Edward Malesic**, Diocese of Cleveland

"This is the book on Flannery I've been waiting for without knowing it: a serious investigation of the Thomistic inflections and foundations that give form to O'Connor's fiction. Undertaken without the academician's tedious jargon, but always substantial and stimulating, *Understanding the Hillbilly Thomist* allows these friends across the centuries to clarify one another. Ference's cross-pollination cultivates our own depth perception, inviting us to adhere to the heart of reality which both beheld so unflinchingly."

—**Joshua Hren**, founder of Wiseblood Books, author of *Infinite Regress* and *Contemplative Realism: A Theological-Aesthetical Manifesto*

"There is no one so well-versed in Flannery O'Connor's philosophical background as Fr. Damian Ference. In his attentive exploration into Flannery's art and the thought behind the work, especially her reading and absorption of Thomas Aquinas, Fr. Ference illuminates the soul of O'Connor's fiction. This book accomplishes all its goals: readers understand more about O'Connor's stories and her Thomism, befriend these intellectual giants, and walk away with increased gratitude for the gifts of God."

—Jessica Hooten Wilson, author of *Giving the Devil His Due: Flannery O'Connor and The Brothers Karamazov*

"Congratulations to Fr. Damian Ference, who has written a fine Flannery O'Connor volume undertaken with the parameters of Thomism, the first study of its kind. Ference neither understates nor overstates St. Thomas' fundamental role in shaping O'Connor's literary genius. His approach also means that O'Connor's work is studied—unapologetically—within the context of her deep Catholic faith, just as it should be. Fr. Ference's book is not to be missed by anyone with an interest in, and appreciation for, O'Connor's writing."

—Henry T. Edmondson III, author of *Return to Good and Evil: Flannery O'Connor's Response to Nihilism*

"*Understanding the Hillbilly Thomist* introduces readers to the intellectual universe of one of the twentieth century's most interesting American Catholics. With the clarity of a gifted teacher, Fr. Ference demonstrates how the philosophical vision of St. Thomas Aquinas grounded Flannery O'Connor's confidence in her own sensory powers as a narrative artist— freeing her fiction from sentimental piety and helping her to imagine grace at work in the strangest places, from snorting hogs and tattooed skin to the smug ladies and violent misfits who fill her stories."

—Edward P. Hahnenberg, Jack and Mary Jane Breen Chair in Catholic Theology at John Carroll University

"For over half a century, the Hillbilly school of Thomism counted but one member, and one whose ears for music were made of tin, unlike every subsequent member of the school. Flannery O'Connor was friends, it is true, with a convent of Dominican Sisters who lived some hundred miles up the road from her home in Milledgeville, Georgia. Her readers might well wonder by what possible right she could ever have styled herself a Thomist, even in jest. Not for a moment does Fr. Damian Ference pretend that O'Connor was something she was not: a scholarly exegete of the Angelic Doctor. What he does instead is to show how much O'Connor's narrative art was shaped by her study of Aquinas and of mid-twentieth century Thomists such as Étienne Gilson and Jacques Maritain. Fr. Ference's love for his subject is evident from the outset. It is also infectious. In simple, straightforward prose, and with reference to a wide variety of texts, he provides a highly insightful presentation of the 'Thomistic inclinations, indications, intuitions, presumptions, and themes,' in his words, that inform O'Connor's writing. Fr. Ference helps readers to see how much the comic charity of the first and the greatest of the Hillbilly Thomists originates in clear, tough-minded judgment"
—John C. McCarthy, Dean and Associate Professor of Philosophy at Catholic University of America

"In this extraordinary book, we finally meet Flannery O'Connor the philosopher. Fr. Ference leads us to a deeper and richer understanding of O'Connor's fiction by examining its philosophical and theological underpinnings in the writings of St. Thomas Aquinas and others. Whether you are a longtime fan or a new reader, there are profound insights here for anyone who wishes to appreciate one of the greatest fiction writers of the twentieth century."
—Jennifer Frey, Dean of the Honors College at the University of Tulsa, host of the *Sacred and Profane Love* podcast

UNDERSTANDING THE HILLBILLY THOMIST

UNDERSTANDING THE HILLBILLY THOMIST

THE PHILOSOPHICAL FOUNDATIONS OF FLANNERY O'CONNOR'S NARRATIVE ART

FR. DAMIAN FERENCE

FOREWORD BY
THOMAS JOSEPH WHITE, OP

Published by Word on Fire,
Elk Grove Village, IL 60007
© 2023 by Word on Fire Catholic Ministries
Printed in the United States of America
All rights reserved

Cover design, typesetting, and interior art direction
by Rozann Lee, Cassie Bielak, and Nicolas Fredrickson

First printing, August 2023

ISBN: 978-1-68578-016-6

Library of Congress Control Number: 2021922720

*To Sr. Mary Kevin Clutterbuck, OP, and the
Dominican Sisters of Hawthorne,
Servants of Relief for Incurable Cancer*

CONTENTS

Foreword

Thomas Joseph White, OP

Flannery O'Connor is marked by a gentle but persistent twofold alienation that appears both in her personal letter-writing and in her fiction. One is the alienation of a devout Catholic who is aware of the inner distance between her own vision of the world and the ambient ethos of secularization and religious oblivion emergent in the modern American culture of her time. She perceived the expression of this modern stance of religious indifference in everyday culture but also was attuned to it from the intellectual formation she received at university and by reading deeply in the Catholic tradition. The other form of alienation she exhibits is, paradoxically, typically modern in kind: that of persons seeking explanatory meaning and existential orientation against the backdrop of a world in which the metaphysical certitudes of a bygone era seem to have faded into shadows and become irretrievable, at least for many people. Her art may be thought of as an attempt to tell the truth about both of these forms of alienation simultaneously: of modern people seeking meaning, not sure if and where it might abide, and of people finding an unforeseen resolution to the mystery of life in the revelation of the Holy Spirit, one that introduces a new separation of the human being from the world. Holiness has "separation" as one of its root meanings, and the characters of Flannery O'Connor's work are frequently borne away to the separation of life in God by grace that comes in forms that are both violent and comic.

Why should we say that her work is comic? In a sense, her characters are typically comic and tragic all at once. They are comic in part due to their narrowness and provincialism (expressive of our own), which they embody in slightly caricatural ways. These limitations, however humorous, still have sharp edges. The stories of O'Connor can cause our souls to bleed, even if the bloodletting may be good for our health. They are funny, but the humor cuts deep. They are also tragic in that these same limitations, which are many-sided and impressive, often lead to horrific or violent outcomes. However, this, too, is very human and perhaps especially so. Her characters evoke our own vulnerability, and it is precisely here—when, for example, one has a stroke due to the verbal abuse of a child ("Everything That Rises Must Converge") or another is humiliated by a savvy charlatan ("Good Country People")—that the work of the Spirit emerges. Tragic events have an abyssal feel to them in the fiction of O'Connor, but they never have the last word. Rather, they are like openings in the gulf of human existence that the Holy Spirit is seen to be entering, moments of brutal clarity where the truth can enter and come home to the character and to the reader. Indeed, the ironies that emerge in this space, between where the character is in his or her tragedy and where God is in his action of mercy, is comic in tone. God makes use even of our follies and blindness to realize our salvation and his epiphany of mercy and power in the service of the truth of Christ.

O'Connor's life was marked by the study of theology and philosophy, not in an expert way, but in a deep way that is required of anyone, including an expert, if that study is to have any real impact in the world. She was a reader, and she read works about Aquinas, and of Aquinas. Fr. Damian Ference has done us a wonderful service in this important work, *Understanding the Hillbilly Thomist*, uncovering and exploring with clarity and depth the Thomistic influence on Flannery O'Connor's work. He understands her philosophical influences well, having visited her original library in Andalusia Farm to see the books she actually read. He shows the deep imprint in her thinking of the vision of Étienne Gilson and his diagnostic characterizations of the modern age, as contrasted with the theocentric humanism of

Aquinas. Fr. Ference helps us appreciate her sacramental vision of reality, a world in which physical things can be the bearers, signs, and instruments of grace communicated to a world previously unaware of God. He shows that O'Connor's notions of God the Creator, of providence, and of the human being as a spiritual animal are deeply marked by the Catholic Scholastic tradition. Most especially, he does all of this while appealing to the stories themselves, and in the process he makes the stories more intelligible, even as he connects them to her letters and personal essays.

What results then is an animated and passionate work that serves to greatly advance our understanding of this most enigmatic and religiously forceful of modern American literary authors. We are greatly in debt to Fr. Ference for his book, as we are as well to Flannery O'Connor, who has helped us to resolve so many human mysteries by the pregnant symbols of her fiction, even as she has also helped us enter more fully into others of divine origin.

Acknowledgments

I was first introduced to Flannery O'Connor in a poetry workshop taught by George Bilgere at John Carroll University in the spring of 1998. Dr. Bilgere had each of us write two original poems per week that semester, and during each class he would pick one of our poems and ask another student to read the chosen poem aloud; then, we would "workshop" it. One memorable week, my poem was chosen, and, after a classmate had read it aloud with an unmistakably horrified look on her face, Dr. Bilgere said, "Damian's poem sounds like Flannery O'Connor." I assumed this was a compliment, but I wasn't sure who this Flannery O'Connor guy was. My interest piqued, I wrote his name in my notebook. That evening, I was surprised to learn that this Flannery O'Connor guy was in fact a woman. That summer, I began making my way through her short stories and then her novels, enjoying her narrative art but also aware that there was a depth of meaning to her fiction that, at that time, was beyond my understanding.

Two years later, I began reading O'Connor's essays and lectures in *Mystery and Manners* and her letters in *The Habit of Being*, and I quickly came to understand that this woman who thought of herself as "a hillbilly Thomist" was, in fact, a devout Catholic, an intellectual juggernaut, a postmodern prophet, a narrative artist whose brilliance was matched only by her humor, and a most faithful friend. As it turned out, Flannery O'Connor had befriended a community of Dominican sisters who operate homes for terminal cancer patients (which was founded by the daughter of Nathaniel Hawthorne), with one of them located in my hometown of Cleveland, Ohio.

My mom was a resident at Holy Family Home when I was reading *The Habit of Being* and repeatedly encountering letters in which O'Connor mentioned a Sr. Evangelist and the Dominican sisters who ran Our Lady of Perpetual Help cancer home in Atlanta. So, one afternoon while visiting my mom, I told her nurse, Sr. Kevin, about this book I was reading and how the author mentioned what I thought was her religious order. In her unmistakable New York accent, Sr. Kevin said, "Are ya readin' Flannery?" Surprised that she knew O'Connor's name, I told her that I was, and Sr. Kevin informed me that when she was a young sister, she had worked at the home in Atlanta and knew Flannery, and had even visited Andalusia a few times. The next time I came to see my mom, another Dominican nurse on the floor, Sr. Benedict, having heard of my conversation with Sr. Kevin a few days earlier, told me that she, too, knew Flannery from her time in Atlanta as a young sister. Something was going on here.

A few months after these conversations about Flannery with Sr. Kevin and Sr. Benedict, my mom died; it was a little over a year before I would be ordained a priest. As much as it stung, I figured this loss was somehow part of God's mysterious plan for me, especially the part about two Hawthorne Dominicans who knew Flannery O'Connor and who took great care of my mom in her final days in this life and helped prepare her for the life to come. Upon my ordination, I received some gifts from the Dominican Sisters—a few copies of *A Memoir of Mary Ann* (Flannery wrote the introduction), some original pictures of Mary Ann (a girl diagnosed with terminal cancer who miraculously lived years longer than expected with the Dominican sisters in Atlanta), and even a couple of photographs of Flannery herself. Again, something was going on here.

At my first parish assignment, I ran an intergenerational summer book club. We would read all sorts of books during June, July, and the first part of August, and I managed to fit two O'Connor stories into the mix, to the joy of some of my fellow readers and to the disappointment of others. The more I read O'Connor, especially with others, the more I understood her.

When I started teaching philosophy at Borromeo Seminary a little while later, two of my best students (who are now priests) asked if I would offer an independent study on "O'Connor and Philosophy" for them, and I obliged. In addition to reading selections from O'Connor's fiction and prose, our course included a pilgrimage to O'Connor's Milledgeville, where we visited her farm, her parish, and her grave at Memorial Hill Cemetery. I remember praying there for her, but I also remember praying for myself and for whatever kind of work I was being called to in terms of O'Connor scholarship, figuring that she might be out of purgatory by now and might have some mysterious hand in my future.

When I was assigned to doctoral studies, I had three major decisions to make. First, I had to figure out where to study; second, I had to figure out my topic; and third, I had to find a director who would take an interest in my topic. I had studied with the Jesuits in college and never with the Dominicans, but after considering the connection between the Hillbilly Thomist and the Dominicans, I chose the philosophy faculty at the Pontifical University of St. Thomas Aquinas in Rome, known simply and affectionately as the Angelicum. Seeing that it had been almost a decade since I had earned my licentiate from The Catholic University of America, I needed a new thesis topic, and, led by what I take to be the power of the Holy Spirit and Flannery O'Connor herself, I felt called—truly, an intellectual vocation—to write a dissertation on the philosophical foundations of Flannery O'Connor's narrative art, as it was a major void in O'Connor scholarship. But then came the tricky part: finding a director. As it turned out, around the same time that I arrived in Rome, the man who would become my director—a Georgia native, a convert to the faith (spurred on in part by his reading of O'Connor), a Dominican friar, and a member of a bluegrass band called the Hillbilly Thomists—happened to be starting his new assignment in the Eternal City as well, as the new director of the Thomistic Institute. I wrote Fr. Thomas Joseph White, OP, to explain my project and to ask if he would consider directing my dissertation. His response came quickly and in the generous and humble formulation of "How could I refuse?" I took Fr. White's *fiat* as confirmation of the intellectual mission that had been given to me. Something indeed was going on here, and that something is called divine providence.

I figured that the best way to write about Flannery O'Connor would be to write like Flannery O'Connor, so I adopted her strict schedule, writing from 9:00 a.m. to 12:00 p.m. Monday through Saturday. (O'Connor wrote on Sundays too, but she was dying of lupus and she knew it, so she gets a pass for working on the Lord's Day.) I wrote my first two chapters at the Casa Santa Maria, but as I was finishing up my research for my third chapter, COVID-19 hit. The pandemic sent me—wearing a mask and dragging seventy-five pounds of books in two suitcases and a carry-on bag—back to Cleveland indefinitely. There is a little place back home called Casa Wojtyła where I spent my days away with three brother priests, and thanks to their kindness and understanding, I wrote my third chapter at the dining room table under quarantine. Eventually, we were allowed back into the seminary, and with the help of Mr. Alan Rome, I set up a little writing station in the loft of our library, where I wrote my fourth chapter during the summer months. Upon returning to the Casa Santa Maria, I wrote my fifth and final chapter in the fall, staying faithful to O'Connor's strict writing schedule, whether I wrote one paragraph in a day or three pages. I mention this discipline of writing for three uninterrupted hours per day because I am convinced that while one does need a minimal degree of intelligence to write a dissertation, the truth is that discipline, mortification, and work ethic are what actually get the job done. Like the Grandmother in O'Connor's "A Good Man Is Hard to Find," you need to write as if someone is there to shoot you every minute of your life—at least I do.

Speaking of work ethic, it is a gift that I received from my dad, Eddie Ference, who was an elevator mechanic. He left high school early, joined the Navy, and fought in World War II; if he were alive today, he would think it funny that I have a doctorate in philosophy, but he would also be happy and proud. My mom, Joan Ference, never knew me as a priest, let alone a philosopher, but she was dedicated to the truth, and she taught me at a very early age to love it, respect it, and tell it. I echo the words of Gillian Welch: "I had a real good mother and father." (I have a good brother and extended family too.)

I express my heartfelt thanks to my brothers and sisters of the Diocese of Cleveland for all their support and prayers, to her former shepherd Archbishop Nelson Pérez for assigning me to doctoral studies, and to her current shepherd, Bishop Edward Malesic, for allowing me to finish my academic mission, encouraging me to turn my dissertation into a book and taking great interest in my scholarship, and appointing me as the first Vicar for Evangelization in the Diocese of Cleveland.

When Bishop Robert Barron asked me to be a contributor to the Word on Fire Blog over a decade ago, I never imagined that one day there would be a Word on Fire imprint and that I would write a book for it on two of Barron's *Pivotal Players*, but God's providence is a strange and surprising thing. I am so very grateful to Bishop Barron and the Word on Fire family, especially Fr. Steve Grunow, Brandon Vogt, Matthew Becklo, Daniel Seseske, Jason Paone, Rozann Lee, and Cassie Bielak, for making this book a beautiful reality.

Special thanks go to my dear friends and former students who accompanied me on many memorable pilgrimages to O'Connor's Georgia over the years. Reading an author's work is one thing, but visiting her land is another, especially when that writer is from the South and you are from the North. My love, understanding, and appreciation of Flannery O'Connor and her narrative art only increased through repeated visits to her childhood home in Savannah and to Andalusia, her farmhouse in Milledgeville. I am forever grateful for the generous hospitality and fraternity of

Fr. Young Nguyen, the pastor of Sacred Heart Parish (O'Connor's home parish), and for the kindness of all his faithful parishioners, particularly the Campus Catholics of Georgia College and Ms. Louise Florencourt.

Although writing a book demands a great deal of solitude and isolation, it remains a communal act, and I am grateful to the following friends for discussing O'Connor's narrative art with me for this project: Dr. Beth Rath, Dr. Joel Johnson, Dr. Steve Brule, Fr. Pat Anderson, Fr. Mark Riley, Fr. Dominic Buckley, Fr. Alex Gibbs, Fr. John Paul Mitchell, Br. Tommy "Pranzo" Piolata, OFM Cap., and Mr. Gregg Stovicek. I would be entirely remiss if I did not thank my brilliant and humble friend Mr. Danny O'Brien, not only for his most careful proofreading of this work, but also for his helpful and clarifying comments, questions, and suggestions.

I reserve my deepest thanks for the Triune God who is and who was and who always will be. I hope and pray that this scholarly work gives readers a new or renewed sense of your glorious mystery. And to Our Lady, whose *fiat* made the Incarnation possible, thank you for being my friend and for always protecting me.

Abbreviations

CS: *The Complete Stories*
HB: *The Habit of Being*
MM: *Mystery and Manners*
NE: *Nicomachean Ethics*
PG: *The Presence of Grace*
PJ: *A Prayer Journal*
SCG: *Summa contra Gentiles*
ST: *Summa theologiae*
WB: *Wise Blood*

Breaking a Remarkable Silence

In May of 1955, Flannery O'Connor was preparing to travel from her home in Milledgeville, Georgia, to New York City, where she would appear as a guest on the NBC television program *Galley Proof*, hosted by *New York Times* book editor Harvey Breit.[1] O'Connor was already a successful writer, having published her novel *Wise Blood* in 1952, and would eventually be regarded as perhaps the greatest Catholic fiction writer America has ever produced, but the occasion for her appearance on *Galley Proof* was the upcoming release of her first collection of short stories, *A Good Man Is Hard to Find*. As she anticipated the trip and interview, O'Connor mused in a letter to a friend about how she—a thirty-year-old female Catholic fiction writer with a southern accent—might be perceived by the national television audience. Amid a series of tongue-in-cheek speculations (her self-deprecating tone conveying an understandable mix of excitement and discomfort about stepping into the limelight) came the now-famous quip: "Everyone who has read *Wise Blood* thinks I'm a hillbilly nihilist, whereas I would like to create the impression over the television that I'm a hillbilly Thomist."[2]

The fact is that O'Connor, an educated woman descended from a well-to-do Southern family and a committed religious

1. "Galley Proof: A Good Man Is Hard to Find," in *Conversations with Flannery O'Connor*, ed. Rosemary Magee (Jackson, MS: University Press of Mississippi, 1987), 5.
2. *HB*, 81.

believer, was neither a hillbilly nor a nihilist. But, in a turn typical of her wit, she conceded and repeated the first part of that imagined epithet ("hillbilly," the part presumably more likely to scandalize or alienate the New York literary establishment) while making a point to reject the second part, which to her would be the more offensive misunderstanding. In other words: they could call her a hillbilly if they must, but "nihilist" was where she drew the line. Rightly understood, *Wise Blood* had painted a "terrifying"[3] picture of a modern world marked by self-centeredness, disregard for mystery, and the subordination of reason. In narrating the personal journey of protagonist Hazel Motes —a wild detour through evangelical atheism culminating in a dramatic (and violent) spiritual awakening—O'Connor had in fact confronted and condemned nihilism forcefully and artistically, but not didactically. "A serious fiction writer," she told Breit in her interview, "describes an action only to reveal a mystery."[4]

While some 1950s-era readers may have been perplexed by the mystery of *Wise Blood*, it is no secret nowadays that O'Connor's worldview, which she described as "Christian Realism," was heavily influenced by St. Thomas Aquinas and her preconciliar, Thomistic-laden Catholicism.[5] Her letters and prose are filled with generous mentions of the thirteenth-century Italian Dominican philosopher, whom she regarded with both the respect due to an intellectual hero and the warmth of a faithful friend. In August of 1955—a few months after calling herself a "hillbilly Thomist"—O'Connor said of Aquinas' *Summa theologiae*:

> I read it for about twenty minutes every night before I go to
> bed. If my mother were to come in during this process and say,
> "Turn off that light. It's late," I with lifted finger and broad bland

3. "Her picture of the modern world is literally terrifying" (Caroline Gordon, "May 15 ls Publication Date of Novel by Flannery O'Connor, Milledgeville," in *Conversations*, 3).

4. O'Connor, *Conversations*, 9.

5. *HB*, 92.

beatific expression would reply, "On the contrary, I answer that the light, being eternal and limitless, cannot be turned off. Shut your eyes," or some such thing. In any case, I feel that I can personally guarantee that St. Thomas loved God because for the life of me I cannot help loving St. Thomas.[6]

O'Connor's personal library, currently housed in the Special Collections at Georgia College in Milledgeville, contains a complete edition of Aquinas' *De Veritate*, but not an unabridged set of the *Summa*.[7] However, the library does have O'Connor's cherished (and marked up and underlined) copy of Anton Pegis' *Introduction to St. Thomas Aquinas*, which includes almost seven hundred pages of articles from the *Summa theologiae* and *Summa contra Gentiles*, along with notes and commentary by Pegis. Knowing that this distilled compilation served as O'Connor's primary reference on Thomism and was most likely the volume she read at bedtime helps explain another self-deprecating comment: in a 1961 letter to John Hawkes, O'Connor wrote, "I am a Thomist three times removed and live amongst many distinctions. (A Thomist three times removed is one who doesn't read Latin or St. Thomas but gets it by osmosis.)"[8] This description demonstrates her intellectual humility, but it also suggests, accurately, that O'Connor, while not a trained philosopher, was nonetheless practically swimming in Thomism—her collection is replete with works by Aristotle, Jacques Maritain, Étienne Gilson, Josef Pieper, Frederick Copleston, and Victor White, all of whom helped form her understanding of Aquinas and his thought. O'Connor read and understood these scholars, engaged with their ideas, and talked about them in her letters.[9]

---

6. *HB*, 93–94.
7. Arthur Kinney, *Flannery O'Connor's Library: Resources of Being* (Athens, GA: The University of Georgia Press, 1985), 15.
8. O'Connor, quoted in Kinney, *Flannery O'Connor's Library*, 439.
9. Bennet notes, "Her most important tutors were the neo-Thomist heavyweights who shaped her understanding of modernistic numinousness" (Eric

In the following pages, I will argue that with varying degrees of directness—at times straight from the writing of St. Thomas himself; more frequently mediated through interpreters like Pegis and Gilson; gradually over time by continual "osmosis" from the wider community of Catholic philosophers formed by, explaining, and building on Aquinas; and perhaps most importantly, if hardest to define, through her upbringing in the preconciliar Catholic culture of her time—Thomism exerted a philosophical influence on O'Connor that is difficult to overstate and that sheds a great deal of light on her narrative art.[10]

To date, the vast majority of scholarship surrounding Flannery O'Connor has been carried out by English professors, literary critics, biographers, and theologians, with but only a select few approaching O'Connor's work philosophically. The three most prominent philosophical commentators on O'Connor are the late Marion Montgomery, Henry Edmondson, and Christina Bieber Lake.[11] Brian Barbour's 2018 essay on O'Connor and Thomism

Bennett, "O'Connor and the Dogma of Creative Writing," in *Reconsidering Flannery O'Connor*, ed. Alison Arant and Jordan Cofer [Jackson, MS: University Press of Mississippi, 2020], 222).

10. Cf. Anton C. Pegis, *Introduction to St. Thomas Aquinas* (New York: Modern Library, 1948).

11. Montgomery was a professor of English at the University of Georgia and a friend and correspondent of Flannery O'Connor who authored two books on her: *Why Flannery O'Connor Stayed Home* (La Salle, IL: Sherwood, Sugden and Company, 1981) and *Hillbilly Thomist: Flannery O'Connor, St. Thomas and the Limits of Art*, vols. 1–2 (Jefferson, NC: McFarland and Company, 2006). He shares this memory: "When Dot and I were first married, we joined a group of senior faculty at the University of Georgia here, a little reading group. And we called ourselves the St. Thomas Aquinas and Rabbit Hunters Club. You have to remember we did actually hunt rabbits on occasion, and had little rabbit fries, as it were. But at any rate, we were reading this little volume here. We started with this. And I discovered much later that Flannery was reading the same work. And in my copy, it's rather heavily underlined all through there. It's called *Introduction to St. Thomas Aquinas*, and it is from the *Summa Theologica*. I went down to Milledgeville once and compared my copy to hers, and noted passages she had underlined, and some of them corresponded. It was very interesting" (Montgomery, in *At Home with Flannery O'Connor: An Oral History*, ed. Bruce Gentry and Craig Amason [Milledgeville, GA: The Flannery O'Connor-Andalusia Foundation, 2012], 59–60).

Edmondson is a political scientist and the author of *Return to Good and Evil: Flannery O'Connor's Response to Nihilism* (Lanham, MD: Lexington Books, 2002), references Montgomery, but surprisingly he makes no mention of Edmondson or Bieber Lake. Barbour notes,

> Despite its intrinsic importance, Flannery O'Connor's Thomism is not a topic that receives much attention. Nor is its existence much taken for granted or subsumed in the many exegetical discussions of her fiction. On what would seem to be an important, indeed central, topic, a remarkable silence obtains.[12]

This book seeks to break that "remarkable silence" by offering a thorough and long overdue treatment of the Thomistic philosophy upon which O'Connor's narrative art stands and with which her fiction may best be understood.[13]

***

In the fall semester of 2019, Eleonore Stump gave a public lecture at the Angelicum in Rome, and in the question-and-answer session following her talk, she mentioned that to her mind the greatest Thomist of all time was Dante.[14] Like O'Connor, Dante was not a professionally trained philosopher or theologian but a narrative artist whose work was highly informed by the books that he read. In his introduction to Dante's *Inferno*, Anthony Esolen writes

and the editor of *A Political Companion to Flannery O'Connor*, ed. Henry T. Edmondson (Lexington, KY: University Press of Kentucky, 2017).

Bieber Lake is an English professor but is well-versed in the history of philosophy, especially as it relates to Flannery O'Connor. She is the author of *The Incarnational Art of Flannery O'Connor* and wrote a most important essay, "Future Flannery, or, How a Hillbilly Thomist Can Help Us Navigate the Politics of Personhood in the Twenty-First Century," in Edmondson's *Political Companion*.

12. Brian Barbour, "'His Trees Stood Rising Above Him': Philosophical Thomism in Flannery O'Connor," *Renascence* 70, no. 4 (Fall 2018): 245.

13. My approach to O'Connor's narrative art is that of the "intentionalist" rather than the "textualist" tradition. See Alison Arant and Jordan Cofer, "Recovering Interpretive Possibilities in the Fiction of Flannery O'Connor: An Introduction," in *Reconsidering Flannery O'Connor*, 5.

14. Eleonore Stump, "Fearfully and Wonderfully Made: Creation, Science, and the Second Personal" (lecture, Thomistic Institute at the Angelicum, Rome, October 4, 2019).

the following: "For there are three principles regarding created things that I find fundamental to Dante's view of the world and its beauty. . . . They are these: *Things have an end. Things have meaning. Things are connected.*"[15] These three principles are all Thomistic in nature and, as we shall see, are all on display in the narrative art of Flannery O'Connor as well. In fact, one may argue that O'Connor's project is to reject the antitheses of these three principles, particularly as they show up in modernity and postmodernity. Flannery O'Connor may not be the greatest Thomist of all time, but I argue that her contribution to the Thomistic revival of the twentieth century is indeed great.

This philosophical work is composed of four chapters. Chapter 1 offers a general introduction to Flannery O'Connor. I highlight O'Connor's intellectual formation and present an overview of her vocation as a narrative artist and then offer an account of the unique relationship between philosophy and literature. In chapter 2, I address the metaphysics of Flannery O'Connor's worldview, beginning with God's existence, then moving to a philosophical understanding of the goodness of God's creation, while also explaining the nature of evil, O'Connor's use of the grotesque, and how symbols operate philosophically in O'Connor's fiction. The chapter concludes with a philosophical analysis of "The River." Chapter 3 is devoted to O'Connor's epistemology, starting not with the mind but with a general study of life—moving from vegetative, to sensitive, to intellectual life—then demonstrating the important distinction between *man as knower* and *man as thinker.* Special attention is given to O'Connor's own underlinings in Pegis' *Introduction*, evidently her primary source for understanding Thomistic epistemology, with specific emphasis on the role of the senses in the process of knowing. The most original philosophical argument in this book comes in reading Betty Edwards' *Drawing on the Right Side*

15. Anthony Esolen, introduction to Dante's *Inferno* (New York: Modern Library, 2005), xvii.

of the Brain through a Thomistic lens and then applying her thesis to O'Connor's Hillbilly Thomism. This chapter also includes a defense of O'Connor's philosophical attraction to Teilhard de Chardin, a French Jesuit who proved to be one of O'Connor's great intellectual heroes. Chapter 3 concludes with a philosophical analysis of O'Connor's "Parker's Back." The fourth and final chapter explores O'Connor's ethics, beginning with a general understanding of the (natural and supernatural) end of man, and then showing how one achieves that end through the operation of the intellect and will, in accord with the natural law, through the practice of virtue, and with the help of friends. I then demonstrate how these Thomistic themes are on display in O'Connor's fiction as well as in her life, giving special attention to her understanding of natural law, human sexuality, and friendship. This chapter concludes with an analysis of O'Connor's longest short story, "The Displaced Person."

Walker Percy once wrote, "The thought crossed my mind: why not do what French philosophers often do and Americans almost never—novelize philosophy, incarnate ideas in a person and a place, which latter is, after all, a noble Southern tradition."[16] Flannery herself presents a notable exception to Percy's "almost never" claim. For in Flannery O'Connor, the Hillbilly Thomist, we find an American narrative artist with a unique ability to novelize philosophy with tremendous effect.

I argue within these pages that although one may study O'Connor's fiction through a variety of intellectual traditions and interpretive lenses, the Thomistic tradition offers the most complete view of her artistic project, and that any other approach to O'Connor's work must contend with her ubiquitous Thomistic intuitions.

My hope is that Thomists in particular will come to appreciate the way in which O'Connor employs Thomistic philosophy as

16. Walker Percy, *Signposts in a Strange Land* (New York: Farrar, Straus and Giroux, 1991), 382.

the foundation of her stories and come to see how her fiction can be a starting point for philosophy, especially in the classroom. In other words, this book seeks to give philosophical justification to O'Connor's literary art as a manifestation of philosophical ideas, showing that O'Connor's fiction matters to philosophy and that philosophy—specifically Thomistic philosophy—matters to O'Connor's fiction.

I hope that by becoming aware of certain Thomistic ideas that directly influenced O'Connor, along with others that are less directly expressed by her but no less illuminating, you will grow in your understanding and enjoyment of what's going on in her stories and how they work—the metaphysical premises that anchor them, the resources of meaning that O'Connor saw when she stared at the world around her, the "nature and aim" of her artistic choices—in short, that your own imagination will be better equipped to absorb and appreciate the brilliant narrative art of our Hillbilly Thomist.

CHAPTER ONE

Foundations

A BRIEF BIOGRAPHY

Mary Flannery O'Connor, the only child of Edward and Regina (Cline) O'Connor, was born in Savannah, Georgia, on March 25, 1925, the Feast of the Annunciation, which is the day Christians celebrate God becoming man in the womb of the Virgin Mary in the person of Jesus Christ, heralded by the angel Gabriel.[1] Flannery O'Connor (she dropped the "Mary" from her name in graduate school in order to be taken seriously by her mostly male professors, colleagues, and future editors) was raised in a devout Catholic home and remained a faithful daughter of the Church her entire life. Her notable contribution to the mind of the Church was not to discourse on truth as a philosopher, but rather to incarnate truth as an artist through the medium of fiction, particularly the short story.

It is likely literally—not just metaphorically—the case that Flannery O'Connor was, as has often been said, "conceived in the shadow of the cathedral." As her biographer Brad Gooch notes, "Looming through her parents' bedroom windows were always its pale green twin spires, topped by gold crosses—visible, indeed for miles around."[2] O'Connor was baptized and received her First Holy Communion in that very cathedral, her family's

---

1. See Luke 1:26–38.
2. Brad Gooch, *Flannery: A Life of Flannery O'Connor* (New York: Little, Brown and Company, 2009), 18.

home parish under the patronage of St. John the Baptist. She spent her first five years of school at St. Vincent's Grammar School for Girls, run by the Sisters of Mercy, which Gooch describes as a school "which maintained a nearly medieval aura of Latinate order and spirituality."[3] As early as first grade, it became clear that O'Connor had a penchant for life's most foundational questions. Her highest grades were in catechism, "where she scored 96 in her first year and 98 in her second,"[4] while her lowest grades were in arithmetic and spelling. In the 1930s, the *Baltimore Catechism* was the text of the day in American parochial schools, and "it was organized in a simple Q-and-A format, leading students to memorize rote answers to fundamental questions in a singsong litany with nuns."[5] Memorizing answers to these *fundamental questions* was not simply a classroom exercise for O'Connor but became the foundation of her intellectual worldview. She was being formed in the classic tradition that taught her that God exists, that God made her, that her purpose—and that of the entire human race—was to "know him, to love him, to serve him in this world and to be happy with him forever in the next,"[6] and that Jesus is God and he teaches us through the Catholic Church.[7] O'Connor's mother transferred her from St. Vincent's to Sacred Heart School in sixth grade, where she continued to develop her love of reading (and her disdain for mathematics) until her family moved from Savannah to Milledgeville, due to her father's work situation, where she enrolled in Peabody Elementary School for the last two months of her seventh-grade year.[8] The O'Connor family moved again to Atlanta and then back to Milledgeville, where O'Connor attended Peabody High School, during which

3. Gooch, 29.
4. Gooch, 32.
5. Gooch, 32.
6. Gooch, 33.
7. *Saint Joseph Baltimore Catechism: The Truths of Our Catholic Faith Clearly Explained and Illustrated* (New York: Catholic Book Publishing Co., 1969), 9.
8. Gooch, *Flannery*, 49.

time her beloved father died of lupus. In 1942, she graduated from high school and then matriculated at Georgia State College for Women (GSCW), where she began her course work that very summer.

Gooch reports that it was during that first summer at GSCW that O'Connor enrolled in the first part of the Survey of Humanities course taught by fellow Catholic Dr. Paul Boeson, whom "she trusted as her first guide to the world of philosophical ideas."[9] A year later, O'Connor "took the second half of his survey, buying the editions of Plato, Aristotle and the *Selected Essays* of Montaigne that she would keep her entire life."[10] And although O'Connor was a social science major, "the most important class O'Connor took at GSCW turned out to be one of her last, Social Science 412: Introduction to Modern Philosophy."[11] This course would prove to have a lasting influence on O'Connor, as in many ways it offered a foil to what would become her Hillbilly Thomism. A fellow student recalls, "Once O'Connor went up to the blackboard to diagram, in detail, what she saw as the contrast between Aquinas and modernism."[12] And her professor, Dr. George Beiswanger, observed, "She knew Aquinas in detail, was amazingly well read in earlier philosophy, and developed into a first rate '*intellectual*' along with her other accomplishments."[13] Because O'Connor took classes during the summers, she completed college in three years and graduated in June of 1945. In a poignant letter to Alfred Corn dated May 30, 1962, O'Connor reflects back on her college years:

> What kept me a sceptic in college was precisely my Christian faith. It always said: wait, don't bite on this, get a wider picture, continue to read.

9. Gooch, 85.
10. Gooch, 85.
11. Gooch, 112.
12. Gooch, 114.
13. Gooch, 114.

If you want your faith, you have to work for it. It is a gift, but for very few is it a gift given without any demand for equal time devoted to its cultivation. For every book you read that is anti-Christian, make it your business to read one that presents the other side of the picture; if one isn't satisfactory read others. Don't think that you have to abandon reason to be a Christian.[14]

O'Connor spent her next two years earning a master of fine arts (MFA) in creative writing at the Iowa Writers' Workshop and then moved to Yaddo, an artists' colony in upstate New York, where she described herself to a fellow artist one evening as "a thirteenth century Catholic," referring to the century of St. Thomas Aquinas.[15] Although her formal philosophical education was complete by this time, O'Connor continued to read philosophy:

> The most "thirteenth-century" book she was reading, and avidly underlining, at the time was *Art and Scholasticism*, by Jacques Maritain, a French Thomist, who was teaching at Princeton and helping to make the thought of Thomas Aquinas relevant in forties America. Its eighth chapter, "Christian Art," was a thunderclap to O'Connor; she drew line markings next to the passage "Do not make the absurd attempt to sever in yourself the artist and the Christian."[16]

Many of the artists at Yaddo did not share O'Connor's Catholic convictions, but rather embraced communism and atheism. Eventually, O'Connor left Yaddo for a short stint in New York City and then moved in with her good friends and fellow Catholics Robert and Sally Fitzgerald and their growing family in Connecticut, where she wrote much of her first novel, *Wise Blood*.

14. *HB*, 477.
15. Gooch, *Flannery*, 156.
16. Gooch, 156.

She returned to Milledgeville for Christmas in 1950 to visit her mother and her doctor, who diagnosed her with lupus, the same disease that had taken her father's life when she was fifteen.

O'Connor would spend the next fourteen years of her life living on a 544-acre farm called Andalusia just outside of Milledgeville, and this is where she did her best writing and her most important reading. Many scholars have noted that O'Connor lived a life of religious practices akin to a monk or a Dominican sister, keeping a strict *horarium* that included daily Mass, prayer, work (three hours of writing every morning), and spiritual reading. Gooch's description of her evening ritual is most insightful:

> Sundown and bedtime were nearly synonymous for Flannery. "I go to bed at nine and am always glad to get there," she told a friend. Occasionally she recited Compline, the last office of the day, from her *Breviary*, set between a Sunday missal and her Bible on a low bedside table. More reliably, her habitual nighttime reading was the lofty, lucent prose of Thomas Aquinas. For just as significant as ordering peacocks as a signal of her intention to settle, was her obtaining her own copy of the seven-hundred-page Modern Library selection *Introduction to Saint Thomas Aquinas*, which she signed and dated "1953." . . . Even resting in bed, Flannery was replenishing her writing. "I read a lot of theology because it makes my writing bolder," she once explained to a friend.[17]

Just as her reading of theology made her writing bolder, her reading of philosophy—by which she cultivated her worldview—made her fiction stronger.

Flannery O'Connor died on August 3, 1964, of complications from lupus. A funeral Mass was offered the next day at Sacred Heart Parish, and her body was buried at Memorial Hill Cemetery,

17. Gooch, 228.

where it awaits the resurrection. As the famous byline states on the back covers of all her works of fiction, "When she died at the age of thirty-nine, America lost one of its most gifted writers at the height of her powers."[18]

O'CONNOR AS (HILLBILLY) THOMIST

G.K. Chesterton, in his 1933 biography of St. Thomas, writes, "The Thomist philosophy is nearer than most philosophies to the mind of the man in the street."[19] Following Aristotle, Aquinas taught that human knowledge begins with the senses (*principium nostrae cognitionis est a sensu*),[20] that the senses are trustworthy, and that they are the natural way for human beings to encounter the world. If we see that the sky is dark, feel drops of water falling on us, and hear thunder cracking, we know it is raining; there is no reason to be skeptical about that fact. From the earliest ages of human experience, we trust that our senses tell us the truth. Infants and toddlers are constantly looking at things, touching things, and tasting things (often things that are not edible) because this is the natural way that human beings come to know the world. From that foundation, Thomism also holds that the information provided by our senses is intelligible—able to be understood and to lead us to real knowledge. It takes no great exertion of mental will to encounter the world in this way—trusting our senses is natural and normative. What is forced and unnatural is the modern philosophical "twist" by which we might choose to doubt our senses—a choice that strikes the proverbial "man in the street" as absurd.

18. Flannery O'Connor, *Wise Blood* (New York: Farrar, Straus and Giroux, 1998).

19. G.K. Chesterton, *Saint Thomas Aquinas: The Dumb Ox* (New York: Image Books, 1956), 79.

20. Thomas Aquinas, *Summa theologiae* 1.84.6. (All quotations from the *Summa theologiae* and *Summa contra Gentiles* will be taken from O'Connor's edition of *Introduction to Saint Thomas Aquinas*, ed. and intro. Anton C. Pegis [New York: Modern Library, 1948].)

While O'Connor's philosophy professor Dr. Beiswanger "took for granted that the Renaissance and the Age of Enlightenment set the Western mind free from the benightedness of Medieval thought (from Thomas Aquinas, etc.)," his student did not; on the contrary, Beiswanger remembers that O'Connor made it clear that "she didn't believe a word I was saying."[21] O'Connor was more amenable to the perspective of Étienne Gilson, a leading voice in the Thomistic revival of the twentieth century. In *The Unity of Philosophical Experience* (which O'Connor called "indispensable to an understanding of the modern age"[22]), Gilson methodically dissected how every modern attempt to reinvent philosophy in the image of other sciences had resulted only in the "loss of confidence in our ability to achieve philosophical truth" at all—that is, in deeper skepticism.[23]

René Descartes—the purported "hero" of Beiswanger's course—began his philosophical method by doubting his own senses.[24] Thomism resists this unnatural Cartesian twist, holding instead to what Gilson calls "the solid, down-to-earth realism of the classical metaphysics of being."[25] This reference to "down-to-earth realism" is an excellent and appropriate description of Hillbilly Thomism and likely would have appealed to O'Connor.

The Oxford Dictionary entry for "hillbilly" is as follows: "an unsophisticated country person, as associated originally with the remote regions of the Appalachians."[26] O'Connor's use of the term "hillbilly" is not meant to be derogatory but does suggest that even country folk with no formal background in

21. Gooch, *Flannery*, 113–114.

22. Flannery O'Connor, *The Presence of Grace and Other Book Reviews by Flannery O'Connor*, ed. Carter W. Martin (Athens, GA: The University of Georgia Press, 1983), 129.

23. Desmond J. FitzGerald, foreword to Étienne Gilson, *The Unity of Philosophical Experience* (San Francisco: Ignatius, 1999), x–xi.

24. Gooch, *Flannery*, 113–114.

25. Étienne Gilson, *Painting and Reality: The A.W. Mellon Lectures in the Fine Arts* (New York: Pantheon Books, 1957), x.

26. "Hillbilly," Oxford Reference Dictionary, oxfordreference.com.

philosophy nevertheless reflect Thomistic epistemology: they use their common sense and trust that their senses are telling them the truth about reality. As Robert Sokolowski puts it, "There *can be* a hillbilly Thomist, but there could not be a hillbilly Kantian or Hegelian, let alone a hillbilly Derridean."[27] In other words, the insights of Aquinas "can be expressed in a simple, straightforward manner,"[28] a manner that even a hillbilly would understand, but the same cannot be said of Kant, Hegel, and Derrida because their philosophies all reject the starting point of common sense.

Borrowing Chesterton's language, we might take "Hillbilly Thomism" as another way of saying "man-in-the-street Thomism." Perhaps this seems almost redundant—why not just say "Thomism"? But Chesterton goes on to lament that only rarely in practice is the common sense of Thomism expressed in a common manner. For the average person, untrained in philosophy, the difficulty of engaging with St. Thomas' language (whether in Latin or in translation), combined with a lack of imagery to illustrate his logical method, constitutes "a very high brick wall" that unfortunately serves to separate "normal men" from "normal philosophy."[29] For most of us, overcoming the barrier requires the help of a great teacher—or perhaps a great artist. O'Connor managed, as did Dante,[30] to climb the wall, see what was on both sides, and vividly illustrate for others the relationship between the two.

Knowledge begins in the senses, but it does not end there. Thomists are not mere empiricists, and a Thomistic novelist is not simply a journalist. In chapter 3, we will look closely at the Thomistic account of how human beings use their sensory powers

27. Robert Sokolowski, "The Role of Philosophy in Priestly Formation" (keynote address, Mount St. Mary's Seminary, Emmitsburg, MD, May 24, 2010).

28. Sokolowski.

29. Chesterton, *Thomas Aquinas*, 82.

30. Dante was no hillbilly. But his choice to write his *Comedy* in vernacular Italian rather than Latin (the conventional language of both epic poetry and academic philosophy) was a conscious move to include the common "man in the street" within his audience.

to "abstract" the spiritual nature of things from their appearances and come to know universal truths not by disembodied reason but by observing particular truths in the world. When we emphasize that Flannery O'Connor trusted, both in philosophy and in art, the authority and intelligibility of her sensory powers, this is not a trivial point. The cultural consequences of modern philosophy we see in our own day, from the techno-futurist enthusiasm for a coming virtual "metaverse" to the rise of what Bishop Barron has called the "culture of self-invention," demonstrate that not all human beings are—or want to be—in touch with this most human way of being in the world.

Neither is O'Connor's exhortation that artists must "be humble in the face of what-is" an unremarkable or reliably conventional outlook, even among Catholics.[31] In the culture of her time, she observed and frequently denounced a strong current of "vapid Catholicism," a safe, sanitized abstraction of the faith that led to bad art filled with superstition and sentimental cliché. "When the Catholic novelist closes his own eyes and tries to see with the eyes of the Church," O'Connor warned, "the result is another addition to that large body of pious trash for which we have so long been famous."[32]

O'Connor had no interest in turning out "pious trash" on behalf of an abstract idea (even if it was a good idea). She was concerned with *recta ratio factibilium*—"right reason in the order of making things"—beginning with the sensory data from the world, whether that data be pleasing, painful, or perverse; looking deeply, in order to know the invisible reality given initially through sense experience; and then, by careful artistic craft, drawing the reader into its beauty, power, and startling mystery. This approach—taking the world as she found it, then looking for the deeper reality it signified even in all its messiness and

---

31. Flannery O'Connor, *Mystery and Manners: Occasional Prose*, ed. Sally and Robert Fitzgerald (New York: Farrar, Straus and Giroux, 1969), 146.

32. *MM*, 179.

distortions—was not just Catholic but Thomistic, and she saw it as Thomistic.

O'CONNOR AS (ANTI)INTELLECTUAL

Throughout her prose, Flannery O'Connor writes with great confidence about her vocation as a narrative artist, but she hesitates to include herself in a community of "interleckchuls,"[33] and she often goes out of her way to poke fun at professional academics. She told her friend William Sessions, "I hope you are working in a diligent manner so that you can become a Ph.D. and then go ignorant for the rest of your life,"[34] and to Louise and Tom Gossett she wrote, "Congratulations on having finally got educated. Now you can regress at your leisure."[35] In a letter to Betty Hester dated June 1, 1956, O'Connor describes her friend Robert Fitzgerald in this way: "Robert was brought up a Catholic but left the Church when he was about eighteen to become an intellectual."[36] She also once confessed, "Anything I can't stand it's a young writer or intellectual."[37] Although often cloaked in humor, O'Connor's critiques are direct and severe, and they are worthy of our attention. She was well aware of the hubris present in the intellectual life and sought to avoid it.

A major reason for O'Connor's often humorous but harsh criticism of intellectuals, and her insistence on distancing her writing from circles of professional academics, is that she often saw their work as crippling rather than fostering one's intellectual, spiritual, and human growth.

When her friend William Sessions attempted to interpret her second novel through a Freudian lens, O'Connor scolded

---

33. Gooch, *Flannery*, 318. (O'Connor was a terrible speller, but this misspelling of "intellectuals" is very much intentional and is evidence of her wit, which we will address below.)
34. Gooch, 509.
35. Gooch, 438.
36. Gooch, 161.
37. Gooch, 153.

him, stating, "Your criticism sounds to me as if you have read too many critical books and are too smart in an artificial, destructive, and very limited way."[38] She also witnessed some of her close friends lose their Christian faith when their experiences in college convinced them they had to choose between reason and faith—a dilemma that O'Connor knew was a false choice. In a May 1962 letter to Alfred Corn, O'Connor makes a noble attempt to encourage her friend who was losing his Christian faith on account of his education:

> As a freshman in college you are bombarded with new ideas, or rather pieces of ideas, new frames of reference, an activation of the intellectual life which is only beginning, but which is already running ahead of your lived experience. After a year of this, you think you cannot believe. You are just beginning to realize how difficult it is to have faith and the measure of a commitment to it, but you are too young to decide you don't have faith just because you feel you can't believe. About the only way we know whether we believe or not is by what we do, and I think from your letter that you will not take the path of least resistance in this matter and simply decide that you have lost your faith and that there is nothing you can do about it.[39]

In addition to the critiques found in her prose, O'Connor offers an impressive collection of characters in her fiction who become representative of the type of "intellectual" that she so disdains. With the exception of Catholic priests,[40] the vast majority of educated characters in O'Connor's fiction are presented as arrogant, dysfunctional, unsettled, insecure, and pitiable individuals who are trapped in their own heads and unable to act in the world. Consider the school teacher George Rayber in

38. *HB*, 407.
39. *HB*, 477.
40. See "The Enduring Chill" and "The Displaced Person."

The Violent Bear It Away,[41] who could turn a teenage boy into "a piece of information inside his head"; or the philosopher Joy/Hulga Hopewell from "Good Country People,"[42] whose mother, Mrs. Hopewell, "thought of her as a child though she was thirty-two years old and highly educated"; or Julian from "Everything That Rises Must Converge,"[43] whose uneducated mother reports, "My son just finished college last year. He wants to write but he's selling typewriters until he gets started"; or Asbury from "The Enduring Chill," who inspired his mother to say, "The more education they got, they less they could do";[44] who is described as a "lying stinking atheist";[45] they are all targets of meaningful mockery for O'Connor.

Perhaps a distinction is in order. On the one hand, we have *the intellectual life*, which O'Connor took very seriously, and on the other hand, human beings can fall prey to conventional forms of *intellectualism*, which is the attitude of the academic culture presented in the criticisms mentioned above. O'Connor's approach to the intellectual life was humble but confident. While she was not always confident in herself, she seems to have been forever confident in the intellectual tradition of which she found herself a part. This confidence explains her most impressive library, for example, which was filled with an expansive variety of books that were constantly broadening and deepening her understanding of and appreciation for the Catholic intellectual tradition as well as intellectual movements in fiction and nonfiction. This same confidence animated her in all the ongoing intellectual conversations in which she was engaged both in person and through

41. Flannery O'Connor, *The Violent Bear It Away* (New York: Farrar, Straus and Giroux, 1996), 16.
42. Flannery O'Connor, "Good Country People," in *The Complete Stories* (New York: Farrar, Straus and Giroux, 1971), 274.
43. Flannery O'Connor, "Everything That Rises Must Converge," in *CS*, 411.
44. Flannery O'Connor, "The Enduring Chill," in *CS*, 361.
45. Flannery O'Connor, "The Lame Shall Enter First," in *CS*, 480.

correspondence with artists, novelists, theologians, professors, and well-educated clergy, religious, and lay people.

In the opening line of her essay "Novelist and Believer," Flannery O'Connor writes, "Being a novelist and not a philosopher or theologian, I shall have to enter this discussion at a much lower level and proceed along a much narrower course than that held up to us here as desirable."[46] One might presume by such an introduction that the remainder of this essay would stand bereft of any real intellectual firepower, but O'Connor's familiarity with the Western intellectual tradition is on full display throughout this essay as she makes an implicit reference to the epistemology of Thomas Aquinas, and explicit references to the theology of Augustine and Pascal, as well as the atheism of Albert Camus. "Novelist and Believer" is philosophical and theological in nature but written in her own Hillbilly Thomist style: "lucid . . . straightforward, nonacademic, above cant or jargon and professionally innocent of theory."[47] Carter Martin also notes that "her forte is spare precision" and that it seems to be part of O'Connor's genius that she does not waste words in naming reality.[48] This style is reminiscent of the kind of philosophy Sokolowski argues should be taught in seminaries—what he calls *streamlined Thomism*—which "consists in making strategic elementary distinctions"[49] in a "simple, direct, and understandable"[50] manner.

Although O'Connor once wrote, "I'm not an intellectual and have a horror of making an idiot of myself with abstract statements and theories,"[51] Robert Giroux presents an alternative perspective, stating, "She was completely intellectual and

---

46. *MM*, 154.
47. *PG*, 1.
48. *PG*, 7.
49. Robert Sokolowski, "Philosophy in the Seminary Curriculum," in *Christian Faith and Human Understanding: Studies on the Eucharist, Trinity, and the Human Person* (Washington, DC: The Catholic University of America Press, 2006), 305.
50. Sokolowski, 306.
51. *HB*, 202.

cerebral. She was a thinker. And in those days encountering a philosophical woman thinker was rarer."[52] These two statements, taken together, offer an excellent example of O'Connor's approach to the intellectual life. She knew that it was her duty and her vocation to study, to read, to think, to be both theological and philosophical, but O'Connor was also convinced that engaging in such intellectual activities should make one more human rather than less human, understandable rather than confusing, concrete rather than abstract, plainspoken rather than tangled up in jargon, and simple (in the way God is simple) rather than (unnecessarily) complex.

Flannery O'Connor's style is highly informed and intelligent yet humble, refreshingly free of the arrogance and in-house debates that often discourage nonacademics from engaging life's most important and fundamental questions; it manifests a type of intellectual style in the contemporary age that is both relevant and accessible.

O'CONNOR AS COMIC

Flannery O'Connor once candidly acknowledged how much she enjoyed reading her own stories: "The truth is I like them better than anybody and I read them over and over and laugh and laugh, then get embarrassed when I remember I was the one wrote them."[53] This confession presents to us two important truths. Firstly, that O'Connor is both witty and clever,[54] and that this

---

52. Gooch, *Flannery*, 156.
53. *HB*, 80–81.
54. In a recently discovered college journal, O'Connor wrote the following entry on December 29, 1943: "One new quarter of college has begun. I have achieved a nice success in Eng. 360 by making a rather humorous remark and then not laughing at it while the others did. This is quite unusual for me; however, I guess I deserve no great amount of credit. I didn't think the remark extravagantly clever when I made it. It achieved quite a nice effect though. I must try to do it again. That is the sort of me I strive to build up—the cool, sophisticated, clever wit. The inarticulate, confused blunderer overwhelms the CSCW most of the time, however" (Flannery O'Connor, "Higher Mathematics: Flannery O'Connor's College Journal," *Image*, no. 94 [Fall 2017]: 67).

combination is on display not just in her letters but throughout her canon.[55] And secondly, that her fiction, if properly understood, should result in occasional laughter. O'Connor's natural, reflexive use of humor within her narrative art is consistent with Aristotle and Thomas' definition of humor and serves as an important aspect of her Hillbilly Thomism.

Mary Barbara Tate, a close friend and correspondent of O'Connor, recalls the following anecdote:

> One night, my husband asked if he could read us one of her stories, and she said no, but she would read us one. If it was going to be read, she would read it. And she read us "The Enduring Chill," which she could hardly read for laughing. She had told us that she considered herself a comic writer. She certainly did enjoy her own wit and cleverness, as did we.[56]

According to Aristotle and Thomas Aquinas, humans are the only animals who are truly risible because we human beings are the only animals with intellect.[57] Noël Carroll argues that although there are a variety of theories about why this is so, the *incongruity theory* best accounts for the link between rationality and risibility.[58] Noël explains, "According to the incongruity theory, what is key to comic amusement is a deviation from some presupposed norm—that is to say, an anomaly or an incongruity

---

55. In her prayer journal, O'Connor makes two important mentions of cleverness in forty short pages: "But I do not mean to be clever although I do mean to be clever on 2nd thought and like to be clever & want to be considered so," and, "I say many many too many uncharitable things about people everyday. I say them because they make me look clever. Please help me to realize practically how cheap this is" (Flannery O'Connor, *A Prayer Journal*, ed. W.A. Sessions [New York: Farrar, Straus and Giroux, 2013], 6, 19).

56. Mary Barbara Tate, in Marion Montgomery, *At Home with Flannery O'Connor: An Oral History,* ed. Bruce Gentry and Craig Amason (Milledgeville, GA: The Flannery O'Connor-Andalusia Foundation, 2012), 27–28.

57. "In homine aliud est quod est animal rationale mortale, aliquid quod est risibile" (*ST* 1-2.2.6).

58. Noël Carroll, *Humour: A Very Short Introduction* (Oxford: Oxford University Press, 2014), 17.

relative to some framework governing the way in which we think the world is or should be."[59] In order to understand some kind of incongruity, we first have to be able to know what things are, and then make distinctions between different things, and this activity all depends upon our ability to grasp concepts. For example, in O'Connor's short story "Good Country People," Manley Pointer tells Hulga Hopewell a joke:

> Then on what seemed an insuck of breath, he whispered, "You ever ate a chicken that was two days old?"
>
> The girl looked at him stonily. He might have just put this question up for a meeting of a philosophical association. "Yes," she presently replied as if she had considered it from all angles.
>
> "It must have been mighty small!" he said triumphantly and shook all over with little nervous giggles, getting very red in the face, and subsiding finally into his gaze of complete admiration, while the girl's expression remained exactly the same.[60]

This joke is an example of an *anomalous juxtaposition* because the meaning of "two days old" in the punchline deviates from the meaning anticipated in the setup. Moreover, although Hulga did not laugh at Manley's joke, she understood it, which makes her response to the joke funny to the reader, as the reader experiences not only the joke but the divergent responses to the joke by Hulga and Manley, which present another level of incongruity. She is alienated by her elitism and humiliated by this hillbilly cleverness, which is itself both humorous and foreboding. This is but one of many examples of how O'Connor's wit marks her art.

According to Aristotle, wittiness (εὐτραπελία) is a social virtue that involves saying and listening to the right things in the

---

59. Carroll, 17.
60. O'Connor, "Good Country People," in *CS*, 283.

right way in regard to humor or amusement.[61] In typical fashion, Aristotle defines this virtue by its extremes, with boorishness (αγροίκος) as its deficiency and buffoonery (βωμολόχος) as its excess. He describes the boorish as people "who would never say anything themselves to raise a laugh, and even object when other people do it,"[62] and buffoons as those who "stop at nothing to raise a laugh, and care more about that than about saying what is seemly and avoiding pain to the victims of the joke."[63] The witty person, however, is one who is neither stiff nor vulgar but knows how to "joke well."[64] In his commentary on this section of the *Nicomachean Ethics*, Thomas Aquinas notes that wittiness "pertains to the mean habit of virtue to speak and to listen to what is becoming in jesting."[65] So according to both Aristotle and Thomas, humor and laughter have a proper place in human living, and the witty person is the one who shows us how to be virtuous in regard to joking and risibility. The witty person will laugh at the right things, in the right way, at the right time, and for the right reason, and will do the same in regard to the telling of jokes. The witty person knows what is funny and what is not, and always employs humor for the sake of the good, for the sake of human flourishing, and never in a manner that is base or vulgar.

Wittiness, as we have said, is a virtue that is found throughout O'Connor's canon, and within her fiction in particular; she uses it not only for the sake of the good but as part of her pedagogy, which makes her virtually unique among writers coming out of the Thomistic tradition. This aspect of her thought is intimately related, of course, to the literary form in which she writes. Often, the most significant moments in her fiction are also the funniest,

---

61. Aristotle, *Nicomachean Ethics*, trans. W.D. Ross (London: Oxford University Press, 1925), 1128a2–4.

62. *NE* 1128a8–10.

63. *NE* 1128a6–7.

64. *NE* 1128a26.

65. Thomas Aquinas, *Commentary on Aristotle's Nicomachean Ethics*, trans. C.I. Litzinger (Notre Dame, IN: Dumb Ox Books, 1993), §858.

as she uses humor to break into the mind and heart of her reader. What is O'Connor's point of mixing a most serious philosophical and theological question with humor?[66] Charles Campbell notes, "The imagery used for laughter is similar to imagery that is often used to describe the gospel itself. Like laughter, the gospel *fractures*; it *interrupts*; it *breaks* in."[67] O'Connor uses humor, then, to *break into* a modern sensibility that often refuses to consider life's most important questions. Since risibility is linked to rationality, "joking well" in a story is an effective way to activate the reader's intellect toward consideration of the aspects of reality most central to human living. O'Connor's skillful employment of humor for the sake of human flourishing is the very embodiment of the virtue of wit.

O'CONNOR AS NARRATIVE ARTIST

Thomas Aquinas defines art as *recta ratio factibilium*[68]—that is, right reason in the order of making things. We note immediately that the medieval understanding of art is radically different from a modern notion of art as self-expression or as creating one's own world or universe. On the contrary, Thomas and the medievals understood art not as setting oneself apart from or conquering nature but as an act of alignment and harmony with nature and the created world.

Flannery O'Connor understands herself as an artist inspired by such thirteenth-century standards; her art is writing fiction,

---

66. In cinema, the Coen brothers and Quentin Tarantino are similar to Flannery O'Connor in this regard. Their dark or grotesque humor, like O'Connor's, catches viewers off-guard by making them laugh at things that under normal circumstances do not lead to laughter—such as death—in order to encourage a deeper reflection on what is. O'Connor explains, "In my own experience, everything funny I have written is more terrible than it is funny, or only funny because it is terrible, or only terrible because it is funny" (*MM*, 105).

67. Charles L. Campbell, "Ministry with a Laugh," *Interpretation: A Journal of Bible and Theology* 69, no. 2 (2015): 197.

68. *ST* 1-2.57.4.

and her concern is writing fiction well.[69] She is out to write good stories, and she is convinced that the only way to accomplish this end is to resign herself to the "demands and inconveniences"[70] of the art of fiction writing. O'Connor explains, "St. Thomas Aquinas says that art does not require rectitude of the appetite, that it is wholly concerned with the good of that which is made. He says that a work of art is a good in itself, and this is a truth that the modern world has largely forgotten."[71] In "The Nature and Aim of Fiction," O'Connor offers her most detailed reflection on the nature of art and the artist:

> Now I'd better stop here and explain how I'm using the word art. Art is a word that immediately scares people off, as being a little too grand. But all I mean by art is writing something that is valuable in itself and that works in itself. The basis of art is truth, both in matter and in mode. The person who aims after art in his work aims after truth, in an imaginative sense, no more and no less. St. Thomas said that the artist is concerned with the good of that which is made; and that will have to be the basis of my few words on the subject of fiction.[72]

Although O'Connor's philosophy of art is undeniably Thomistic, we have no evidence that she read Thomas directly on the matter, although we know that her study of Jacques Maritain, Étienne Gilson, Victor White, and William Lynch all contributed significantly to her understanding of art and the vocation of the artist.

---

69. "Non enim pertinet ad laudem artificis, inquantum artifex est, qua voluntate opus faciat; sed quale sit opus quod facit" (*ST* 1-2.57.3).
70. *MM*, 171.
71. *MM*, 171.
72. *MM*, 65.

VOCATION AND DISCIPLINE

Throughout her essays and letters, O'Connor refers to her fiction writing as a *vocation*, a call from God.[73] She believed that God equipped her with particular artistic potentialities or gifts[74] that were hers to nurture, develop, and actualize, and then return to him in the making of good art, which in her case was the writing of good fiction. In her essay "The Nature and Aim of Fiction," O'Connor shares a pithy but significant anecdote:

> Last spring I talked here, and one of the girls asked me, "Miss O'Connor, why do you write?" and I said, "Because I'm good at it," and at once I felt a considerable disapproval in the atmosphere. I felt this was not thought by the majority to be a high-minded answer; but it was the only answer I could give. I had not been asked why I write the way I do, but why I write at all; and to that question there is only one legitimate answer.[75]

O'Connor is forever concerned with writing well, with writing good fiction, with being not just an artist but a good artist, because she understands art to be her vocation. Jacques Maritain's *Art and Scholasticism*,[76] which O'Connor mentions and recommends frequently in her correspondence, was most influential in her understanding of art and of herself as an artist,

---

73. Although O'Connor understood writing as her vocation, she did not think that everyone who wrote had a vocation to writing. In fact, it could be argued that the following lines from "The Nature and Aim of Fiction" define the *anti-vocation* of the writer: "I know well enough that very few people who are supposedly interested in writing are interested in writing well. They are interested in publishing something, and if possible in making a 'killing.' They are interested in seeing their names at the top of something printed, it matters not what" (*MM*, 64).

74. "There is no excuse for anyone to write fiction for public consumption unless he has been called to do so by the presence of a gift" (*MM*, 81).

75. *MM*, 81.

76. Jacques Maritain, *Art and Scholasticism with Other Essays*, trans. J.F. Scanlan (Minneapolis, MN: Filiquarian, 2007), 81. (O'Connor's personal copy of this book: Jacques Maritain, *Art and Scholasticism: With Other Essays*, trans. J.F. Scanlan [New York: Charles Scribner's Sons, 1930].)

particularly in terms of her self-discipline as an artist. Maritain writes,

> The Artist is subject, in the sphere of his art, to a kind of asceticism, which may require heroic sacrifices. He must be thoroughly undeviating as regards the end of his art, perpetually on guard not only against the banal attraction of easy execution and success, but against a multitude of more subtle temptations, and against the slightest relaxation of his interior effort, for habits diminish with the mere cessation of their acts, even more, with every relaxed act, every act which is not proportionate to their intensity. He must pass through spiritual nights, purify himself without ceasing, voluntarily abandon fertile regions for regions that are barren and full of insecurity.[77]

Any mention of asceticism, limitation, or restriction in regard to art or the artist may seem to offend our modern notions of artistic freedom, self-expression, and creativity, but O'Connor's philosophy of art is Thomistic and has an inner logic to it. She explains, "Vocation implies limitation but few people realize it who don't actually practice an art."[78] O'Connor thinks limitation is important to the artist in two ways: first in terms of personal discipline and second in terms of vision. We will address the artist's vision below, but here we will direct our attention to O'Connor's personal habits and practices as an artist. In a letter to Cecil Dawkins dated November 19, 1960, O'Connor writes:

> You ought to set aside three hours every morning in which you write or do nothing else; no reading, no talking, no cooking, no nothing, but you sit there. If you write all right and if you don't all right, but you do not read; whether you start something different every day and finish nothing makes no difference; you

77. Maritain, *Art and Scholasticism*, 81.
78. *HB*, 221.

sit there. It's the only way, I'm telling you. If inspiration comes you are there to receive it, you are not reading. And don't write letters during that time. If you don't write, don't do anything else. And get in a room by yourself. If there are two rooms in that house, get in the one where nobody else is.[79]

This advice to Dawkins is based upon O'Connor's own daily discipline of writing,[80] which she first established in graduate school and maintained throughout her life.[81] In a letter written three years earlier, O'Connor defends her own writing disciplines to Dawkins:

I'm a full-time believer in writing habits, pedestrian as it all may sound. You may be able to do without them if you have genius but most of us only have talent and this is simply something that has to be assisted all the time by physical and mental habits or it dries up and blows away. I see it happen all the time. Of course you have to make your habits in this conform to what you *can* do. I write only about two hours every day because that's all the energy I have, but I don't let anything interfere with those two hours, at the same time and the same place. This doesn't mean I produce much out of the two hours. Sometimes I work for months and have to throw everything away, but I don't think any of that was time wasted. Something goes on that makes it

---

79. *HB*, 417–418.

80. Depending upon O'Connor's health, she wrote two to three hours daily, although in graduate school she reports writing for four hours every morning (*HB*, 16).

81. Even in the final weeks of her life, O'Connor continued writing. In a letter to Thomas Stritch dated June 28, 1964, she reports, "I do what amounts to two hours of work a day and that is about as good as I ever did anyway. I asked the doctor if I could sit up at the electric typewriter and work. You can work, says he, but you can't exert yourself. I haven't quite figured this out yet; anyway I am confined to these two rooms and the porch so far and ain't allowed to wash the dishes. I guess that is exerting yourself where writing is officially not" (*HB*, 588).

easier when it does come well. And the fact is if you don't sit there every day, the day it would come well, you won't be sitting there.[82]

We have noted that the artist's need to enforce restrictions and limitations upon himself in order to make good art may seem counterintuitive. Yet O'Connor insists in her commentary on her own writing habits and in her advice to others that the artist requires an exceptional amount of discipline to develop his craft and actualize his potential. Maritain was not alone in teaching O'Connor that art requires asceticism; her friend and regular correspondent William Lynch, SJ, noted in his own work that art "is a highly professional act which makes severe demands on a particular form of the professional intelligence and which has always been held in high honor by human civilization. It demands great sacrifice and a rigorous asceticism."[83]

Flannery O'Connor imposed strict disciplines upon herself in order to bring out the best of herself as an artist. She writes, "A gift of any kind is a considerable responsibility. . . . Usually the artist has to suffer certain deprivations in order to use his gift with integrity."[84] O'Connor was convinced that her vocation was to be an artist, and she responded to that call with great discipline, responsibility, and integrity, actualizing the potential that was given to her and becoming a virtuous writing model for others to emulate.[85]

---

82. *HB*, 242.

83. William Lynch, *The Image Industries* (New York: Sheed & Ward, 1959), 137.

84. *MM*, 81.

85. O'Connor would have been familiar with the following words of Maritain regarding the responsibility of the artist: "In our day natural gift is lightly taken for art itself, especially if it is covered over with facile faking and a voluptuous medley of colors. However, natural gift is only a prerequisite condition for art, or again a rough outline (*inchoatio naturalis*) of the artistic habitus. This inborn disposition is clearly indispensable; but without cultivation and a discipline which the ancients held should be long and patient and honest, it will never develop into art properly speaking. Thus art, like love, proceeds from a spontaneous instinct, and it must be cultivated like friendship; for it is a virtue like friendship" (*Art and Scholasticism*, 44).

THE HABIT OF ART

As much as O'Connor is concerned with self-discipline and personal writing habits, as we have seen above, she is even more interested in *the habit of art*. According to O'Connor, the artist is one who sees reality, understands what-is, and then is able to imitate it; as Aristotle said, "Art imitates nature."[86] Gilson explains this activity: "Man looks at the way God does things in nature in order to learn, as a good pupil, how to do his own works; but the two domains remain distinct because the works of nature are no works of art."[87] Only God can *create*, according to Thomas, but human beings can *make*, and art is the making of things according to right reason. The habit of art, then, is both about *knowing* and *making*. It is not simply about creating one's own world, universe, or reality, but about seeing reality as it is and imitating it, presenting what-is through what the artist makes. Christina Bieber Lake notes, "By exercising the habit of art, the artist finds meaning in things. By looking at the created world both through her eyes and the eyes of the church, she discovers that all being is beautiful, and she designs her work to participate in that beauty, to continue it."[88]

According to the habit of art, then, every work of art must be logical—not simply an expression of emotion or creativity but aligned through reason with reality. O'Connor offers a most insightful reflection:

> St. Thomas called art "reason in making." This is a very cold and very beautiful definition, and if it is unpopular today, this is because reason has lost ground among us. As grace and nature have been separated, so imagination and reason have been

---

86. Aristotle, *Physics*, in *Selections*, trans. Terence Irwin and Gail Fine (Indianapolis, IN: Hackett, 1995), 194a20.

87. Gilson, *Painting and Reality*, 291.

88. Christina Bieber Lake, *The Incarnational Art of Flannery O'Connor* (Macon, GA: Mercer University Press, 2005), 163.

separated, and this always means an end to art. The artist uses his reason to discover an answering reason in everything he sees. For him, to be reasonable is to find, in the object, in the situation, in the sequence, the spirit which makes it itself. This is not an easy or simple thing to do. It is to intrude upon the timeless, and that is only done by the violence of a single-minded respect for the truth.[89]

It is likely that O'Connor's observations above were inspired by Maritain, who notes that art "must be steeped in logic: not in the pseudo-logic of clear ideas, and not in the logic of knowledge and demonstration, but in working logic, always mysterious and disconcerting, the logic of the structure of the living and of the intimate geometry of nature."[90] This is not to deny the significant role of the passions or emotions in the life and work of the artist, but it is to say that "the intellect has primacy in the work of art."[91] In fact, Maritain argues that art has the ability to purify passions.[92]

Flannery O'Connor's Thomistic understanding of art and of being an artist were undeniably influenced by Jacques Maritain, and although she writes as a narrative artist and not as a philosopher, her following account of Maritain's thesis is highly philosophical and represents his thought well:

I think the answer to this is what Maritain calls "the habit of art." It is a fact that fiction writing is something in which the whole personality takes part—the conscious as well as the unconscious mind. Art is the habit of the artist; and habits have to be rooted deep in the whole personality. They have to be cultivated like any other habit, over a long period of time, by experience; and

---

89. *MM*, 82–83.
90. Maritain, *Art and Scholasticism*, 54.
91. Maritain, 53.
92. Maritain, 53.

teaching any kind of writing is largely a matter of helping the student develop the habit of art. I think this is more than just a discipline, although it is that; I think it is a way of looking at the created world and of using the senses so as to make them find as much meaning as possible in things.[93]

Two important truths are on display in this quotation. The first involves *looking* and the second involves *meaning*, and the two are related. In O'Connor's view, we first come to know things through our senses, and if one's ability to see is obscured or deficient in some way, then one's understanding will be distorted and one will miss out on the meaning of things—that is, the *true* meaning of things. The artist, according to O'Connor, must be able to see things clearly in order to present them clearly, according to how things actually are and what they mean. The artist makes things according to how they are by presenting the form of things in his or her art. Maritain explains, "If the delight in the beautiful work comes from a truth, it does not come from the truth of imitation as reproduction of things, it comes from the perfection with which the work expresses or manifests the form, in the metaphysical sense of this word, it comes from the truth of imitation as manifestation of form."[94] An essential element of the habit of art, then, is being able to see what-is and then being able to show what-is by making something that contains the form of what-is, while always remaining within the boundaries of what-is. O'Connor explains,

What the fiction writer will discover, if he discovers anything at all, is that he himself cannot move or mold reality in the interests of abstract truth. The writer learns, perhaps more quickly than the reader, to be humble in the face of what-is. What-is is all he has to do with; the concrete is his medium; and he will realize

93. *MM*, 101.
94. *MM*, 60.

eventually that fiction can transcend its limitations only by staying within them.[95]

At the heart of the habit of art is reality, or what O'Connor constantly refers to as *what-is*. Although Maritain was the major influence on O'Connor in regard to the habit of art, she also learned from William Lynch that "it is precisely as artist, and not despite his art, that he is a master of reality."[96] Lynch does not mean "master of reality" in the Cartesian sense that one conquers reality, but in the Thomistic sense that one becomes a master of seeing reality, of knowing reality, and then of presenting the form of reality in what one makes. In her review of Lynch's *The Image Industries*, O'Connor summarizes his thesis as being about "the task of reality against fantasy,"[97] which is another way of stating that the vocation of the artist is to remain within the boundaries of reality in order to make things well and according to right reason.

A CATHOLIC ARTIST WITH PROPHETIC VISION

In a journal entry dated April 14, 1947, Flannery O'Connor wrote the following: "I must write down that I am to be an artist. Not in the sense of aesthetic frippery but in the sense of aesthetic craftsmanship. . . . I want to be the best artist it is possible for me to be, under God."[98] O'Connor rejected the notion that her Catholic faith was a hindrance to her art; in fact, she believed that being a Catholic saved her "a couple of thousand years in learning to write."[99] She was convinced that her Catholicism allowed her to see reality, which is most necessary for an artist whose job it is to make things according to right reason. But O'Connor was

95. *MM*, 145–146.
96. Lynch, *Image Industries*, 34.
97. *PG*, 75.
98. *PJ*, 29.
99. *HB*, 114.

also convinced that Catholicism only made one a better artist if one was first an artist, and this notion deserves some attention.

In her essay "Catholic Novelists," O'Connor states, "A novelist is, first of all, a person who has been given talent to do a particular thing."[100] She delivered stinging critiques of those who attempted to use fiction as a means toward evangelization rather than practice the art of storytelling for its own sake. O'Connor thought that artists should make art, and evangelists should evangelize, and that if somehow an artist's work contributed to the work of evangelization, it was not because the artist was making an effort to evangelize but because the artist was making good art. She explains her understanding of the artist's vocation: "The artist has his hands full and does his duty if he attends to his art. He can safely leave evangelizing to the evangelists. He must first of all be aware of his limitations as an artist—for art transcends its limitations only by staying within them."[101]

There is an important principle at work in here, and it is that "not all are called to be artists in the specific sense of the term."[102] O'Connor argues that "the Catholic novelist doesn't have to be a saint; he doesn't even have to be a Catholic; he does, unfortunately, have to be a novelist."[103] As we have seen, O'Connor is both an artist and a Catholic, and although she recognizes a definite relation between her art and her Catholicism, she also insists on holding the distinction for the good of the Church and for the good of art and artists.

John Paul II, in his *Letter to Artists*, echoes Flannery O'Connor's point when he writes, "It is one thing for human beings to be the authors of their own acts, with responsibility for their moral value; it is another to be an artist, able, that is, to respond to *the demands of art* and faithfully accept art's specific dictates.

100. *MM*, 170.
101. *MM*, 171.
102. John Paul II, *Letter to Artists* (Boston: Pauline Books and Media, 1999), §2.
103. *MM*, 172.

This is what makes the artist capable of producing *objects*, but it says nothing as yet of his moral character."[104] So, according to Flannery O'Connor and John Paul II, an artist can make good art without being Catholic; or, if he is Catholic, can make good art without being a *good* Catholic, because the goodness of art is found in the objects made and not in the moral fiber or moral actions of the artist. But for both O'Connor and John Paul II, the artist always needs to be an artist.[105] This principle is Thomistic in that it focuses on what is essential to the nature of an artist.

There is very strong evidence that O'Connor learned this principle or at least deepened her understanding of it by her reading of Victor White's *God and the Unconscious*,[106] a book she references four different times in *The Habit of Being*. In a letter to Betty Hester dated December 25, 1959, O'Connor writes,

> I have found a lucky find for me in St. Thomas's sections of the *Summa* and the *De Veritate* on prophecy. I haven't seen them in the original because that section of the *Summa* is not in the Modern Library volume I have and I don't have the *De Veritate*; this is only from a commentary of Victor White, O.P. Anyway, St. T. says that prophetic vision is dependent on the *imagination* of the prophet, not his moral life; and that there is a distinction that must be made between having prophetic vision and the proclamation of the same. More of this later.[107]

This principle that one does not have to be good (morally speaking) in order to *do* good (in speaking a prophetic word or in making good art) is constantly on display in O'Connor's fiction

---

104. John Paul II, *Letter to Artists*, §2.

105. For an example of this reality, see Damian Ference, "Springsteen's Catechist: Flannery O'Connor's Influence on Bruce Springsteen," *Flannery O'Connor Review* 17 (2019): 129–146.

106. Victor White, *God and the Unconscious* (London: Fontana Books, 1952), 127.

107. *HB*, 367.

and in her letters, and it appears that she pulls it directly from White's text:

> More shocking still perhaps to the sweet reasonableness is St. Thomas's emphasis that prophetic revelation is as such independent of good morals—let alone of personal sanctity (*De Ver.* Xii. 5: 1-11. 172, 4). For prophecy is required, he says tersely, not "goodness of morals" (*bonitas morum*) but "goodness of imagination" (*bonitas imaginationis*). . . . Aristotle, St. Thomas reminds us, had already remarked on the fact that it is not the best people who have the best dreams.[108]

O'Connor sees a relation between the artist and the prophet: each must do the work essential to his vocation, but neither the artist nor the prophet need be morally virtuous or holy for that work to be accomplished. O'Connor thinks that the true artist sees with what she calls *prophetic vision*, and she thinks it comes with tremendous responsibility. She explains,

> The fiction writer should be characterized by his kind of vision. His kind of vision is prophetic vision. Prophecy, which is dependent on the imaginative and not the moral faculty, need not be a matter of predicting the future. The prophet is a realist of distances, and it is this kind of realism that goes into great novels. It is the realism which does not hesitate to distort appearances in order to show a hidden truth.[109]

Although Flannery O'Connor was indeed a devout Catholic, she did not close her eyes and trust the Church to see for her, but knew that she had tremendous responsibility as an artist to hone her own craft and to *look*,[110] and then "to reproduce, with words,"

108. White, *God and the Unconscious*, 127.
109. *MM*, 179.
110. See chapter 3 for more on the relation between looking and knowing.

what she saw.[111] She believed that it was the job of the artist to see, and then to make, according to right reason, in order to allow others to see what she first saw with her prophetic vision.

LITERATURE AS A HANDMAID TO PHILOSOPHY

As a philosopher and theologian, St. Thomas Aquinas never wrote a treatise on art or aesthetics; however, he did compose beautiful hymns that are sung to this day within the Catholic liturgy. Among the most well-known are *O Salutaris Hostia* and *Tantum Ergo Sacramentum*, the latter of which is the only direct quote of Aquinas in O'Connor's fiction. In "A Temple of the Holy Ghost,"[112] two fourteen-year-old Catholic school girls, Susan and Joanne, enter into what might be called a "battle of hymns" on the front porch of their aunt's house with two Protestant boys, Cory and Wendell, who accompany their singing with guitar and harmonica. We enter the scene immediately after Wendell has sung two verses of "I've Found a Friend in Jesus." The story's protagonist, an unnamed twelve-year-old girl, observes all the action while standing on a barrel pushed between some bushes on the side of the house:

> The girls looked at each other and held their lips stiff so as not to giggle but Susan let out one anyway and clapped her hand on her mouth. The singer frowned and for a few seconds only strummed the guitar. Then he began "The Old Rugged Cross" and they listened politely but when he had finished they said, "Let us sing one!" and before he could start another, they began to sing with their convent-trained voices,
>
> > "*Tantum ergo Sacramentum*
> > *Veneremur Cernui:*

111. *MM*, 177.
112. Flannery O'Connor, "A Temple of the Holy Ghost," in *CS*, 236–248.

Et antiquum documentum
Novo cedat ritui:"

The child watched the boys' solemn faces turn with perplexed frowning stares at each other as if they were uncertain whether they were being made fun of.

"Praestet fides supplementum
Sensuum defectui
Genitori, Genitoque
Laus et jubilatio
Salus, honor, virtus quoque . . ."

The boys' faces were dark red in the gray-purple light. They looked fierce and startled.

"Sit et benedictio;
Procedenti ab utroque
Compar sit laudatio.
Amen."

The girls dragged out the Amen and then there was a silence.

"That must be Jew singing," Wendell said and began to tune the guitar.

The girls giggled idiotically but the child stamped her foot on the barrel. "You big dumb ox!" she shouted. "You big dumb Church of God ox!" she roared and fell off the barrel and scrambled up and shot around the corner of the house as they jumped from the banister to see who was shouting.[113]

---

113. *CS*, 240–241.

I have noted this extended quotation for two reasons. First, to highlight the fact that although Aquinas himself was a philosopher and theologian, not an artist *per se*, he recognized the need to convey truth through other forms of expression beyond dialectic—in his own case, through the poetic art of hymnody. A philosophical or theological truth that can be stated can also be demonstrated—often more powerfully—in a story, poem, or song, as Plato, Aristotle, and Aquinas all understood. Second, we can see in this passage O'Connor's admiration not only for the philosophical and theological acumen of Aquinas but also for his ability to compose beautiful hymns that have stood the test of time. O'Connor makes the connection abundantly clear in her protagonist's two exclamations of "big dumb ox," a clever and intentional nod to Aquinas' famous nickname.

In his introductory remarks to *A Political Companion to Flannery O'Connor*, Henry Edmondson notes, "Fiction may at times convey philosophical ideas in a way that philosophy cannot due to the limitations of philosophical discourse."[114] Although Aquinas' *Tantum Ergo* is religious poetry, not fiction, it shares in literature's ability to convey profound philosophical and theological truths without entering into explicit philosophical and theological discourse. This sort of thinking about poetry and literature as potential bearers of philosophical truth is at the heart of this book. Flannery O'Connor's fiction is not philosophy *per se*, but it is literature grounded in philosophical ideas, and as such it has the capacity to illustrate truth in a manner that supplements the work of the philosopher.

THE PHILOSOPHY OF INCARNATIONAL ART

In their recent work, *When Fiction and Philosophy Meet*, E. Jane Doering and Ruthann Knechel Johansen remind us that "the

---

114. Henry T. Edmondson, introduction to *A Political Companion to Flannery O'Connor*, ed. Henry T. Edmonson (Lexington, KY: The University Press of Kentucky, 2017), 10.

two thinkers to whom O'Connor refers most frequently in her essays and in her letters about her ideas on art, the artist, reality, and mystery are St. Thomas Aquinas and Jacques Maritain."[115] In particular, both Aquinas and Maritain convinced O'Connor of the necessity of making *incarnational art*. This particular kind of art is unique to Christianity, in that Christians believe that God became a human being in the person of Jesus Christ—that is, that God took on flesh, God became incarnate. Matter, then, according to Catholic Christianity, is never understood as bad, but as good, not only because it is part of creation, but because God chose to take on flesh in the person of Jesus Christ. Therefore, if God has mediated himself in history to humanity in and through matter, with a human body, and not as an abstraction but as the Incarnation, then the best kind of art, according to O'Connor, will follow that model and be incarnational; it will be concrete and sensual.[116]

Throughout her letters and her essays, O'Connor repeats a major principle of her incarnational art: *the narrative artist should show, not tell.* Here are some varying iterations of the principle:

- "Show these things and you don't have to say them."[117]
- "The fiction writer doesn't state, he shows, renders."[118]
- "Fiction has to be largely presented rather than reported."[119]
- "Fiction writing is very seldom a matter of saying things; it is a matter of showing things."[120]

---

115. E. Jane Doering and Ruthann Knechel Johansen, *When Fiction and Philosophy Meet: A Conversation with Flannery O'Connor and Simone Weil* (Macon, GA: Mercer University Press, 2019), 58.

116. By "sensual" here I mean in the Aristotelian-Thomistic tradition of knowledge beginning in the senses.

117. *HB*, 84.

118. *HB*, 143.

119. *MM*, 73–74.

120. *MM*, 93.

God did not simply tell the world that he was love; he showed the world that he was love in the Incarnation of Jesus Christ. In the same way, O'Connor thinks that the best art will be incarnational, in that it will be known not abstractly but concretely. In "The Nature and Aim of Fiction," O'Connor stresses the artist's need to recognize the goodness of matter and to work within the reality of being, never apart from it:

> The Manicheans separated spirit and matter. To them all material things were evil. They sought pure spirit and tried to approach the infinite directly without any mediation of matter. This is also pretty much the modern spirit, and for the sensibility infected with it, fiction is hard if not impossible to write because fiction is so very much an incarnational art.[121]

O'Connor's Roman Catholicism is incarnational and sacramental; it is a faith that insists that God has worked in and through his creation to the point of taking on flesh, becoming incarnate. This faith also insists that God continues to communicate himself through water, oil, bread, wine, and human bodies in the seven sacraments of the Catholic Church, and it should not come as a surprise that this sacramental and incarnational worldview profoundly influences O'Connor's philosophy of art.

O'CONNOR'S WRITINGS

Flannery O'Connor is best known for her fiction, consisting of thirty-two short stories and two novels, *Wise Blood* and *The Violent Bear It Away*. O'Connor's essays, which are mostly comprised of lectures she delivered to "university groups, Catholics, Georgians, [and] writing classes,"[122] are found in *Mystery and Manners*, selected and edited by O'Connor's dear friends Sally and Robert Fitzgerald, who note,

121. *MM*, 67–68.
122. *MM*, viii.

It is clear that discourse, even here, had secondary importance for the author, who felt that her principal calling was to write stories and that her stories contained what she had to offer. On the other hand, she knew that those concentrations of experience and invention had their place in real contexts, literary, regional, and religious, that could and should be examined and discussed. She had a gift for this, too. Her papers not only complement her stories but are valuable and even seminal in themselves.[123]

The majority of O'Connor's published letters are found in *The Habit of Being*, selected and edited by Sally Fitzgerald. A new batch of O'Connor's letters has recently been published in two separate volumes, one edited by Benjamin B. Alexander[124] and the other by Christine Flanagan,[125] while other, unpublished letters are housed in the Flannery O'Connor archive at Emory University. In addition to writing fiction, prose, and letters, O'Connor also wrote book reviews for her diocesan newspaper, which are contained in *The Presence of Grace*:

> She chose a broad range of works, reviewing 143 titles in 120 sep-
> arate reviews between 1956 and 1964. The works were distributed
> as follows: 50 religious and homiletic, 21 biographies and saints'
> lives, 19 sermons and theology, 17 fiction, 8 literary criticism,
> 6 psychology, 6 philosophy and science, 4 history, 4 letters, 4
> periodicals, 3 intellectual history and criticism, 1 art criticism.[126]

In the last decade, two personal journals belonging to O'Connor have also been published. The first, *A Prayer Journal*,

---

123. *MM*, ix–x.
124. Flannery O'Connor et al., *Good Things Out of Nazareth: The Uncollected Letters of Flannery O'Connor and Friends*, ed. Benjamin B. Alexander (New York: Convergent, 2019).
125. Flannery O'Connor and Caroline Gordon, *The Letters of Flannery O'Connor and Caroline Gordon*, ed. Christine Flanagan (Athens, GA: The University of Georgia Press, 2018).
126. *PG*, 3.

is a collection of prayers written by O'Connor from January 1946 to September 1947, while she was living in Iowa City as a graduate student at the Writer's Workshop. The second, "Higher Mathematics," was published in the Fall 2017 issue of *Image* and contains twenty-nine journal entries from December 29, 1943, through February 6, 1944, written during her time at Georgia State College for Women. And although she did not write *Conversations with Flannery O'Connor*, this book does contain O'Connor's own words in transcript form, edited by Rosemary Magee, who notes that "these interviews add a new dimension to an appreciation of O'Connor and, as a result, to an understanding of her fiction."[127] Finally, in 2010, a book of cartoons drawn by O'Connor for her college newspaper was published in a collection titled *The Cartoons of Flannery O'Connor at Georgia College*, and two years later a complete collection of her cartoons was released, simply titled *Flannery O'Connor: The Cartoons*.

O'CONNOR'S PHILOSOPHICAL INFLUENCES

Flannery O'Connor was an exceptionally well-read woman, and much of her personal library is accessible to scholars in Special Collections at Georgia College. In 1985, Arthur Kinney published *Flannery O'Connor's Library: Resources of Being*, a catalog of O'Connor's library with detailed accounts of any and all marks that O'Connor made in each book. Kinney explains,

> By our standards, she owned many books and kept them unusually well, with dust jackets intact even with heavy usage, and she talked to them, drawing lines in the margins, underlining, starring passages, checking (and even numbering) points seriatim, and writing marginalia of agreement, joy, bafflement, irritation,

---

127. Rosemary Magee, introduction to *Conversations with Flannery O'Connor* (Jackson, MS: University Press of Mississippi, 1987), viii.

scorn, or mockery. Together they illuminate the shape of her mind and some essential components of her reading interests.[128]

As impressive as this collection of 712 volumes is, it does not contain every book O'Connor read; indeed, it omits some of the books she cherished most, such as Romano Guardini's *The Lord*. Kinney reports that "Only 90 of the 130 books she reviewed are accounted for"[129] and that since O'Connor also borrowed books regularly from the Georgia College library, received books from the Atlanta library through the mail from Betty Hester, and "may have loaned other books that have never been returned,"[130] we do not have a complete account of the books that informed O'Connor's philosophy. Nonetheless, what we do have is rather significant.

It is absolutely certain that the writings of St. Thomas Aquinas had a profound influence on O'Connor's thought, as she references him constantly in her letters and papers,[131] on three occasions even referring to him by the very familiar "St. T."[132] However, it is difficult to determine how much of O'Connor's philosophy was formed by Thomas' own writings, as O'Connor's library is short on volumes of Aquinas himself. In fact, although Kinney lists eleven entries under "Aquinas, St. Thomas" in his index, only six of the books listed are the actual writings of Aquinas, and three of those six volumes make up O'Connor's copy of *De Veritate*. We do know that O'Connor's copy of *Introduction to Saint Thomas Aquinas*, containing some of the most salient sections of the *Summa theologiae* and *Summa contra Gentiles*, was the volume she claimed to have to read for twenty minutes every night, and

128. Arthur Kinney, *Flannery O'Connor's Library: Resources of Being* (Athens, GA: The University of Georgia Press, 1985), 5.
129. Kinney, 4.
130. Kinney, 5.
131. O'Connor mentions St. Thomas Aquinas twenty-three different times in *HB*.
132. *HB*, 110, 368, 370.

that editor Anton G. Pegis' introduction was heavily marked by O'Connor's pen. However, by O'Connor's own admission, much of what she knows of Thomas and his philosophy she gains through secondary sources, specifically Étienne Gilson, Jacques Maritain, Josef Pieper, Victor White, and Eric Voegelin, not to mention her preconciliar Catholic upbringing.

It serves well to conclude this section with two examples from O'Connor's letters where she mentions her reading of St. Thomas and Thomistic thinkers, and to allow her words to speak for themselves. In a letter to Fr. John McCown dated May 9, 1956, O'Connor writes, "The novel is an art form and when you use it for anything other than art, you pervert it. I didn't make this up. I got it from St. Thomas (via Maritain)."[133] And in a letter to Betty Hester she reports,

> If you are going to read 1500 pages of St. Thomas and 650 pages of Aristotle, you will at least be an ossified jellyfish when you get through—if such is possible. I am currently reading Étienne Gilson's *History of Christian Philosophy in the Middle Ages* and I am surprised to come across various answers to Simone Weil's questions to Fr. Perrin. St. Justin Martyr anticipated her in the 2nd century on the question of the Logos enlightening every man who comes into the world. This is really one of her central questions and St. Justin answered it in what I am sure would have been her own way. Gilson is a vigorous writer, more so than Maritain; the other thing I have read of his is *The Unity of Philosophical Experience*, which I am an admirer of.[134]

133. *HB*, 157.
134. *HB*, 107.

CHAPTER TWO

The Metaphysics of Flannery O'Connor

Our concern in this chapter is not the current debate over the nature of metaphysics or a survey of the history of metaphysics, but rather a speculative study of the role of metaphysics in the narrative art of Flannery O'Connor. For these purposes, we can assume the relevance of the traditional definition of the "science" of metaphysics as the study of being, since this is the understanding that O'Connor herself imbibed directly or indirectly from the Thomistic authors she frequently read.

As we have stated repeatedly, O'Connor is first and foremost a narrative artist and not a philosopher, yet her reading of philosophy affected her fiction in profound and remarkable ways. Gilson notes, "Philosophers start from art in the hope that its study will open new vistas on philosophical problems to them, whereas artists, when they philosophize, do so in the hope of clearing up for themselves difficulties inherent in their art."[1] Our task in this chapter, then, is not only to present a general understanding of O'Connor's fundamental view of reality and its foundational structures by studying her narrative art as philosophers, but also to study the way in which O'Connor's philosophizing clarifies her narrative art. To avoid any suspense, we should state from the start that O'Connor partakes in what Gilson calls "the rediscovery

1. Étienne Gilson, *Painting and Reality: The A.W. Mellon Lectures in the Fine Arts* (New York: Pantheon Books, 1957), x.

of the solid, down-to-earth realism of the classical metaphysics of being as interpreted by St. Thomas Aquinas."[2] However, whereas Aquinas intentionally places before any interested reader a highly sophisticated and systematic presentation of his approach to metaphysics, O'Connor's must be discovered by gleaning the various clues scattered across her fiction, letters, essays, lectures, book reviews, and journal entries.

GOD

It is abundantly clear that Flannery O'Connor believes in God; it is evident, therefore, that she thinks theism is philosophically reasonable. It is less apparent that she arrived at her belief through the kind of intellectual work proper to a philosopher or theologian such as Aquinas. She never offers demonstrative arguments for it, and at times it may even seem as if O'Connor has no intellectual grounding for her belief in God, stating, "When I ask myself how I know I believe, I have no satisfactory answer at all, no assurance at all, no feeling at all. I can only say with Peter, Lord I believe, help my unbelief. And all I can say about my love of God, is, Lord help me in my lack of it."[3] Yet O'Connor constantly references her Catholic faith as a credible authority grounding her philosophical and theological positions, and she never hesitates to encourage her friends, correspondents, and general audience to consider the intellectual tradition according to which she lives and in which she places her trust.[4] She confidently notes, "I am no disbeliever in spiritual purpose and no vague believer. I see from the standpoint of Christian orthodoxy. This means that for me the meaning of life is centered in our Redemption by Christ and what I see in the world I see in its relation to that."[5] O'Connor displays an edifying intellectual humility in that while doing her

2. Gilson, x.
3. *HB*, 92.
4. See O'Connor's letter to Cecil Dawkins (December 23, 1959) for a prime example (*HB*, 363–366).
5. *MM*, 32.

very best to explain what she knows and understands in matters of God and Christian faith, she also freely admits when a line of argumentation is beyond her area of expertise, as is on display in her words to Alfred Corn: "I find it reasonable to believe, even though these beliefs are beyond reason. If you are interested, the enclosed book [*Creative Evolution* by Teilhard de Chardin] will give you one general line of reasoning about why I do. I'm not equipped to talk philosophically; this man is."[6] She also acknowledges that belief in God and practicing one's Catholic faith constitute not a static but a dynamic reality, one grounded in truth but constantly opening up to a deeper understanding of things, as she notes in her letter to Betty Hester dated August 28, 1955: "What one has as a born Catholic is something given and accepted before it is experienced. I am only slowly coming to experience things that I have all along accepted."[7]

GOD'S EXISTENCE

Brian Davies notes that although from the modern point of view, Thomas has become "famous for thinking that the existence of God can be proved by a rational argument," in the context of his own time, he was "not at all worried about making out a case for God's existence."[8] Indeed, Davies notes, "It is most unlikely that he ever encountered an atheist in the modern sense. Nor does he maintain that anyone has an obligation to weigh up the evidence for theism."[9] Aquinas thinks it is perfectly proper to take God's existence for granted as a matter of supernatural faith, which is the position of Flannery O'Connor and, for that matter, the vast majority of believing Christians.[10] However, although Thomas may not be worried about making a philosophical case for God's

6. *HB*, 479–480.
7. *HB*, 97.
8. Brian Davies, *The Thought of Thomas Aquinas* (New York: Oxford University Press, 1992), 21.
9. Davies, 21.
10. See Davies, 22.

existence, "at another level he takes [the question] very seriously. And his answer is unequivocal. His view is that God exists and that reasons can be given for saying so—reasons which ought to be acceptable to any fair-minded or impartial person."[11] Flannery O'Connor was certainly familiar with Thomas Aquinas' teaching on God, as Marion Montgomery reports that they read the same copy of the *Summa*, and they would likely have commenced their study at the beginning of Aquinas' classic text.[12]

In the very first question and the very first article of the *Summa theologiae*, Thomas asks whether another science is needed beyond that of philosophy. In his answer, he offers the initial part of his famous argument for the harmony of faith and reason: "It was necessary for man's salvation that there should be a knowledge revealed by God, besides the philosophical sciences investigated by human reason."[13] Thomas explains that humans naturally desire to know the first cause directly, but intimacy with God is beyond the access of natural human reason and is therefore dependent upon grace and divine revelation.[14] He thinks there are certain truths about God (including God's existence) that can be known to human beings by reason alone, but that God also willed to make these truths known by divine revelation, since otherwise they "would only be known by a few, and that after a long time, and with the admixture of many errors."[15] While some individuals might manage to grasp God's existence and attributes by reason alone, the majority of human beings do not—or cannot—prioritize the devotion of time and intellectual effort

---

11. Davies, 22.

12. Marion Montgomery, in *At Home with Flannery O'Connor: An Oral History*, ed. Bruce Gentry and Craig Amason (Milledgeville, GA: The Flannery O'Connor-Andalusia Foundation, 2012), 59.

13. *ST* 1.1.1.

14. The grace of faith, as Aquinas explains it in *ST* 2-2.1–2, is adhered to not from merely natural motives but from supernatural motives. As a good Catholic, O'Connor seems to have a non-reflective instinct of this reality.

15. *ST* 2-2.1–2.

required to do so; therefore, another science besides philosophy is necessary. Thomas explains,

> In order that the salvation of men might be brought about more fitly and more surely, it was necessary that they be taught divine truths by divine revelation. It was therefore necessary that, besides the philosophical sciences investigated by reason, there should be a sacred science by way of revelation.[16]

According to Aquinas, human beings can come to know that God exists and that he has certain attributes because such knowledge is accessible through human reason (philosophy) *and also* because God has revealed these truths about himself to humanity through divine revelation. Flannery O'Connor—and most people who believe in God's existence and in his divine attributes—do so not because they themselves have done all the philosophical work of making arguments and coming to such conclusions, but because they believe what God has revealed about himself to be true and find this revelation to be reasonable. Regarding O'Connor specifically, her trust in the credible authority of the Catholic Church to mediate God's revealed truth precedes and complements her reliance on her own reason.[17]

In the second question of the *Summa*, Thomas presents three articles regarding God's existence. The first asks whether the existence of God is self-evident, the second considers whether God's existence can be demonstrated, and the third contains

---

16. *ST* 2-2.1-2.

17. "The good Catholic acts upon the beliefs (assumptions if you want to call them that) that he receives from the Church and he does this in accordance with his degree of intelligence, his knowledge of what the Church teaches, and the grace, natural & supernatural, that he's been given" (*HB*, 345). "I believe what the Church teaches—that God has given us reason to use and that it can lead us toward a knowledge of him, through analogy; that he has revealed himself in history and continues to do so through the Church, and that he is present (not just symbolically) in the Eucharist on our altars. To believe all this I don't take any leap into the absurd. I find it reasonable to believe, even though these beliefs are beyond reason" (*HB*, 479).

Thomas' famous five "ways" for God's existence.[18] O'Connor certainly would have been familiar with this well-known section of the *Summa*, yet we have no evidence that she took great interest in these arguments. Nowhere in O'Connor's canon does she make an argument for God's existence, and, as we have seen, Aquinas affirms that she need not do so.[19] Demonstrating rational proofs for God's existence is the proper task of a philosopher; as a narrative artist, O'Connor knows her task is to tell stories. So she trusts St. Thomas and, even more, the teaching authority of the Catholic Church to tell her the truth about God and the world:

> Catholics believe that Christ left the Church with a teaching authority and that this teaching authority is protected by the Holy Ghost; in other words that in matters of faith and morals the Church cannot err, that in these matters she is Christ speaking in time. So you can see that I don't find it an infringement of my independence to have the Church tell me what is true and what is not in regard to faith and what is right and what is wrong in regard to morals. Certainly I am no fit judge. If left to myself, I certainly wouldn't know how to interpret Romans IX. I don't believe Christ left us to chaos.[20]

We recall that in graduate school, O'Connor referred to herself as a "thirteenth century Catholic," and perhaps one way to understand this identification is to note that in the thirteenth century it was virtually impossible not to believe in God.[21] It is likely, therefore, that O'Connor never bothers to offer rational

18. The five "ways to God" or "proofs of God's existence" are as follows: *motion, causality, necessity, gradation,* and *governance of the world* (*ST* 1.2.3). Excellent summaries and commentaries on the five ways can be found in a number of sources, but those of Wippel, Davies, and Feser are especially good.

19. "Nevertheless, there is nothing to prevent a man, who cannot grasp a proof, from accepting, as a matter of faith, something which in itself is capable of being scientifically known and demonstrated" (*ST* 1.2.2).

20. *HB*, 489.

21. Charles Taylor, *A Secular Age* (Cambridge, MA: The Belknap Press of Harvard University Press, 2007), 25.

proofs for God's existence because she thinks, along with the Psalmist, that "fools say in their hearts, 'There is no God'" (Ps. 53:1),[22] and, as Alfred Corn reports, "She was not easily tolerant of people's foolishness."[23]

GOD AS CREATOR

Before O'Connor's philosophical and theological positions were influenced by Thomas Aquinas, her initial intellectual formation came by way of her Catholic upbringing, particularly the liturgy and prayers of the Church and the basic teachings found in the *Baltimore Catechism*. For instance, the very first line of the Apostles' Creed states, "I believe in God, the Father almighty, Creator of heaven and earth."[24] God's existence is affirmed as well as his unity, the first person of the Trinity is named and given the attribute of omnipotence, and he is identified as the one who creates (everything visible and invisible).[25] And in the very first lesson in the *Baltimore Catechism*, entitled "On the End of Man," the first two questions are as follows:

1. Q. Who made the world?
   A. God made the world.

---

22. Cf. *ST* 1.2.1. (In the *sed contra*, Thomas cites Psalm 53 as evidence that the claim "God exists" is not self-evident. It is a rare example of humor in the *Summa*, but perhaps one with which O'Connor was familiar.)

23. Alfred Corn, in *At Home with Flannery O'Connor*, 50.

24. *The Roman Missal* (New Jersey: Catholic Book Publishing Co., 2010), 379.

25. Louise Abbot shares this anecdote: "Well, talking about books became a very prominent part of our relationship. I thought I was a fairly good reader. But, in all honesty, when I read the collection *A Good Man Is Hard to Find*, I really couldn't figure out whose side she was on. And at that time, I was a thorough-going agnostic and had felt that I was going to meet a fellow traveler, and she set me straight right away. And I'm sure my face was burning, I was so embarrassed. She set me very straight, reciting the Apostles' Creed to me. 'I believe that,' then recited. She recited the entire Apostles' Creed, and I was in a rocking chair, and she was in one, but I can tell you, I stopped rocking, I wanted to slink away" (Abbot, in *At Home with Flannery O'Connor*, 8).

2. Q. Who is God?

A. God is the Creator of heaven and earth, and of all things.[26]

These simple but important theses from the Creed and the catechism would have formed O'Connor's understanding of God from a very young age. Their frequent repetition in the context of liturgical practice and religious instruction seems to have naturally imparted to the child Mary Flannery that certain metaphysical premises—God exists, and he is Creator—could be taken for granted in her worldview. As she matured, O'Connor learned how the teaching of the Church supported and deepened the basic formulations she had long accepted. Although O'Connor may not have depended upon philosophical arguments to ground her own belief in God as the Creator of heaven and earth, she likely would have become familiar with Thomas' account of God and Creation in his response to question 44 of the *Summa*:

> It must be said that everything, that in any way is, is from God. For whatever is found in anything by participation must be caused in it by that to which it belongs essentially, as iron becomes heated by fire. Now it has been shown above, when treating of the divine simplicity, that God is self-subsisting being itself, and also that subsisting being can only be one; just as, if whiteness were self-subsisting, it would be one, since whiteness is multiplied by its recipients. Therefore all beings other than God are not their own being, but are beings by participation. Therefore, it must be that all things which are diversified by the diverse participation of being, so as to be more or less perfect, are caused by one First Being, Who possesses being most perfectly.[27]

26. *Saint Joseph Baltimore Catechism: The Truths of Our Catholic Faith Clearly Explained and Illustrated* (New York: Catholic Book Publishing Co., 1969), Lesson One, Questions 1–2.

27. *ST* 1.44.1.

Within this response, Thomas makes an argument for God as the sheer act of existence, for the unity and simplicity of God, and for the claim that anything that has being does so because it participates in God. According to Thomas, human beings and other animals can "make," but only God can create because creation always implies the notion of *ex nihilo*.[28] Human beings and animals can build and make from what is already in existence, while God alone brings things into existence by creating from nothing.

In addition to Aquinas himself, O'Connor's reading of Étienne Gilson also influenced her understanding of God as Creator, specifically in what is known as Gilson's "metaphysics of Exodus."[29] According to Gilson, the God who revealed himself to Moses (Exod. 3:14) as "I AM"—the first cause, the One who is pure act, whose essence is to exist—is also the answer to modern man's existential questions about being. Anything that has being, that has existence, does so only because it participates in the One who is existence itself, the Creator who is uncreated, the One who *is*.

As much as O'Connor may have been familiar with Thomas' arguments for God as Creator—they are all contained in her Modern Library copy of the *Summa*—an important aspect of O'Connor's Hillbilly Thomism is that she trusts Catholic thinkers, and St. Thomas in particular, to provide proper philosophical arguments for God's existence and for God as Creator, and she accepts them as valid and true. She is quite comfortable simply asserting such positions without making actual philosophical arguments for them.

Within two weeks' time, in January of 1956, O'Connor wrote two important letters to her friend Betty Hester in which she makes some important distinctions about her understanding of God as Creator. First, she notes, "I am not a pantheist and do

28. See Davies, *Thought of Thomas Aquinas*, 34.
29. See Étienne Gilson, *The Christian Philosophy of St. Thomas Aquinas*, trans. L.K. Shook (Notre Dame, IN: University of Notre Dame Press, 1994), 84–95.

not think of the creation as God, but as made and sustained by God."[30] Spinoza championed the theory that God and nature are one. O'Connor rejects this position outright and explains her own position: creation is not God; rather, it comes from God and is sustained by God, meaning that God is something other (and greater) than his creation. O'Connor is making a philosophical assertion, not an argument, but she is well aware that the arguments explaining and defining this distinction have been made by Thomas.

Creation, Matter and Form, Substance and Accidents

In the second chapter of Genesis, the biblical author recounts that "the LORD God formed man from the dust of the ground, and breathed into his nostrils the breath of life; and the man became a living being."[31] Philosophically speaking, the author of Genesis points to the reality that living things are composed of a visible and an invisible part—"dust and breath" was taken by the medieval theologians to be a poetic way of saying body and soul, matter and form. This biblical account is a helpful example in understanding the way in which O'Connor's metaphysics was informed, not strictly through reading medieval philosophy, but often through (biblical) narrative, which in the Catholic tradition is understood to be latent with ontological truth.

In *De Anima*, Aristotle argues that all living things have souls and that souls have different powers depending on the type of living thing; Aquinas readily accepts this position. The soul is the form of the body of a living thing, according to Aquinas; it makes a living thing what it is.[32] A human being is a body-soul composite, while a human corpse is, properly speaking, no longer a human body—without a soul, without form, without life, it is a material substrate that was a living body. The same can be said of the

30. *HB*, 126.
31. Gen. 2:7.
32. *ST* 1.75.1.

carcass of a dog or a peacock, although a human soul is immortal while the souls of animals and plants are not. Nonliving things also have invisible parts or forms, although they are not considered "souls," since such things lack life. For example, a rock or a cloud would be said to have a form but not a soul, yet both rocks and clouds still have material potency and component parts that are united within a whole that provides *substantial unity*—that is, they are composed of matter and form.

This matter/form, visible/invisible understanding of the world is more metaphysically robust than the Cartesian, Spinozan, or Comtean approaches to reality. For Aquinas' view of things is not mechanistic, materialistic, or positivistic—philosophical approaches to reality that limit human understanding to attributes that can be measured by the natural sciences. The Thomistic approach to reality is forever and always imbued with the study of being, which cannot be measured by the natural sciences.

In addition to this distinction between matter and form, Thomas also follows Aristotle in making a distinction between *substance* and *accidents*. In the Thomistic tradition, substance is *the thing itself*, while the accidents are not *what* but *how* a thing is, or *how much*, or *where*, etc.[33] Aristotle and Thomas make a further distinction between *primary substance* and *secondary substance*. Primary substance refers to a concrete, particular instance of something, a given existing object on whose specificity all other senses of *be* or *what is* with respect to it depend (e.g., this particular woman, this particular peacock); while secondary substances are the genera of the primary substance (e.g., rational animal, animal), so that the universal is known through the particular.[34] Aristotle and Thomas' prioritization of primary substance (i.e., concrete and particular things)—rather than prioritizing universals and

33. See Aristotle, *Categories* 4.1b25–2a11, in *Selections*, trans. Terence Irwin and Gail Fine (Indianapolis, IN: Hackett, 1995); John F. Wippel, *The Metaphysical Thought of Thomas Aquinas: From Finite Being to Uncreated Being* (Washington, DC: The Catholic University of America Press, 2000), 204–206.
34. See Aristotle, *Categories* 5.2a12–19.

abstractions—illuminates the concreteness of O'Connor's vision and her focus on particularity. This prioritization of substance coupled with the matter/form distinction accounts for what has been termed O'Connor's "sacramental vision" and the "Christian realism" in her narrative art, which particularizes materiality without succumbing to materialism.[35]

The next chapter will present a thorough study of Thomistic epistemology as it relates to O'Connor, but at this point it is worth noting a basic truth about human understanding according to Thomas, since doing so offers insight into his metaphysics. Because human beings are body-soul composites, they come to know the world in both a sensate-animal and intellectual-personal way simultaneously, according to their material and immaterial composition, and according to the substance/accident distinction.[36] Substantial things in the world have both material and formal components, and human beings come to know what a thing is through the perception of both. For example, when one sees a peacock, one sees a peacock of a particular size, in a particular place, in a particular position, acting in a particular way, but the knowledge one has of "peacock" itself is not something that is particular (although *this* peacock is particular), but is rather a recognition of a universal (through abstraction)—the concept "peacock"—which in itself is not material but immaterial or spiritual; this immaterial, universal concept allows us to grasp the form of peacock, which is common to every individual substance of this kind. According to Thomas, humans come to know the world and substances in the world as composite beings, meaning that both their bodies and souls—the visible and invisible parts of themselves—are involved in cognition, thereby affording them insight, beyond what can be measured by the natural sciences,

---

35. See section 2.3.3 for a review of O'Connor's understanding of modernity's distrust of the concrete.

36. "That which is received is received according to the mode of the receiver" (*ST* 1.75.5).

into the reality of how things exist, participate in existence, are distinct from other things that exist, and relate to the cause of existence.

As we conclude this section, it may prove helpful to offer a brief explanation of how these metaphysical realities operate in what O'Connor called "the center of existence for me"[37]—that is, the Eucharist. Flannery O'Connor believed in the doctrine of *transubstantiation*, which is the term Catholics use to explain the metaphysical change that takes place at Mass when the bread and wine become the Body and Blood of Jesus Christ, not just symbolically, but actually. Transubstantiation is a mystery of faith, but it can be understood by appealing to a robust Thomistic metaphysics as a mystery that the Creator can enact by his omnipotence, without acting in "contradiction" with the ordinary structure of reality.[38] This basic idea of mystery present in the midst of the natural world that the Creator sustains in being and that in some way expresses the Creator is essential to the metaphysics of Hillbilly Thomism.

According to Aquinas, "bread" is the substance of the object that is mostly white, unleavened, on a paten, composed of wheat and water, is a little bigger than a half-dollar, tastes bland, is made by cloistered nuns, and is pulled from a package of other hosts just like it from a small refrigerator in a sacristy. In this case, the bread is a substantial artifact, a concrete being with ontological unity, in which whiteness or size are present as properties ("accidents"). The same can be said about the wine. The substance of wine is what it is: an artificial being, having a unity and a nature, composed of properties, like its quantity, qualitative taste, and so forth. This is why we can also speak of the wine as being red, cold, from the same fridge as the hosts, currently in a cruet, about to be poured

37. *HB*, 125.
38. Although Catholics have always believed that Jesus is truly present in the Eucharist, it was Thomas Aquinas who clarified this teaching with the assistance of Aristotelian metaphysics.

into a chalice, and having a dry, not fruity, taste. But the wine essentially as a unified being is not simply identical with these properties that we use to describe it; wine is the substance, while these properties are the accidents that inhere in the substance or pertain to it. What Catholics believe happens at every validly celebrated Mass is that through the power of the Holy Spirit acting in concord with the words of the priest at the consecration, the substance "bread" and the substance "wine" actually change in being and essence so as to become another substance—namely, the Body and Blood of Jesus—while the nonsubstantial aspects (the accidents or quantitative and qualitative properties of bread and wine) remain, which we perceive in the Eucharist's shape, position, temperature, taste, etc.[39] The Eucharist is a direct encounter with Jesus as he is through these accidents here and now on the altar—there is no more bread. The only what-is, the only substance we encounter, is the very Body and Blood of Christ, indeed the whole Christ.

The Catholic doctrine of transubstantiation, then, presents a very particular example for thinking about Thomistic metaphysical distinctions. It does not pertain to a natural example but to something mysterious that God does by his omnipotence within the domain of creation and that is distinct in kind. The Catholic tradition teaches that only those who cooperate with the grace of supernatural faith are able to recognize the real (substantial) presence of Christ in the Eucharist, and consequently there is no merely philosophical way to demonstrate or disprove the reality of this mystery. However, this teaching not only does not contradict but in fact presupposes more generally a reasonable metaphysical understanding of natural realities that Thomas inherited from Aristotle. This is the idea that all material substances are composed of form and matter, and that correspondingly each substance possesses accidents, like qualities

---

39. Cf. Aristotle, *Categories* 4.1b25–2a4; Thomas Aquinas, *ST* 3.75.1–8.

and quantity, which are properties of its being. This is a doctrine with which O'Connor was most familiar and one that she believed most firmly. Moreover, the concrete and particular nature of the Eucharist offers a helpful image of the concrete and particular metaphysics of O'Connor's narrative art.[40]

Creation and the Four Causes

Aristotle is famous for his teaching on the four causes, which he presents in *Physics*[41] and *Metaphysics*[42] and which Aquinas re-presents in *On the Principles of Nature*[43] and in his commentaries on the *Physics*[44] and *Metaphysics*.[45] The four causes answer the most basic questions about the reality of things. Riding on the metaphysical principles of the previous section, the four causes answer questions both about matter and form, and although O'Connor never mentions the causes anywhere in her canon, it

40. In addition to this example of transubstantiation, another worthy example from O'Connor's own writings comes from her understanding of the unity of the Church in her July 18, 1956, letter to Dr. T.R. Spivey: "We mean entirely different things when we each say we believe the Church is Divine. You mean the invisible Church with somehow related to it many forms, whereas I mean one and one only visible Church. It is not logical to the Catholic to believe that Christ teaches through many visible forms all teaching contrary doctrine. You speak of the well-known facts of Christ's life—but these facts are hotly contested—the virgin birth, the resurrection, the very divinity of Christ. For us the one visible Church pronounces on these matters infallibly and we receive her doctrine whether subjectively it fits in with our surmises or not. We believe that Christ left the Church to speak for him, that it speaks with his voice, he the head and we the members. If Christ actually teaches through many forms then for fifteen centuries, he taught that the Eucharist was his actual body and blood and thereafter he taught part of his people that it was only a symbol. The Catholic can't live with this kind of contradiction" (*HB*, 341). O'Connor's Thomistic understanding of the nature of the Church rides on her belief in the one invisible form for the one visible Church.

41. Aristotle, *Physics*, trans. R.P. Hardie and R.K. Gaye (Oxford: Clarendon, 1930), 2.3.194b16–195a2.

42. Aristotle, *Metaphysics*, trans. W.D. Ross (Oxford: Clarendon, 1930), 5.2.1013a24–35.

43. Thomas Aquinas, *On the Principles of Nature*, in *Opuscula I Treatises*, trans. Cyril Vollert et. al. (Green Bay, WI: Aquinas Institute, 2018), c. 3.

44. Thomae Aquinatis, *Commentaria in octo libros Physicorum Aristotleis* (Romae: S.C. de Propaganda Fide, 1889), 3.5.1–11.

45. Thomas Aquinas, *Commentary on the Metaphysics of Aristotle*, trans. John P. Rowan (Chicago: Henry Regnery, 1961), 5.3.777–794.

is probable that she was familiar with them from her undergraduate philosophy courses at GSCW as well as from her reading of Gilson and Maritain. Her doctrine of symbolism, inherited in part from Victor White, also seems to be clearly influenced by formal and exemplary causality, while her doctrine of the sacraments demonstrates a sense of instrumental or efficient causality. Consequently, an understanding of the four causes, even an intuitive understanding or subconscious awareness, is helpful for understanding O'Connor's narrative art.

The four causes are *formal, material, efficient,* and *final.* The formal cause and the material cause deal directly with the content of the previous section, as the formal cause is what a thing is and the material cause deals with the matter that makes a thing what it is. For example, the formal cause of a copy of *Wise Blood* is "book." In this case, the being in question is an artifact. The form is concerned with the essential aspect of the thing, the "what-it-is" as a whole. The material cause is composed of those visible elements that constitute *Wise Blood* as it is: paper, pages, ink, spine, front and back covers, etc. The efficient cause answers the question about what brings something into being, so in the case of the copy of *Wise Blood*, the answer would be O'Connor, her editor, and the publishing house that printed the book. And the final cause answers the question about why a thing exists—that is, its end, its goal, its purpose. The copy of *Wise Blood* exists primarily to be read and enjoyed by the one who reads it.

Aristotle and Thomas both think that in combination, "these [four] causes provide a complete explanation of a thing."[46] According to Feser, this is not to say that once one has answered these foundational questions there are no further questions to ask, but it is to say that "the answers to [additional] questions will all be just further instances of material, formal, efficient, and final causes."[47]

46. Edward Feser, *Aquinas: A Beginner's Guide* (London: Oneworld, 2009), 16.
47. Feser, 16–17.

The shift that occurs in modern philosophy, particularly in Descartes, keeps human beings from access to formal cause and final cause as such, since Descartes deemed Aquinas' understanding of "natures"—those "secret energies" ascribed to bodies—to be confused and obscure.[48] To know what a thing is and what a thing is for is beyond the scope of Descartes' mathematically based epistemology, which limits human beings to the clear and distinct knowledge of only material cause and efficient cause.

As we mentioned at the beginning of this section, although O'Connor never writes specifically about the four causes, her writing displays a knowledge and understanding of this Aristotelian-Thomistic metaphysical doctrine. She writes in her opening lines to "Catholic Novelists and Their Readers,"

> Whenever I think of the Catholic novelist and his problems, I always remember the legend of St. Francis and the wolf of Gubbio. This legend has it that St. Francis converted a wolf. I don't know whether he actually converted this wolf or whether the wolf's character didn't just greatly improve after he met St. Francis. Anyway, he calmed down a good deal. But the moral of this story, for me at least, is that the wolf, in spite of his improved character, always remained a wolf.[49]

When O'Connor states the wolf always remained a wolf, she is understanding the wolf as a Thomist understands a wolf, acknowledging that although the wolf's behavior changes, the wolf does not become something other than what it is; the wolf's formal cause and final cause do not change. In Aristotelian-Thomistic terms, she is illustrating the act/potency distinction,[50] showing that what actually happens in the case of the wolf's "conversion" is that it

---

48. Étienne Gilson, *The Unity of Philosophical Experience* (San Francisco: Ignatius, 1999), 162.
49. *MM*, 169.
50. Aristotle, *Metaphysics* 1048b1–3.

becomes more of what it was supposed to be, by its nature, having its potential actualized through its encounter with St. Francis, rather than becoming something other than a wolf. The point of the metaphor is obvious: grace heals nature and does not destroy it. The saint is more human than others, not less.

We note that of the four causes, the two that are most important are also the most metaphysical: formal and final. Knowing what a thing is and what it is for takes philosophical precedence over its origin or material composition. For example, if someone walking along a riverside happens upon a three-month-old baby lying in a papyrus basket lined with bitumen and pitch caught up in a cluster of reeds, the one finding this baby does not need to know who the parents of this child are (efficient) or anything about human anatomy (material) to know that this baby is a fellow human being (formal) who needs to be rescued in order to survive (final). Or, to take a less dramatic example, a person seeking the proper tool to drive a nail into a wall needs first and foremost to know what a hammer is (formal) and what a hammer is for (final). Whether the hammer in one's garage was made in the United States of America or Mexico or China (efficient), and whether the hammer is made out of steel, aluminum, or brass (material), are much less important to the task than knowing that one is holding a hammer and not a handsaw. One can find a hammer and drive a nail without ever knowing who made the hammer or its material constitution.

Significantly, the two causes that hold metaphysical priority for Aristotle and Thomas—formal and final—are the same causes that Descartes initially considers inaccessible according to his method. O'Connor's narrative art, by contrast, insists that we can and must take all four causes into account if we are to understand reality; her fiction challenges the reader to practice a more complete metaphysics than the limitations of modernism permit.

GOD AS PERSONAL AND RELATIONAL

In her review of Eric Voegelin's *Order and History: Volume One*, O'Connor writes, "In the Hellenic world man was seeking God, in the Hebrew world God was seeking man. Real history begins when man accepts the God Who is, Who seeks him."[51] This notion of a personal and relational God is key to understanding O'Connor and her narrative art. Again, O'Connor does not take it upon herself to offer philosophical proofs for her belief in God, as she trusts Catholic philosophers, especially Thomas Aquinas, to make those arguments for her, but she does rely upon her own experience of being in relationship with God, which is on display in so much of her correspondence, interviews, her prayer journal, and her general "habit of being" as a practicing Catholic. In "Novelist and Believer," O'Connor makes a distinction between herself as a believer and other novelists who lack Christian belief. She writes,

> What I say here would be much more in line with the spirit of our times if I could speak to you about the experience of such novelists as Hemingway and Kafka and Gide and Camus, but all my own experience has been that of the writer who believes, again in Pascal's words, in the "God of Abraham, Isaac, and Jacob and not of the philosophers and scholars." This is an unlimited God and one who has revealed himself specifically. It is one who became man and rose from the dead. It is one who confounds the senses and the sensibilities, one known early on as a stumbling block. There is no way to gloss over this specification or to make it more acceptable to modern thought. This God is the object of ultimate concern and he has a name.[52]

51. *PG*, 60.
52. *MM*, 161.

O'Connor believes in the God who calls himself "I Am": the God who reveals himself to Moses in the burning bush; who becomes man, suffers, dies, and rises again; who says, "I am the way, and the truth, and the life."[53] The God O'Connor believes in is good[54] and noncompetitive.[55] When God reveals himself to Moses as "I Am" in the burning bush, although the bush was on fire, it was not consumed. The fire, symbolic of God, does not compete with, consume, or destroy the bush, which is symbolic of nature and creation, but the fire exists with the bush in a noncompetitive manner. The reason for this state of affairs is that God is not a being like other created beings, but God is Being itself. God is pure act, the first cause, the uncaused cause, and the Creator of all that is, and so to be in competition with his creation would mean being somehow in competition with himself, which is a contradiction.

O'Connor also believes in a God who desires to bring salvation to the human race, and she thinks that "the Catholic writer, insofar as he has the mind of the Church, will feel life from the standpoint of the central Christian mystery: that it has, for all its horror, been found by God to be worth dying for."[56] O'Connor believes these things on faith, but a faith that is in accord with reason, a faith that she shares with a most intelligent cast of thinkers, including Augustine, Aquinas, Guardini, Gilson, Maritain, and Edith Stein, which gives her the confidence to write, "I feel that if I were not a Catholic, I would have no reason to write, no reason to see, no reason ever to feel horrified or even to enjoy anything. I am a born Catholic, went to Catholic schools in my early years, and have never left or wanted to leave the Church."[57]

53. John 14:6.
54. *ST* 1.5.1–6.
55. Cf. Davies, *Thought of Thomas Aquinas*, 33–35; Robert Sokolowski, *The God of Faith and Reason: Foundations of Christian Theology* (Washington, DC: The Catholic University of America Press, 1995), 36.
56. *MM*, 146.
57. *HB*, 114.

As a child, Aquinas was fascinated with the question "What is God?"[58] O'Connor is less concerned with the question "What is God?" than with the question "Who is God?"—a question more of revelation and faith (although not at all unreasonable). The following entry from her prayer journal offers an important account of the way in which O'Connor understood herself to be in relationship with God, how O'Connor invested in that relationship, and how difficult she found it to remain faithful to that relationship within the academic culture of her time: "Dear God, I don't want to have invented my faith to satisfy my weakness. I don't want to have created God to my own image as they're so fond of saying. Please give me the necessary grace, oh Lord, and please don't let it be as hard to get as Kafka made it."[59]

O'Connor was convinced that belief in God in the twentieth century was certainly more difficult than it had been in the thirteenth century. She follows Gilson in thinking that this difficulty arises from a certain kind of post-Enlightenment scientism, since Descartes appeals to God primarily as the foundation of his study of physics in the extended world, and Spinoza equates God with nature, abolishing any distinction between God and creation.[60]

Davies claims that Aquinas never encountered an atheist in the modern sense,[61] but O'Connor was personally acquainted with a host of modern atheists, especially in her artistic community, and she corresponded with many of them. She perceived herself to be in the minority, stating, "The general intelligent reader today is not a believer."[62] Yet she found it both reasonable and right to believe in a relational God, although she readily acknowledged that such belief was not without difficulty. In one of her most compelling letters, written to her friend Louise Abbot, O'Connor

58. Davies, *Thought of Thomas Aquinas*, 40.

59. *PJ*, 17–18.

60. Jonathan I. Israel, *Radical Enlightenment: Philosophy and the Making of Modernity 1650–1750* (Oxford: Oxford University Press, 2001), 162.

61. Davies, *Thought of Thomas Aquinas*, 21.

62. *MM*, 181.

makes her case for belief in a personal and relational God while at the same time revealing the difficulty of such belief in a modern age:

> What people don't realize is how much religion costs. They think faith is a big electric blanket, when of course it is the cross. It is much harder to believe than not to believe. If you feel you can't believe, you must at least do this: keep an open mind. Keep it open toward faith, keep wanting it, keep asking for it, and leave the rest to God.[63]

Robert Giroux, O'Connor's editor and friend, once said of her, "She was 100% Catholic, philosophically speaking."[64] This pithy quotation is a worthy summary of O'Connor's understanding of God and his creation, as the Hillbilly Thomist follows the orthodox formulations of Catholic Christianity and finds it reasonable to do so, even if at times doing so may prove to be difficult and unpopular. But O'Connor thought that the alternative to the Catholic view of things would eventually lead one down a road to nihilism, so in that regard, according to O'Connor, the truly unreasonable position would be to hold that God did not exist or that God was dead.

NIETZSCHE AS A THOMISTIC FOIL

There are no books by Friedrich Nietzsche in Flannery O'Connor's personal library, and O'Connor mentions Nietzsche only twice by name in *The Habit of Being*, but she was well aware of the German thinker and his philosophy of nihilism.[65] Edmondson explains that O'Connor's introduction to Nietzsche would likely have been in her "Introduction to Modern Philosophy" course at

---

63. *HB*, 354.
64. Robert Giroux, in *At Home with Flannery O'Connor*, 90.
65. O'Connor did have a copy of Copleston's *St. Thomas and Nietzsche* in her library, along with a volume entitled *The Disinherited Mind: Essays in Modern German Literature and Thought*, but no titles by Nietzsche himself.

GSCW—the same course that introduced her to the thought of Descartes—by way of the primary text for that class, *The Making of the Modern Mind* by John Randall.[66] While O'Connor's reading of Nietzsche himself may have been limited, responding to his substantial influence on modern culture became a major theme of her work.

O'Connor once noted, "If you live today you breathe in nihilism. In or out of the Church, it's the gas you breathe. If I hadn't had the Church to fight it with or to tell me the necessity of fighting it, I would be the stinkingest logical positivist you ever saw right now."[67] This quotation suggests an inner dialogue in O'Connor of some importance in which she understands the influence of Nietzsche as either fueled by or as responding to the threat of nihilism. She clearly thinks this threat is compounded in our time by logical positivism (Comte) and is widespread in the general culture and even in the culture of the Church. Yet, at the same time, she claims that it is precisely the Church—and, we may argue, her Hillbilly Thomism—that keeps her from surrendering to these attractive and influential intellectual movements.

In an oft-quoted letter to Betty Hester dated July 20, 1955, O'Connor offers a striking metaphor for her understanding of Nietzschean philosophy:

> The moral sense has been bred out of certain sections of the population, like the wings have been bred off certain chickens to produce more white meat on them. This is a generation of wingless chickens, which I suppose is what Nietzsche meant when he said God was dead.[68]

---

66. Henry Edmondson, *Return to Good and Evil: Flannery O'Connor's Response to Nihilism* (Lanham, MD: Lexington Books, 2002), 20.
    67. *HB*, 97.
    68. *HB*, 90.

Chickens, by their nature, have wings, so being "wingless" speaks to a defect in the chicken, in this particular case an intentional defect brought about by human manipulation of what-is. O'Connor understands Nietzsche to promote a philosophy of artistic freedom that intentionally seeks to conquer and re-create what-is; to displace, abandon, and even strike the pretended structures of nature and its God from the world in order to bring about a new kind of world and a new kind of humanity in the same way that modern scientists breed chickens without wings for the sake of producing more white meat.

Throughout her canon, O'Connor repeatedly professes her belief in and dependence upon both God and Catholic Christianity as the most basic grounding for her metaphysical vision, which assists her in coming to know what-is and in navigating her way through the real world, explaining, "I think that the Church is the only thing that is going to make the terrible world we are coming to endurable."[69] Nietzsche, however, sees the detritus of Christianity in the modern world as a hollow corpse that must be displaced if we are to face the stark challenge of finding meaning under new, modern conditions. O'Connor's alternative modern vision is first and foremost related to her faith: "I see from the standpoint of Christian orthodoxy. This means that for me the meaning of life is centered in our Redemption by Christ and what I see in the world I see in its relation to that."[70] Nietzsche retorts, "I call Christianity the one great curse, the one great intrinsic depravity, the one great instinct of revenge, for which no means are venomous enough, or secret, or subterranean and small enough—I call it the one immortal blemish upon the human race."[71] Nietzsche, then, is arguably the most important

---

69. *HB*, 90.
70. *MM*, 32.
71. Friedrich Nietzsche, *The Anti-Christ*, trans. H.L. Mencken (Tucson, AZ: See Sharp, 1999), 91.

philosophical foil to O'Connor's Hillbilly Thomism and to her metaphysics in particular.[72] Edmondson explains,

> O'Connor concluded, however, that despite Nietzsche's brilliance in recognizing the weaknesses of Western civilization, he failed to offer anything of constructive value to replace what he sought to overthrow. Quite the contrary, a distillation of Nietzsche's thought yields little more than a dangerous product of crude sex, raw power, and aimless destruction. O'Connor did agree, however, with Nietzsche's complaint that the modern age is populated by "last men," individuals without faith, vision, purpose, or valor. Her solution, unlike Nietzsche's, was a recovery of the concepts of good and evil, not their rejection. The return to good and evil means that man must recognize anew his need for God and for the operative principle of God's dealings with man, grace. When grace is absent the vacuum will be filled with evil. Thus, far from transcending good and evil, O'Connor believed that nihilism would lead us into a chasm of evil—hence the single-minded urgency of her literary mission.[73]

As we noted above, O'Connor presents her philosophical vision as a narrative artist, a Hillbilly Thomist. In her fiction, where God is rejected by her characters in distinctively modern ways, the distinctively modern defects and grotesqueness of such a worldview become manifest. This approach is on display in O'Connor's first novel, *Wise Blood,* in the character of Hazel Motes

---

72. William Murray finds more compatibility between O'Connor and Nietzsche than I do, stating, "Like the German philosopher, she promotes an inexplicable sense of mystery that extends beyond visible comprehension. Her work, therefore, avoids crusading for a narrow set of values that are singularly aligned with any one doctrine or any final version of good and evil" (William Murray, "Friedrich Nietzsche, O'Connor, and the Limiting Power of Certainty," in *Reconsidering Flannery O'Connor,* ed. Alison Arant and Jordan Cofer [Jackson, MS: University Press of Mississippi, 2020], 36.). On my read, the "mystery" in O'Connor's narrative art is God, not some generic mystery, and, as I demonstrate in chapter 4, she embraced the natural law tradition of values.
73. Edmondson, *Return to Good and Evil,* xi–xii.

and his "Church Without Christ," the embodiment of a view that Caroline Gordon calls "terrifying." But O'Connor's characterization of the "Nietzschean" worldview is also on display in two of her short stories: the well-known "Good Country People" and the lesser-known "The Partridge Festival." In both stories, a protagonist who thinks herself intellectually superior—on account of her disbelief in God and her embrace of nihilism considered as a form of realism—comes face to face with a yet more realistic embodiment of nihilism and realizes the consequential terror of such a metaphysical position. Marion Montgomery notes,

> From Miss O'Connor's point of view, then, we may see a culmi-
> nation of certain intellectual currents coming to spectacular
> pressure in Nietzsche's mind, making him of particular dramatic
> interest to such a searching intellectual eye as Miss O'Con-
> nor's. Either Christ or Antichrist one might say, focusing one
> heroic branch of that current of thought from Kierkegaard to
> Nietzsche.[74]

O'Connor's fiction appeals to fundamental distinctions between being and nonbeing, life and death, good and evil, meaning and meaninglessness, God and nothing; we find such dichotomies consistently foregrounded in her artistic design. And these stark distinctions make Nietzsche a better philosophical foil to O'Connor's Hillbilly Thomism than Descartes, Spinoza, or Comte, since Nietzsche's far more radical thought questions the very use of these distinctions and their basis in human experience. Whereas Descartes continued to profess belief in God, and Spinoza's God became nature but remained God, and Comte's views culminated in what he considered a more perfect religion, Nietzsche goes directly, intentionally, and vehemently to the heart of traditional metaphysics with the goal of rendering the study of being—or

74. Marion Montgomery, *Why Flannery O'Connor Stayed Home* (La Salle, IL: Sherwood Sugden and Company, 1981), 387.

God—dead and the world ultimately inexplicable ("meaningless," in classical terms), beckoning an elite class of humans to create a new kind of world and a new kind of human being, with a new kind of meaning and a new kind of freedom, after the demise of the Christian/Classical European intellectual tradition. Such views function as a foil for O'Connor, with some qualification:

> Her works are not an attempt to refute directly the Nietzschean philosophical corpus, point-for-point. She was not an expert in his writing and undoubtedly had no desire to be one, nor was she formally trained as a philosopher. Instead, her work is a general literary response to the pervasive nihilistic influence in philosophy and culture. . . .
>
> O'Connor's interest, then, lies not in a debate with Nietzsche or any other philosopher, but in identifying and refuting the cultural influence of nihilism more generally understood and offering a remedy to a world rapidly falling under its spell. Both O'Connor and Nietzsche would agree that an experience of "nothingness" is the logical consequence of a world that has for centuries rejected God or at least acted as if He were irrelevant to modern life and affairs. O'Connor argues on many occasions that when God is excluded, then even the exercise of reason becomes overburdened, loses its footing, and is rendered unreliable.[75]

In her narrative art, O'Connor seemingly employs a kind of negative or apophatic theology[76] to expose what she considers seriously flawed metaphysical positions. Edmondson explains,

> Flannery O'Connor sees Western civilization in the middle of a kind of cosmic struggle for its fate; a struggle that features, on one side, the menace of nihilism, the latest step in a long

75. Edmondson, *Return to Good and Evil*, 3.
76. See Davies, *Thought of Thomas Aquinas*, 59.

cultural decline that would eradicate the philosophy and religion of the past. Nietzsche justifies this act of destruction by a
yearning for a new world. The nihilistic opportunity has been
staged by the progression of Enlightenment philosophy that,
once divorced from religion, promises the secular perfectibility
of the human species. On the other side of the struggle is the
Judeo-Christian tradition. O'Connor plays the role of literary
interpreter of this struggle and makes the contest intelligible by
her fiction, prose, and correspondence. She is not an impartial
commentator, though; she is, instead, a partisan advocate for
the Thomistic worldview, infused as it is with his synthesis of
Christian theology and classical philosophy.[77]

Indeed, it is difficult to understand O'Connor's metaphysics
without her engagement of Nietzsche as a metaphysical foil.

THE PROBLEM OF EVIL

Every philosopher will eventually have to address the problem of
evil in the world, and O'Connor thinks that every good narrative
artist will do the same. O'Connor's copy of *Introduction to St.
Thomas Aquinas* includes a short article from the *Summa* "On
Evil" with which she was almost certainly familiar,[78] and although
we have no record of O'Connor owning or reading *St. Thomas
and the Problem of Evil* by Jacques Maritain,[79] Edmondson finds
this text to be "especially helpful in understanding O'Connor's
reliance upon Thomas."[80] Maritain makes his thesis clear, setting
out to emphasize two points: "First, the meaning of the existence
of evil in this world; second, the cause of evil where free will is

77. Edmondson, *Return to Good and Evil*, 31.
78. *ST* 1.48.1–3.
79. Jacques Maritain, *St. Thomas and the Problem of Evil*, trans. Gordon
Andison (Milwaukee, WI: Marquette University Press, 1942). This little book
contains the text of "The Aquinas Lecture" given by Maritain in 1942 sponsored
by the Aristotelian Society of Marquette University.
80. Edmondson, *Return to Good and Evil*, 135.

concerned."[81] In this section, we will see how Aquinas influenced Flannery O'Connor's understanding of the problem of evil, as well as her belief in the reality of the devil as a critical aspect of her metaphysics and cosmology.

THE GOODNESS OF BEING (AND CREATION) AND ITS PRIVATION

We have already established O'Connor's belief in God as Creator of all things visible and invisible, so now we will consider another important aspect of Thomistic metaphysics—namely, God's goodness and the goodness of being, hence the goodness of creation. Early on in the *Summa*, Thomas argues that "to be good belongs pre-eminently to God,"[82] that "God is the highest good absolutely,"[83] and that "God alone is essentially good."[84] He then goes on to say that "all things are good inasmuch as they have being,"[85] so that "goodness" and "being" are the same in reference,[86] which means that all of creation is essentially good. Thomas writes,

> For He brought things into being in order that His goodness might be communicated to creatures, and be represented by them. And because His goodness could not be adequately represented by one creature alone, He produced many and diverse creatures, so that what was wanting to one in the representation of the divine goodness might be supplied to another. For goodness, which in God is simple and uniform, in creatures is manifold and divided; and hence the whole universe

81. Maritain, *St. Thomas and the Problem of Evil*, 1.
82. *ST* 1.6.1.
83. *ST* 1.6.2.
84. *ST* 1.6.3.
85. *ST* 1.6.4.
86. See Eleonore Stump, *Aquinas* (London: Routledge, 2003), 368.

together participates in the divine goodness more perfectly, and represents it better, than any given single creature.[87]

This understanding of God's goodness and Thomas' insistence that everything that exists is good because it has being[88] is, in fact, the foundation for his understanding of evil, because Thomas thinks that evil is not *something that is* but *something that is not*. For Thomas, evil is a lack or a defect; it is the privation of being and the privation of goodness.[89] "Evil has no formal cause, but is rather a privation of form. So, too, neither has it a final cause, but is rather a privation of order to the proper end."[90] He uses the example of sight to illustrate his point, noting, "The absence of good, taken in a privative sense, is an evil; as, for instance, the privation of sight is called blindness."[91] But Thomas goes on to note, "The subject of blindness is not *sight*, but *the animal*,"[92] meaning that the privation of sight has a greater context than the eye itself, since seeing is not simply for the eye but for the good of the animal. Maritain explains, "Evil is real, it actually exists like a wound or mutilation of the being; evil is there in all reality, whenever a thing—which, insofar as it is, and has being, is good—is deprived of some being or of some good it should have."[93] Evil, then, Thomistically speaking, can only be understood against the greater context of the goodness of being because evil is not its own subject; rather, "the subject of evil is

---

87. *ST* 1.47.1.
88. Thomas makes an important distinction to clarify his Aristotelian position and a more Platonic approach: "Everything is therefore called good from the divine goodness, as from the first exemplary, effective and final principle of all goodness. Nevertheless, everything is called good by reason of the likeness of the divine goodness belonging to it, which is formally its own goodness, whereby it is denominated good. And so of all things there is one goodness, and yet many goodnesses" (*ST* 1.6.4).
89. This idea was first developed in elaborate fashion by Augustine in response to Manicheanism. See Augustine, *Confessions* 7.2–5.
90. *ST* 1.49.1.
91. *ST* 1.48.3.
92. *ST* 1.48.3.
93. Maritain, *St. Thomas and the Problem of Evil*, 2.

good."[94] It is also worth noting that Thomas thinks "there cannot be a highest evil, for . . . although evil always lessens the good, yet it never wholly consumes it; and thus, since the good always survives, nothing can be wholly and perfectly evil."[95]

THE CAUSE OF EVIL

If God is good and his creation is also good, both because it comes from God and because it participates in being, then what according to Thomas is the cause of evil in the world? Thomas answers this question in two ways. He explains that God is the cause of evil in the sense that some evils are part of the whole *ordo* of the universe (e.g., the death of peacocks because of the predation by mongooses) and that the *whole* is good precisely with the strategic failures and losses of this or that particular individual. Thomas writes, "The order of the universe requires . . . that there should be some things that can and do fail. And thus God, by causing in things the good of the order of the universe, consequently, and, as it were by accident, causes the corruptions of things."[96] Furthermore, on Thomas' view, even the evils committed by the wicked and suffered by virtuous and vicious alike all fall under God's providence. That is, for Thomas, there are no evils except those which God permits, which he incorporates into the order of the world and its history and future as a whole. In the sense of the larger *ordo* of creation, then, God is the cause of evil.

However, in a more specific way, "the creature is the primary cause, but negatively,"[97] meaning that evil comes from creatures endowed with free will, which Thomas understood to be "a natural inclination towards goodness associated with the agent's understanding of goodness."[98] Thomas explains, "In voluntary beings the defect of the action comes from an actually deficient

94. *ST* 1.48.3.
95. *ST* 1.49.3.
96. *ST* 1.49.2.
97. *ST* 1-2.18.1–11; Maritain, *St. Thomas and the Problem of Evil*, 35.
98. Stump, *Aquinas*, 103.

will inasmuch as it does not actually subject itself to its proper rule. This defect, however, is not a fault; but fault follows upon it from the fact that the will acts with this defect."[99] The "proper rule"[100] is the way by which human beings ought to live in accord with the order of the created world, and Thomas points to the lack of the consideration of this rule as a defect of the will. This is why Thomas is able to say, "No being is called evil by participation, but by privation of participation,"[101] meaning that because God is good, and his creation is good, and nature is good, and the order of nature is good, and because the intellect and the will are good, evil is a result of the rational creature choosing not to participate in the goodness of God and his creation along with all the laws that govern the economy of his creation. This "choosing not to participate," therefore, is the result of a good but defective will. Maritain recognizes the profundity of this philosophical implication:

> That is the metaphysical grandeur of the universe of freedom: there, and only there can the creature do something by itself alone, but that something consists in non-being, and that "doing" is an absence of action. All that it does by itself alone is nothingness; namely, the actual non-consideration of the rule, through its free initiative—the non-consideration of that rule without which the act it is about to do cannot be good.[102]

This philosophical implication, we can now state, is also known theologically as *sin*.

---

99. *ST* 1.49.1.

100. In chapter 4, we will go into detail regarding Thomas' understanding of law and the various kinds of law, but for now it is sufficient to note that the rational creature becomes the cause of evil when he fails to make use of reason and divine law.

101. *ST* 1.49.3.

102. Maritain, *St. Thomas and the Problem of Evil*, 34–35. (Cf. *ST* 1-2.112.3 ad. 2.)

Although it is likely that Flannery O'Connor read the few pages dedicated to the topic of evil in her copy of *Introduction to St. Thomas Aquinas*, it is even more likely that her understanding of evil was formed primarily by her reading of the *Baltimore Catechism* and the Bible, as well as her lifelong participation in Catholic liturgy and the fact that she was from the South.[103] O'Connor believed in sin, both original and actual, as well as the fall of the angels, and although these doctrines come by way of divine revelation, they remain a most important component of her metaphysics, and in no way does she find them unreasonable.

Eleonore Stump notes, "On the traditional understanding, all human beings are marred by original sin, which means, among other things, that a post-Fall person has a will which tends to will what he ought not will, and that that inborn defect of will results sooner or later in sinful actions, with consequent moral deterioration."[104] O'Connor shares this belief, and because she understands sin to be a foundational and universal aspect of the human condition, she also thinks it is an integral part of good fiction. She explains,

> The serious writer has always taken the flaw in human nature
> for his starting point, usually the flaw in an otherwise admirable
> character. Drama usually bases itself on the bedrock of original
> sin, whether the writer thinks in theological terms or not. . . .
> The novelist doesn't write about people in a vacuum; he writes
> about people in a world where something is obviously lacking,
> where there is the general mystery of incompleteness and the
> particular tragedy of our own times to be demonstrated, and

103. O'Connor once quoted Walker Percy's explanation for why there were so many good Southern writers: "Because we lost the War." She went on to explain, "He didn't mean by that simply that a lost war makes good subject matter. What he was saying was that we have had our Fall. We have gone into the modern world with an inburnt knowledge of human limitations and with a sense of mystery which could not have developed in our first state of innocence—as it has not sufficiently developed in the rest of the country" (*MM*, 59).

104. *ST* 1.82.1–4, 1.85.1; Stump, *Aquinas*, 374–375.

the novelist tries to give you, within the form of the book, a total experience of human nature at any time.[105]

What Thomas calls a "privation," O'Connor refers to above as "lacking" and "incompleteness," but essentially she and Thomas are saying the very same thing, insisting that the cause of evil in the world is the human tendency to seek happiness by turning away from God and toward some other created good, which can never actually lead to happiness, since God alone is good and apart from him one cannot be happy, as God is the final cause of man.

With all this in mind, we now turn to O'Connor's clarifying words to John Hawkes in a letter dated November 28, 1961, regarding the nature of evil:

> You say that one becomes "evil" when one leaves the herd. I say that depends entirely on what the herd is doing.
>
> The herd has been known to be right, in which case the one who leaves it is doing evil. When the herd is wrong, the one who leaves it is not doing evil but the right thing. If I remember rightly, you put that word, evil, in quotation marks which means the standards you judge it by there are relative; in fact you would be looking at it there with the eyes of the herd.[106]

O'Connor insists that evil is not relative but objective, because evil is always considered in relation to the good, and turning from the good—regardless of what a particular herd is doing or not doing—is the source of evil.

THE ONTOLOGICAL REALITY OF EVIL AND THE DEVIL

O'Connor follows St. Thomas in thinking that the free act of turning away from the good and from God is not limited to human beings. According to Thomas, angels are also intelligent

105. *MM*, 167.
106. *HB*, 456.

beings, different from humans in that they are pure spirits (without bodies), yet like humans in that they have free will.[107] And although today many may view belief in angels as puerile, in the thirteenth century, Thomas found himself part of a pre-Christian philosophical tradition supporting the reality of incorporeal intelligences, a lineage that included the Neoplatonists and Avicenna.[108] Thomas thinks that before the fall of man there came the fall of angels, at least some of them, and that this fall resulted in the spiritual realities of the devil and his demons.[109]

Victor White, a twentieth-century Thomist whose *God and the Unconscious* was a favorite of O'Connor's, presents a basic account of Thomas' position on the devil, which is, unsurprisingly, similar to the position of O'Connor:

> How did Lucifer go bad? How, in metaphorical language, did some angels fall? In their essence, their being, St. Thomas insists, they did not, and (being immaterial, and therefore essentially changeless and incorruptible) could not. But they sinned—their evil was and is a moral, not a physical, evil. But how? St. Thomas argues, by a process of elimination, that a bodiless, timeless, passionless "thinking thought," such as angels are conceived to be, could be capable of only one sin, *superbia* (which is perhaps better translated as uppishness or ambition or even self-complacency, than as pride) with its concomitant, *invidia* or envy. The essentially Satanic sin is thus autonomy over against God, satisfaction with natural endowments and happiness, and consequent refusal to accept the offer of a share in Divine life, grace, bliss and glory.[110]

107. See *ST* 1.50.1–2.
108. Victor White, *God and the Unconscious* (London: Fontana Books, 1952), 195.
109. *ST* 1.63.1–9.
110. White, *God and the Unconscious*, 196–197.

O'Connor was well aware that her belief in the reality of the devil was considered pure superstition by much of her audience, yet she holds this traditional metaphysical view with the utmost seriousness, as she illustrates in her words to John Hawkes:

> My Devil has a name, a history and a definite plan. His name is Lucifer, he's a fallen angel, his sin is pride, and his aim is the destruction of the Divine plan. Now I judge that your Devil is co-equal to God, not his creature; that pride is his virtue, not his sin; and that his aim is not to destroy the Divine plan because there isn't any Divine plan to destroy. My devil is objective and yours is subjective.[111]

According to O'Connor, the devil is an elemental aspect of what-is, since there is a hierarchy of being, ascending from natural nonliving things to living things without sensate knowledge (plants), to living things with sensate knowledge (animals), to rational animals with spiritual souls, and "above" these, to immaterial spirits that are incorporeal. Some of these immaterial spirits have freely dissented from the good, just as human beings, no matter how intelligent or powerful, can do. Jessica Hooten Wilson observes, "Satan rejects being itself. He rejects existence. . . . When Satan attempts to replace being, he loses being, and is thrust from heaven to roam the earth and to feed parasitically off human beings. Satan does not disappear, but his triumphs are limited by the nothingness he serves."[112] Consequently, when one denies the devil's existence, or even attempts to speak of evil in a vague or general way, reducing an actual metaphysical reality to a psychological state, or a superstitious belief, or a literary

---

111. *HB*, 456.
112. Jessica Hooten Wilson, *Giving the Devil His Due: Demonic Authority in the Fiction of Flannery O'Connor and Fyodor Dostoevsky* (Eugene, OR: Cascade Books, 2017), 82–83.

device (as John Hawkes was doing), O'Connor thinks that one misrepresents reality. She makes her case in a number of ways:

> To ensure our sense of mystery, we need a sense of evil that sees the devil as a real spirit who must be made to name himself, and not simply to name himself as vague evil, but to name himself with his specific personality for every occasion.[113]

> Our salvation is a drama played out with the devil, a devil who is not simply generalized evil, but an evil intelligence determined on its own supremacy. I think that if writers with a religious view of the world excel these days in the depiction of evil, it is because they have to make its nature unmistakable to their particular audience.[114]

> The Catholic novel can't be categorized by subject matter, but only by what it assumes about human and divine reality. . . . Its center of meaning will be Christ; its center of destruction will be the devil. No matter how this view of life may be fleshed out, these assumptions form its skeleton.[115]

So although, as Guardini regretfully notes, "modern man has done away with Satan and his realm,"[116] O'Connor refuses to do so, because she thinks that such an approach is an unrealistic and dishonest one. The profound seriousness of O'Connor's position regarding the devil is summarized in a brief but magnificently clever observation she makes in "Catholic Novelists." O'Connor suggests that many Catholics who demand pious or "positive" books find themselves scandalized by much of modern literature,

---

113. *MM*, 117.
114. *MM*, 168.
115. *MM*, 196–197.
116. Romano Guardini, *The Lord*, trans. Elinor Castendyk Briefs (Chicago: Henry Regnery, 1954), 138.

which they assume to be the work of the devil.[117] She agrees, but ironically so, and proceeds to offer a profound metaphysical claim: "Probably the devil plays the greatest role in the production of fiction from which he himself is an absent actor."[118]

THE GROTESQUE

Thus far, we have noted a series of metaphysical positions that are indicative of O'Connor's Christian beliefs about the nature of reality, including her intellectual commitment to the existence of God as a hidden transcendent Creator, the creation of the world, the reality of things visible and invisible, the goodness of all created things, the existence of spiritual personhood in human beings and angels, and even the ontological goodness of the devil. Yet O'Connor was well aware that such a view of reality was readily dismissed in a world dominated by atheism, materialism, and nihilism, so she needed a way to convey to her readers—whom she claimed "are the people who think God is dead"[119]—the basic principles of Christian realism with a credible voice. She developed a strategy:

> When you can assume that your audience holds the same beliefs you do, you can relax a little and use more normal means of talking to it; when you have to assume that it does not, then you have to make your vision apparent by shock—to the hard of hearing you shout, and for the almost-blind you draw large and startling figures.[120]

Simply stated, O'Connor's strategy is to employ the grotesque—that is, to exaggerate and distort reality in such a way that her audience is forced to reconsider their metaphysical

117. *MM*, 188–189.
118. *MM*, 189.
119. *HB*, 92.
120. *MM*, 34.

presumptions. She notes, "Distortion in this case is an instrument; exaggeration has a purpose. . . . This is not the kind of distortion that destroys; it is the kind that reveals, or should reveal."[121] This is also the reason O'Connor's fiction happens to be so violent, with beatings, maulings, drownings, rapes, and murders. It is not for the sake of violence itself, but for the sake of revealing the true metaphysical contours of reality that her audience might otherwise be prone to ignore. O'Connor explains,

> I have found that violence is strangely capable of returning my characters to reality and preparing them to accept their moment of grace. Their heads are so hard that almost nothing else will do the work. This idea, that reality is something to which we must be returned at considerable cost, is one which is seldom understood by the casual reader, but it is one which is implicit in the Christian view of the world.[122]

This is also why there are so many bodily distortions and disfigurements in O'Connor's fiction. Because the spiritual is known through the material—the invisible through the visible—the appearance of a physical disability in O'Connor's narrative always points to a spiritual disability. Whether it is a missing leg, a deformed arm, a clubfoot, blindness, or even a fatherless home,[123] the lack or privation of the physical is always a sign in O'Connor's Thomistically influenced fiction of some spiritual or metaphysical privation. Yet the grotesque is not limited to revealing privation, according to the Hillbilly Thomist.

121. *MM*, 162.
122. *MM*, 112.
123. In a letter written to Flannery O'Connor dated November 13, 1951, Caroline Gordon notes, "But homosexuality, childishness, freakishness—in the end, I think it comes to *fatherlessness*—is rampant in the world today. And you are giving us a terrifying picture of the modern world, so your book is full of freaks" (Flannery O'Connor and Caroline Gordon, *The Letters of Flannery O'Connor and Caroline Gordon*, ed. Christine Flanagan [Athens, GA: The University of Georgia Press, 2018], 24).

In her introduction to *A Memoir of Mary Ann*, O'Connor recalls an afternoon conversation with some of the Hawthorne Dominican sisters who ran the cancer home in Atlanta, one of whom had asked her why she "wrote about such grotesque characters, why the grotesque (of all things) was [her] vocation."[124] She notes that she was struggling to find a proper response when another guest said, "It's your vocation too."[125] What that guest meant was that the Hawthorne Dominicans were around the grotesque every day, as their vocation was tending to those terminally ill with cancer. O'Connor found the conversation to be most revealing:

> This opened up for me also a new perspective on the grotesque. Most of us have learned to be dispassionate about evil, to look it in the face and find, as often as not, our own grinning reflections with which we do not argue, but good is another matter. Few have stared at that long enough to accept the fact that its face too is grotesque, that in us the good is something under construction.[126]

This "good under construction" is another way of referring to O'Connor's metaphysical view that God is good and personal and relational and is constantly at work to bring all things back to being, back to God himself. She thinks that without the use of the grotesque—that is, without distorting and exaggerating reality—it is almost impossible to recognize the need for what she knows in her Christian realism to be the redemption from nonbeing.[127]

---

124. *MM*, 225.
125. *MM*, 225.
126. *MM*, 226.
127. See Marshall Bruce Gentry, *Flannery O'Connor's Religion of the Grotesque* (Jackson, MS: University Press of Mississippi, 1986).

SYMBOLS

Whether it be a horizon, a peacock, a pair of glasses, a statue, or an automobile, Flannery O'Connor frequently relies on symbols in her fiction to present both the profundity and the mystery of reality in a way that invites her readers to reconsider their metaphysical assumptions. According to Victor White, "A symbol, as we say, 'does something to us,' it moves us, shifts our center of awareness, changes our values."[128] A philosopher is charged with explaining how symbols operate, while a narrative artist's job is to actually set them in motion; it is O'Connor's gift that she does both.[129]

O'Connor deals with symbols most directly in "The Nature and Aim of Fiction," where she acknowledges that "the word *symbol* scares a good many people off, just as the word *art* does."[130] In this essay, O'Connor never actually tells us what she thinks a symbol is, but she does tell us what a symbol is not, and then she shows us how a symbol operates using an example from her first novel.[131] She explains that many readers wrongly think of a symbol as if it were a problem in algebra: "Find x. And when they do find or think they find this abstraction, x, then they go off with an elaborate sense of satisfaction and the notion that they have

128. White, *God and the Unconscious*, 233.
129. In the fall of 1961, O'Connor received a book entitled *Myth and Ritual in Christianity* by Alan Watts, along with a copy of a book she already owned, *God and the Unconscious* by Victor White, OP, as gifts from Dr. Spivey (*HB*, 451). Both contain some critical observations about the nature of symbols. In his prologue, Watts writes, "There are ways in which the symbols express their truth more adequately than the more formal and exact language of the doctrine, for the truth in question is not an idea but a reality-of-experience so fundamental and alive that we cannot 'pin it down' and know 'about it' in exact terms" (Alan W. Watts, *Myth and Ritual in Christianity* [Boston: Beacon, 1968], 18–19). And White explains, "The meaning of a true symbol is not exhausted when we have found some rational formula which will define or 'explain' it" (White, *God and the Unconscious*, 233).
130. *MM*, 71.
131. Such an approach is similar to O'Connor's general approach to God, as we saw in the first part of this chapter, in that she doesn't make an argument for God's existence, but she will show us what the world looks like when God is ignored. It is not enough for her to tell; she has to show.

'understood' the story."[132] In contrast to this simplistic mode of analysis, O'Connor argues that symbols "are details that, while having their essential place in the literal level of the story, operate in depth as well as on the surface, increasing the story in every direction."[133] We note that such an approach to symbols—rejecting the algebraic certainty (Descartes) and embracing the mystery of being (Thomas)—is consistent with O'Connor's general view of reality. According to O'Connor, the symbol is not a problem to solve but a way by which a reader is given greater access to the meaning of the story and of reality in general. She notes, "The truer the symbol, the deeper it leads you, the more meaning it opens up."[134]

O'Connor then moves from "telling" how symbols work to actually "showing" how symbols work:

> To take an example from my own book, *Wise Blood*, the hero's rat-colored automobile is his pulpit and his coffin as well as something he thinks of as a means of escape. He is mistaken in thinking that it is a means of escape, of course, and does not really escape his predicament until the car is destroyed by the patrolman. The car is a kind of death-in-life symbol, as his blindness is a life-in-death symbol. The fact that these meanings are there makes the book significant. The reader may not see them but they have their effect on him nonetheless. This is the way the modern novelist sinks, or hides, his theme.[135]

---

132. *MM*, 71. O'Connor makes the same argument in "Recent Southern Fiction," stating, "So many students approach a story as if it were a problem in algebra: find X and when they find X they can dismiss the rest of it" (*Conversations with Flannery O'Connor* [Jackson, MS: University Press of Mississippi, 1987], 73–74).
133. *MM*, 71.
134. *MM*, 72.
135. *MM*, 72.

In 1960, O'Connor was part of a panel discussion with three other fiction writers at Wesleyan College.[136] At one point, the moderator, Louis D. Rubin Jr., posed a question to O'Connor's friend Katherine Anne Porter, asking her to comment about the religious symbolism present in her work. Porter responded,

> Symbolism happens of its own self and it comes out of something so deep in your own consciousness and your own experience that I don't think that most writers are at all conscious of their use of symbols. I never am until I see them. They come of themselves because they belong to me and have meaning to me, but they come of themselves. I have no way of explaining them but I have a great deal of religious symbolism in my stories because I have a very deep sense of religion and also I have a religious training. And I suppose you don't invent symbolism. You don't say, "I am going to have the flowering Judas tree stand for betrayal," but, of course, it does.[137]

Porter's response is important because O'Connor immediately followed it by stating, "I would second everything Miss Porter says,"[138] which is hardly a surprise considering all we know about O'Connor's Catholic upbringing.

A striking example of Porter's claim that good symbols in fiction come from themselves and are not invented is found in the fact that O'Connor wrote one of her most symbolically memorable short stories, "Good Country People," unusually quickly—"in about four days," she reports.[139] In her essay "Writing Short Stories," O'Connor describes how the memorable symbolism in "Good Country People" came to emerge naturally, without any intentional invention:

136. Flannery O'Connor, "Recent Southern Fiction: A Panel Discussion," in *Conversations*, 61–78.
137. *MM*, 72–73.
138. *MM*, 73.
139. *HB*, 160.

I wouldn't want you to think that in that story I sat down and said, "I am now going to write a story about a Ph.D. with a wooden leg, using the wooden leg as a symbol for another kind of affliction." I doubt myself if many writers know what they are going to do when they start out. When I started writing that story, I didn't know there was going to be a Ph.D. with a wooden leg in it. I merely found myself one morning writing a description of two women that I knew something about, and before I realized it, I had equipped one of them with a daughter with a wooden leg. As the story progressed, I brought in the Bible salesman, but I had no idea what I was going to do with him. I didn't know he was going to steal that wooden leg until ten or twelve lines before he did it, but when I found out that this was what was going to happen, I realized that it was inevitable.[140]

Much of what O'Connor states above relates to her understanding of *prophetic vision*, which is beyond the scope of this book but remains an important aspect of O'Connor's narrative art, and which does relate to her metaphysical vision, as we will see at the end of this section.[141]

But—to return to the panel discussion—O'Connor expands on her agreement with Porter by offering what may be the closest she ever comes to an actual definition of a *symbol*:

I really didn't know what a symbol was until I started reading about them. It seemed I was going to have to know about them if I was going to be a respectable literary person. Now I have the notion that a symbol is sort of like the engine in a story and I usually discover as I write something in the story that is taking

140. *MM*, 100.
141. See chapter 7, "Revelation and Unconsciousness," of Victor White's *God and the Unconscious*, 125–157.

on more and more meaning so that as I go along, before long, that something is turning or working the story.[142]

But how, philosophically speaking, does a symbol actually work? We have arrived at a point where we can now answer this question by referring back to the *four causes* and the *matter/form* distinction. We can say that a symbol is something that is charged with signifying power by the artist, often subconsciously, and that offers greater access to the meaning of reality in a narrative by applying the meaning (spiritual and invisible) of one thing upon another thing.

It is most important to remember that even when dealing with symbols, according to O'Connor's Thomistic understanding of reality, one always begins with actual things. She writes, "If you want to say that the wooden leg is a symbol, you can say that. But it is a wooden leg first, and as a wooden leg it is absolutely necessary to the story. It has its place on the literal level of the story, but it operates in depth as well as on the surface."[143] So a symbol, according to O'Connor, always starts with one literal thing as its foundation before more meaning can be given to that particular thing. That is, before something can operate as a symbol, it first has to be what it is, according to its nature. Then, the narrative artist is able to add meaning to a thing by making it symbolic of something else, and that added meaning is not material but formal or spiritual. We turn back to O'Connor's previous example from *Wise Blood* to see how this happens.

Hazel Motes' car is first a car on the literal level, but as the story unfolds, we learn that his car also comes to symbolize his entire self-consciously nihilistic philosophy. In other words, the car on the literal level can be known by its four causes: formal (it is a car); material (it is constructed of metal, rubber, glass, etc.); efficient (it was made in an automobile factory and sold to Hazel

142. O'Connor, *Conversations*, 73.
143. *MM*, 99.

Motes from a used-car lot); and final (its purpose is to provide transportation). The use of symbolism operates, therefore, by starting in our apprehension of ordinary physical things through our senses, then by moving to a consideration of their spiritual meaning or use. That is to say that O'Connor, the narrative artist, starts with a literal thing (Motes' car), but then she brings the form of another, nonliteral thing (Motes' nihilism) to the original literal thing, giving it a greater depth of meaning while maintaining both its original formal and material components (i.e., it is both a car and symbolic of Motes' nihilism). The literal thing remains while also presenting or manifesting the reality of something else, since it signifies, manifests, or embodies this second referent. So, when the patrolman pushes the car over the hill, not only does the life of the car come to a violent end, but so too does Motes' means for the expression of his intentionally post-Christian nihilism. In losing his literal car, Motes also loses his philosophical worldview.

Symbols understood in this way cannot operate on a purely mechanistic or materialistic level, as the meaning given in a symbol is embodied in the very created reality itself, and therefore requires a robust metaphysics that acknowledges the reality of natural goods and meanings in reality. And symbols, as we have seen, are rarely forced in good art, but instead naturally emerge from the way in which the artist understands reality—that is, from the artist's metaphysical vision. O'Connor thinks that "the artist penetrates the concrete world in order to find at its depths the image of its source, the image of ultimate reality,"[144] which reminds us that O'Connor is only able to do what she does as a narrative artist because of her belief in God and the intelligibility of a world that was created and is sustained by him.

144. *MM*, 157.

O'CONNOR'S METAPHYSICS IN "THE RIVER"

We now turn to one story in particular, "The River"[145]—first published in the Summer 1953 issue of the *Sewanee Review*[146]—and show how each of the metaphysical themes we presented above is on display in one of O'Connor's most misunderstood short stories. The story begins in the urban home of Harry Ashfield, who the narrator reports is "four or five," and his bohemian parents, who remain nameless for the entire story. The uncertainty about Harry's actual age is indicative of parental neglect, as his mother and father appear more interested in their dinner parties than in the health and well-being of their only son. The family name literally means "field of ashes," a nod to the impending threat of nihilism that pervades their lives, symbolized by the smell of "dead cigarette butts" and the description of the apartment as dark or dimly lit. In O'Connor's fiction, the city is often presented as a godless or meaningless place, and this is no less true in "The River," with the Ashfield family apartment symbolizing modern domestic life without God and without meaning, where jokes, rather than the truth, are given reverence.

Mrs. Connin[147] is not from the city, but she arrives early in the morning at the Ashfield apartment to pick up Harry in order to watch him for the day. She has never met the boy before but tells his father that she plans to take him down to the river for a healing with the Reverend Bevel Summers. Mrs. Connin notices a piece of art on the wall of the apartment, "a watercolor

---

145. *CS*, 157–174.

146. Margaret Earley Whitt, *Understanding Flannery O'Connor* (Columbia, SC: University of South Carolina Press, 1995), 49.

147. It is not clear why O'Connor named this character Connin, but there are three likely possibilities. First, "conn" is a nautical term for controlling a ship's movements at sea, so perhaps she is steering Bevel toward God and away from the rocky shores of nihilistic materialism. Second, "conn" could indicate the activity of "*conn*ection," as Mrs. Connin is about connecting Bevel to the divine life through education and Baptism. Third, "Conn" is a derivative of Cohen, the priestly class of the Jewish people. The priest is the mediator between God and his people, which is the role that Mrs. Connin takes on in this story, mediating between God and Bevel.

hanging near the phonograph," and she "peer[s] closely at the black lines crossing into broken planes of violent color."[148] Mrs. Connin speaks twice about the abstract art: "I wouldn't have paid for that. . . . I would have drew it myself"; and "I wouldn't have drew it." Like the family name, this piece of formless modern art symbolizes the empty, materialistic landscape of the family home, and Mrs. Connin finds it repulsive. Before Harry leaves the apartment, Mr. Ashfield tells him, "Good-by, old man," and shortly after, Mrs. Connin asks the boy his name. He tells her his name is "Bevel," which is not the truth but a little joke of the sort common in the Ashfield home.

Mrs. Connin is a Christian woman who takes her faith seriously, even stridently; O'Connor, in her typical way, depicts her faith almost comically, underscoring that the ugliness and imperfection of individual Christians does not prevent them from becoming, almost despite themselves, the accidental instruments of a victorious God. She lives with her daughter and three sons in a paper brick house half a mile from the end of the car line. In contrast to the abstract art at the Ashfield apartment, the walls of Mrs. Connin's country home are decorated with pictures and calendars. After explaining to Bevel that one of the photographs is of her (hospitalized) husband, we are introduced to the foil of the abstract painting in the Ashfield's abstract watercolor: "Bevel turned from Mr. Connin to a colored picture over the bed of a man wearing a white sheet. He had long hair and a gold circle around his head and he was sawing on a board while some children stood watching him."[149] Bevel does not recognize the man, but he is intrigued. Just as he is about to ask about the man in the picture, the three Connin boys invite Bevel out to the yard, where they plan to play a little trick on him. Since Bevel is from the city, he has no prior experience with farm animals; the narrator describes his innocence: "Bevel had never seen a real pig but he had seen

148. *CS*, 157.
149. *CS*, 161.

a pig in a book and knew they were small fat pink animals with curly tails and round grinning faces and bow ties."[150] But soon, encouraged by the Connin boys, Bevel pulls back a board from the pigpen and is run over by a charging hog. He is so frightened that even though he is rescued from the prank by Mrs. Connin, "the child scream[s] for five minutes."

Once he calms down, he sits on Mrs. Connin's lap and eats breakfast while the shoat that frightened him climbs the back stairs and looks at him with squinted eyes. Mrs. Connin tells Bevel that the pig reminds her of Mr. Paradise, a nonbeliever whom they will see later that day at the river. Although the hog keeps squinting at Bevel, he remains safe on Mrs. Connin's lap, finishing his breakfast. This is the second time Bevel sits on Mrs. Connin's lap, and it is worth noting because Mrs. Connin, despite her rustic imperfection, is markedly more affectionate, tender, and loving toward the boy than his own mother, helping him to blow his nose, holding his hand, feeding him, educating him, and introducing him to God. Mrs. Connin can be understood as a paradoxical symbol for both Mary, the Mother of God, and Mother Church, and as one who displays God's relational and personal nature to Bevel.

Just as Bevel had thought that pigs were cartoons, as he had never seen a real pig before, so too was he confused about the identity of Jesus Christ:

> You found out more when you left where you lived. He had found out already this morning that he had been made by a carpenter named Jesus Christ. Before he had thought it had been a doctor named Sladewall, a fat man with a yellow mustache who gave him shots and thought his name was Herbert, but this must have been a joke. They joked a lot where he lived. If he had thought about it before, he would have thought Jesus Christ

150. *CS*, 161.

was a word like "oh" or "damn" or "God," or maybe somebody who had cheated them out of something sometime. When he had asked Mrs. Connin who the man in the sheet in the picture over her bed was, she had looked at him a while with her mouth open. Then she had said, "That's Jesus," and she had kept on looking at him.[151]

Soon after this incident, Mrs. Connin picks up a copy of a book entitled "The Life of Jesus for Readers Under Twelve" that belonged to her great-grandmother, and reads it to Bevel. "It was full of pictures, one of the carpenter driving a crowd of pigs out of a man. They were real pigs, gray and sour-looking, and Mrs. Connin said Jesus had driven them all out of this one man. When she finished reading, she let him sit on the floor and look at the pictures again."[152] She treats the existence of the demonic and the miraculous as unproblematic facts. These stories of Jesus awaken something in Bevel that he has not known before—a new meaning, a new reality, a new mystery; this man in the white sheet somehow made him and also has the power to heal people.

In order to get to the river, Mrs. Connin leads Bevel through the woods along a path covered with thick pine needles. Even more than the Connin home, nature—specifically the woods, the sun, and the river itself—comes to symbolize God, who is hidden behind the veil of creation, but present. The trip into this landscape represents an opportunity to participate in God, the source of life itself, which is all new to Bevel. "He had never been in woods before and he walked carefully, looking from side to side as if he were entering a strange country."[153] When they arrive at the river, Mrs. Connin takes Bevel by the hand and leads him to the front of the crowd to have a better view of the preacher, Reverend Bevel Summers, who is standing knee-deep in the water. This

151. *CS*, 163.
152. *CS*, 163.
153. *CS*, 164.

detail of Connin leading Bevel by the hand is indicative of her role as rudimentary handmaid, as she guides Bevel to the source of wisdom, life, and being itself, waiting for him in Baptism.

As Summers preaches to his riverside congregation, Bevel looks up to see "the slow circles of two silent birds revolving high in the air,"[154] reminiscent both of the mighty wind that swept over the waters in the first chapter of Genesis as well as the Holy Spirit's descent upon Jesus at his baptism in the River Jordan.[155] The narrator then contrasts the beauty of the natural surroundings with an ugliness in the distance, noting, "The city rose like a cluster of warts on the side of a mountain."[156] The tension builds and the distinction sharpens between Bevel's home and life in the city and this new way of living and being in this strange country.

Just as Mrs. Connin predicted, Mr. Paradise is at the riverside, not to participate in the healing, but to taunt and ridicule those who are. Mr. Paradise is described as "a huge old man who sat like a humped stone on the bumper of a long ancient gray automobile,"[157] with a grotesque cancerous tumor on his left temple.[158] We are told that his hat is also gray, the same color used to describe the pig that charged Bevel earlier that day, and that his small eyes are "half closed," also reminiscent of the squinting hog. Just as Bevel was afraid of the hog back at the Connin home, he fears Mr. Paradise. "Bevel stared at him once and then moved into the folds of Mrs. Connin's coat and hid himself."[159] In the Catholic tradition, Mary the Mother of God is often called upon to protect her children with her mantle, and here we see Mrs. Connin, the rustic mother figure, playing a similar role protecting Bevel from

154. *CS*, 165.
155. See Gen. 1:2; Mark 1:10.
156. *CS*, 165.
157. *CS*, 166.
158. O'Connor's choice for the symbolic placement of Mr. Paradise's tumor on his left temple is most intentional. In Catholic symbolism the right (*dexter*) side is the good side and the left (*sinister*) side is the wicked side. For example, in the last judgment (Matt. 25:31–46), the sheep are at the right and the goats are at the left. Moreover, Jesus himself sits at the right hand of the Father.
159. *CS*, 166.

both the hog and the gaze of Mr. Paradise. In the meantime, the preacher also hears the taunts of Mr. Paradise and responds. "The boy in the river [Reverend Bevel Summers] glanced at the old man quickly and raised his fist. 'Believe Jesus or the devil!' he cried. 'Testify to one or the other!'"[160]

These words strike the reader as too radically disjunctive and brutal, but they are essential to this story and to O'Connor's metaphysical vision in general, because she thinks that "the greatest dramas naturally involve the salvation or loss of the soul."[161] In other words, the stories that move us derive their power from a metaphysical fact: that one is either moving toward God or away from God, toward life or toward death, toward He Who Is or toward nonbeing, toward the fullness of goodness or toward the unbecoming of evil, toward humility or toward pride. The young Bevel Summers and the river in which he stands represent God, Being, Life, divine Goodness, and humility, while the old, squinting Mr. Paradise and his gray hat and gray car represent the crass rebellion of the devil, nonbeing, death, evil, and pride. One has to decide between the two, and there is no middle ground. The unrefined depiction is seemingly meant to confront us with a most basic truth.

Mrs. Connin lifts the boy up above the crowd and tells the preacher that she is watching him for the day, that his name is Bevel (noting the unlikely coincidence of his sharing a name with the preacher), and that he has never been baptized. The narrator describes Bevel "grinning" each time his name is spoken among the crowd, as his little joke is now extending to a greater audience. Mrs. Connin passes him on up to the preacher. "He held him in the crook of his arm and looked at the grinning face. Bevel rolled his eyes in a comical way and thrust his face forward, close to the

160. *CS*, 166.
161. *MM*, 167.

preacher's. 'My name is Bevvvuuuuul,' he said in a loud deep voice and let the tip of his tongue slide across his mouth."[162]

The mood changes quickly. The preacher is serious, refusing to smile. The only person laughing is Mr. Paradise, causing Bevel to grasp the preacher's collar out of fear. "The grin had already disappeared from his face. He had the sudden feeling that this was not a joke. Where he lived everything was a joke. From the preacher's face, he knew immediately that nothing the preacher said or did was a joke."[163] The preacher asks Bevel if he wants to be baptized, because if he does, he will be able to go to the Kingdom of Christ by way of the deep river of life. Bevel agrees to the Baptism and thinks, "I won't go back to the apartment then, I'll go under the river."[164] Summers then tells him that he "won't be the same again" and that he'll "count,"[165] and then he baptizes the boy rather violently, swinging him upside down and plunging his head into the water. Then, jerking him back up out of the water, Summers tells the boy, "You count now. . . . You didn't even count before."[166]

O'Connor makes it clear that something has happened to Bevel as a direct result of the Baptism; something has changed.[167] The Baptism is "no joke." Having been turned upside down in the river of life, Bevel is different now, and the way that he sees the world is different as well. Bieber Lake notes, "Baptism is so significant a topic in O'Connor's fiction because it enables her to play out the ways in which the spiritual is linked to the corporeal."[168] For the

162. *CS*, 167.
163. *CS*, 167–168.
164. *CS*, 168.
165. *CS*, 168.
166. *CS*, 168.
167. At this point we can speculate about the meaning of the name Bevel. To bevel means to change a squared edge to a more rounded one. In this way, Baptism has beveled Harry's original sin and made him into a new creation. Moreover, the one who metaphysically bevels Bevel—Revered Bevel Summers—has himself been beveled. It is also worth noting that the word bevel is close to "believe."
168. Christina Bieber Lake, *The Incarnational Art of Flannery O'Connor* (Macon, GA: Mercer University Press, 2005), 115.

materialist, such change is inexplicable, but for the Thomist it is unsurprising. Baptism is not a mere symbol of inner grace but in fact communicates the grace effectively as an instrument, from the very working of the act, or as Aquinas says, *ex opere operato*.[169]

Bevel is exhausted by the time Mrs. Connin takes him back to his parents' apartment in the city that evening, where they are entertaining two other couples. The narrator notes that upon his return, Bevel's mother "[doesn't] get up" to greet him but remains lying on the sofa. And as his father goes off to retrieve payment for Mrs. Connin's service, one of the other men refers to the boy again as "old man," just as his father did early on in the story, unaware that his Baptism has in fact made him a "new man,"[170] a spiritual change not noticeable to the senses. Soon, Mrs. Connin realizes that the boy's real name is Harry, not Bevel, and seeing the way in which his parents treat him and mock his religious experience, she leaves the apartment "without taking the money."[171]

Mrs. Ashfield calls Bevel toward her and asks him to tell her about his day as she takes off his coat, soon finding the handkerchief and the book about Jesus in the coat's inner lining.

> She threw the handkerchief down and held the book too high for him to reach and began to read it, her face after a second assuming an exaggerated comical expression. The others moved around and looked at it over her shoulder. "My God," somebody said.
>
> One of the men peered at it sharply from behind a thick pair of glasses. "That's valuable," he said. "That's a collector's item," and he took it away from the rest of them and retired to another chair.[172]

169. *ST* 3.62.1.
170. See Eph. 4:22–24.
171. *CS*, 170.
172. *CS*, 170.

O'Connor presents some very crucial details in these few lines of text. First, the book, which represents God, the source of being and life, is kept from Bevel's reach in a taunting sort of way. Second, his mother's "exaggerated comical expression" indicates that she takes the content of the book to be a joke (in contrast to the Baptism itself, which we were told was no joke). Third, one of the dinner guests says "My God" in disgust, but also—ironically—in truth, since the book is about the Incarnation of the second person of the Godhead. Fourth, another one of the guests calls the book "valuable," which it is, but not simply on the material level as a collector's item; its far greater spiritual value is the truth it contains about God and the meaning of life.

Bevel makes his way down to "the room where he slept"[173]—an interesting detail, indicating that he does not have his own bedroom—and his mother comes in a minute later, pressing him for more information about what happened at the riverside. In striking contrast with the affectionate ways of Mrs. Connin, Bevel's own mother, who is seemingly less rudimentary, treats him roughly, as we are told she "pulled him into a sitting position and he felt as if he had been drawn up from under the river."[174] Then, she "lowered him by the front of his shirt onto his pillow. She hung over him an instant and brushed her lips against his forehead."[175] Bevel's mother and the darkness of the apartment play foil here to the maternal care of Mrs. Connin and "the broken pieces of the sun knocking the water"[176] of the river where he was baptized earlier that day.

When Bevel wakes up the next morning, the apartment is still dark, even though "he didn't wake up early,"[177] which is indicative of his parents' late-night lifestyle, the darkness of their immanentistic worldview, and their distance from God, who, in O'Connor's

173. *CS*, 170.
174. *CS*, 170–171.
175. *CS*, 171.
176. *CS*, 168.
177. *CS*, 168.

view, is the source of light. (The narrator reports, "The sun came in palely, stained gray by the glass."[178]) Bevel's encounter with Mrs. Connin, the book about Jesus, and his Baptism have changed him. He counts now. His life has meaning and significance, and he longs to return to the cause of this change, and this spiritual longing is on display in his bodily hunger. The first thing he eats are "two crackers spread with anchovy paste," perhaps a nod to the Gospel account of Jesus' multiplication of loaves and fishes.[179] He drinks some ginger ale and looks around for his book but cannot find it. He keeps eating, making himself a raisin bread sandwich stuffed with a half jar of peanut butter, washing it down with chocolate milk. Although he satisfies his physical hunger, a spiritual hunger remains.

> He decided he would empty a few of the ashtrays on the floor. If he only emptied a few, she would think they had fallen. He emptied two, rubbing the ashes carefully into the rug with his finger. Then he lay on the floor for a while, studying his feet which he held up in the air. His shoes were still damp and he began to think about the river.
>
> Very slowly, his expression changed as if he were gradually seeing appear what he didn't know he'd been looking for. Then all of a sudden he knew what he wanted to do.[180]

Bevel's act of spilling the two ashtrays and rubbing the ashes into the carpet is symbolically important in three ways. First, he is marking the apartment for what it is and what it has been to him: a field of ashes. He has experienced no real love, comfort, affection, truth, understanding, care, or life here, only signs of spiritual lifelessness, with reality understood as a joke—so he marks the place as such. Second, in the Catholic liturgy on Ash

178. *CS*, 171.
179. Matt. 14:13–21.
180. *CS*, 172.

Wednesday, the faithful are told "Remember you are dust, and to dust you shall return" as their heads are literally marked with ashes, a sign of the beginning of the penitential season that prepares the way for the celebration of Christ's Paschal Mystery. Bevel's spreading of ashes is related, in that he is preparing to enter into a great mystery as well. Third, like the phoenix, the mythical bird that rises from the ashes, which is a "popular symbol for the Resurrection of Christ, the triumph of life over death,"[181] Bevel, after having spent enough time in the dark and lifeless Ashfield apartment, rises and starts making his way back to the river, but not before stopping into his parents' room, where they remain asleep, to take a car-token out of his dad's pocketbook and "half a package of Life Savers,"[182] a foreshadowing of what life-saving action is to come at the river.

On his way back to the river, Bevel passes Mr. Paradise but does not notice him. There is "an orange gas pump" in front of his shack, and he is having "an orange drink."[183] We are also told that Mr. Paradise is "looking out at nothing in particular," and twice his eyes are described as "squinting." These details reveal the symbolic identity of Mr. Paradise as the devil, as "orange" is the color of hellfire, "nothing" is symbolic of his embrace of the presumed primacy of nonbeing, and his "squinting" reveals his relation to pigs, both the pigs possessed by demons in the Scriptures and the particular pig that charged Bevel the day before. (Thomistically speaking, sin, or the embrace of nonbeing, actually darkens one's vision, whether that vision be of an angel or a human being, so the physical "squinting" reveals this spiritual condition.[184]) Moreover, in the first edition of *A Good Man Is Hard to Find and Other Stories*, the collection containing "The River,"

181. Gertrude Grace Sill, *A Handbook of Symbols in Christian Art* (New York: Collier Books, 1975), 25.
182. *CS*, 172.
183. *CS*, 172.
184. *ST* 1.86.1–2.

O'Connor had the following quotation by St. Cyril of Jerusalem placed at the front of the book:

> The dragon is by the side of the road, watching those who pass. Beware lest he devour you. We go to the father of souls, but it is necessary to pass by the dragon.[185]

Mr. Paradise is the dragon by the side of the road in "The River," and he is looking to devour Bevel: "He went in the shack and picked out a peppermint stick, a foot long and two inches thick, from the candy shelf, and stuck it in his hip pocket. Then he got in his car and drove slowly down the highway after the boy."[186] The peppermint stick is a phallic symbol, indicating the way in which Mr. Paradise plans to aggress Bevel sexually.[187] Once Bevel arrives at the river, Mr. Paradise is there in his usual spot, but Bevel still does not see him. The narrator describes Mr. Paradise as "holding an unbaited fishing line,"[188] indicating both that he is not there to catch fish but the boy, and to symbolize his identity as one whose life is pervaded by nothingness.

Bevel has returned to the river because it is the place where yesterday his life took on meaning and significance, as his Baptism made him "count" in a way that he had not counted or mattered before. His first attempt to put himself under the water fails, as does his second, leaving him disappointed. "The river wouldn't have him. He tried again and came up, choking."[189] The reader feels Bevel's frustration as the river, by rejecting him three times—presumably a kind of echo of the threefold immersion of

---

185. Flannery O'Connor, *Three by Flannery O'Connor: Wise Blood; A Good Man Is Hard To Find; The Violent Bear It Away* (New York: Signet Books, 1962), 128.
186. *CS*, 173.
187. There is a child rape in *The Violent Bear It Away*, so this interpretation of the peppermint stick should not be dismissed too easily. Also, we recall that the name the Bible salesman gives himself in "Good Country People" is "Manley Pointer," and in "A Stroke of Good Fortune" Mrs. Gilfeet's husband's name is "Rodman," both phallic references by O'Connor.
188. *CS*, 173.
189. *CS*, 173.

Baptism—appears to treat him as his parents have treated him his entire life. "He stopped and thought suddenly: it's another joke, it's just another joke!"[190] He continues to wallow in his disappointment when

> he heard a shout and turned his head and saw something like a giant pig bounding after him, shaking a red and white club and shouting. He plunged under once and this time, the waiting current caught him like a long gentle hand and pulled him swiftly forward and down. For an instant he was overcome with surprise: then since he was moving quickly and knew that he was getting somewhere, all his fury and fear left him.[191]

The boy drowns in the river (its "long gentle hand" reminiscent of the hand of Mrs. Connin), and Mr. Paradise is left standing there like "some ancient water monster . . . empty-handed."[192] Bevel has passed the dragon without being devoured and has made his way to the father of souls, to God, the source of being and Being itself.

A GROTESQUE DROWNING OF A CHILD

Without a proper understanding of O'Connor's robust metaphysical vision, "The River" can come off as a well-written but terribly tragic story about a boy who seemingly commits suicide in a river as a consequence of the abuse (by neglect) that he receives from his parents. Some readers may even suggest that Mr. Paradise is trying to save the boy from drowning in the final scene, understanding Mr. Paradise as the heroic representation of an enlightened, this-worldly secular humanism that mocks religion but looks compassionately toward humanity. But O'Connor makes her vision clear: "Bevel hasn't reached the age of reason; therefore he

190. *CS*, 173.
191. *CS*, 174.
192. *CS*, 174.

can't commit suicide. He comes to a good end. He's saved from those nutty parents, a fate worse than death. He's been baptized and so he goes to his Maker; this is a good end."[193]

"The River" is not the only example of a child drowning in O'Connor's catalog, for she presents a similar incident in *The Violent Bear It Away*, when young Tarwater drowns Bishop in the lake.[194] In the following quotation, O'Connor explains that action's significance, which can equally be applied to Bevel's drowning in "The River":

> Well, I tell stories that frequently hinge on the things of belief, and the man of our times is certainly not a believer. When I write a novel in which the central action is baptism, I have to assume that for the general reader, or the general run of readers, baptism is a meaningless rite, and I have to arrange the action so that this baptism carries enough awe and terror to jar the reader into some kind of emotional recognition of its significance. I have to make him feel, viscerally if no other way, that something is going on here that counts. Distortion is an instrument in this case; exaggeration has a purpose.[195]

We noted earlier that the grotesque is an exaggeration of what-is, employed in order to alert the reader to a reality that often goes unnoticed or unrecognized. The use of the grotesque is O'Connor's way of shocking her reader to realities that she finds crucial and necessary, which is why she goes to such extremes, shouting and drawing large, startling figures.[196]

193. Flannery O'Connor, "An Interview with Flannery O'Connor," in *Conversations*, 58.

194. Flannery O'Connor, *The Violent Bear It Away* (New York: Farrar, Straus and Giroux, 1955), 202–203.

195. Flannery O'Connor, "Flannery O'Connor: An Interview, by C. Ross Mullins," in *Conversations*, 104–105.

196. See *MM*, 34.

ADDITIONAL SYMBOLS IN "THE RIVER"

Although we addressed many of the story's symbols and their meanings in our analysis above, there are two particular symbols that deserve our attention, as both of them reveal O'Connor's metaphysical vision and, in fact, do not make sense without it.

Mrs. Connin's Handkerchief

Early on in "The River," the narrator tells us about a particular action of Mrs. Connin toward Bevel: "She took a red and blue flowered handkerchief out of her pocket and stooped down and began to work on his nose."[197] The colors named here are not random; they have important theological significance, particularly in O'Connor's Catholic tradition.[198] Blue is the color of the sky; it symbolizes heaven and the divine. Red is the color of flesh and blood; it symbolizes humanity. So blue and red together are symbolic of the Incarnation: God becoming man in the person of Jesus Christ. And although the pattern on the handkerchief is not specified as a particular type of flower, flowers in general are a symbol of life.[199] Consequently, the red and blue flowered handkerchief can be understood as a sign of the Incarnation and a sign of a new life being introduced to Bevel through the tenderness and maternal care of Mrs. Connin. This makes her not only a Marian symbol but also a symbol of *mater ecclesia*, Mother Church. Moreover, Mrs. Connin is "working" on Bevel's nose in response to the brief exchange with his father early on in the story when she notices and mentions that Bevel "ain't fixed right." His father responds, "Well then for Christ's sake fix him." Mrs. Connin's "work" on his nose with her own handkerchief (since Bevel's parents have failed to provide him with one) is doing just that: she is beginning his preparation to be fixed in and by Christ in the river of life.

197. *CS*, 158–159.
198. See Sill, *Symbols in Christian Art*, 29.
199. Sill, 50–53.

Skeletons

Throughout "The River," O'Connor describes Mrs. Connin as a skeleton on four separate occasions. First, when Mr. Ashfield meets her in the doorway of the apartment: "He found her looming . . . a speckled skeleton in a long pea-green coat and a felt helmet."[200] Second, as she sleeps on the streetcar with Bevel on her lap, heading to her home: "She began to whistle and blow like a musical skeleton."[201] Third, as Mrs. Connin walks with her four children and Bevel to the river: "They looked like the skeleton of an old boat with two pointed ends, sailing slowly on the edge of a highway."[202] And fourth, when she drops Bevel back off at the Ashfield apartment: "Mrs. Connin stood a second, staring into the room, with a skeleton's appearance of seeing everything."[203] In addition to these four instances of skeletal imagery, O'Connor twice describes Reverend Bevel Summers in a skeleton-like manner, noting "his face was all bone"[204] and, a few pages later, referencing "his bony face."[205] O'Connor believed that "the creative action of the Christian's life is to prepare his death in Christ,"[206] which is another way of stating the ancient Christian adage *memento mori* (remember your death). The fact that Mrs. Connin, her family,[207] and Bevel Summers are the ones in the story described as skeletons or as "bony" signifies that they understand reality properly; they see that their lives are about more than this world, and they have chosen to spend their lives preparing for their final end with the one who created all ends and is the final end of all being.

200. *CS*, 157.
201. *CS*, 160.
202. *CS*, 162.
203. *CS*, 170.
204. *CS*, 164.
205. *CS*, 167.
206. *MM*, 223.
207. A ship or an ark is a traditional symbol of the Church, which is why the Connin family is described as looking like "the skeleton of an old boat."

CHAPTER THREE

The Epistemology of Flannery O'Connor

Flannery O'Connor's marginal notations and underlinings in her Modern Library edition of *Introduction to St. Thomas Aquinas* are minimal, which is noteworthy since she famously claimed to have read it for twenty minutes every night before going to bed.[1] In fact, the vast majority of her personal markings in this book emphasize not the words of Thomas Aquinas but the words of Anton C. Pegis in the introduction. These markings are significant because they direct us to a primary philosophical source of O'Connor's epistemology, which is undeniably and unapologetically Thomistic. The sentences O'Connor underlined in Pegis' introduction encapsulate philosophical themes that are foundational to her thought and her way of understanding the world, themes we find repeated—almost word for word at times—in her prose and, more importantly, operating in her narrative art. Pegis writes and O'Connor underlines:

> For we are the heirs of generations of philosophic speculations according to which man is a *thinker* and a *mind*. Now it is a fact that the Thomistic man is a knower rather than a thinker, and he is a composite being rather than a mind. In fact, St. Thomas does not even have in his vocabulary a term corresponding to the

1. *HB*, 93.

term thinker: you cannot translate such a term into Thomistic Latin. If we are to judge matters as St. Thomas has done, we are bound to say that the European man became a thinker after he ruined himself as a knower; and we can now even trace the steps of that ruination—from Augustinian Platonism to the nominalistic isolationism of Ockham to the despairing and desperate methodism of Descartes. For what we call the decline of mediaeval philosophy was really a transition from man as a knower to man as a thinker—from man knowing the world of sensible things to man thinking abstract thoughts in separation from existence.[2]

Pegis' "man as thinker" is on full display in O'Connor's fiction in the characters of Rayber, Sheppard, Asbury, Hulga, and Thomas, all of whom find themselves caught up in abstractions and ideas, separated not only from their family members and community but from the world and reality itself. Moreover, O'Connor's constant insistence on recognizing "the world of sensible things" and avoiding mere abstractions apart from concrete being is more than a Thomistic intuition; it *is* fundamental Thomistic epistemology, and the textual evidence for her source is clear.

As we demonstrated in our last chapter, Flannery O'Connor is a metaphysical realist whose philosophical and artistic starting point is not thought or a world of ideas but reality itself, what she calls *what-is*. O'Connor grounds her narrative art in the visible and invisible reality created by God and knowable to human beings who are composed of visible and invisible components, both body and soul, making the human person a knower, not simply a thinker. Although O'Connor is an artist and not a philosopher, she acknowledges in her own way that sound metaphysics and epistemology matter to the writer:

2. Anton C. Pegis, ed., *Introduction to Saint Thomas Aquinas* (New York: Modern Library, 1948), xxiv.

What the fiction writer will discover, if he discovers anything at all, is that he himself cannot move or mold reality in the interests of abstract truth. The writer learns, perhaps more quickly than the reader, to be humble in the face of what-is. What-is is all he has to do with; the concrete is his medium; and he will realize eventually that fiction can transcend its limitations only by staying within them.[3]

AN OVERVIEW OF THOMISTIC EPISTEMOLOGY

Epistemology, metaphysics, and anthropology are generally considered distinct areas of philosophical study, but because they all relate to the nature of being, we should expect a constant and natural overlap when dealing with any of these three areas in the Thomistic philosophical tradition. So although we are primarily concerned with O'Connor's epistemology in this particular chapter, it will be necessary to remember our discussion of O'Connor's metaphysics from the previous chapter and to anticipate some general anthropological themes we will encounter in the next.

Thomas never wrote a treatise on epistemology *per se*, but his theory of knowledge is an integral part of his entire philosophical system and of the history of philosophy in general. (Descartes wanted to replace Aristotelian and scholastic theories of knowledge when writing both his *Discourse on Method* and his *Meditations*.) Thomistic epistemology has been highly developed and systematized over the centuries and remains relevant and influential, even in postmodernity.[4] The purpose of this section is not to present an exhaustive account of Thomistic epistemology but to offer a basic overview of the system in order to help us better understand O'Connor's narrative art.

3. *MM*, 145–146.
4. See James D. Madden, *Mind, Matter, and Nature: A Thomistic Proposal for the Philosophy of Mind* (Washington, DC: The Catholic University of America Press, 2013).

Life

It is noteworthy that the starting point for Thomas' epistemology is not epistemology per se but metaphysics. In other words, rather than begin with some equivalent to the *cogito*, Aquinas first considers being, which offers the necessary Thomistic context for knowing. Whereas Descartes would say, "I think, therefore I am," Aquinas would respond, "I am, therefore I think," or better, "I am, therefore I know." For Aquinas, being always has priority over thinking because thinking (and any other activity of the soul) is dependent upon being. It is also important to note that Descartes' "I" (his *res cogitans*) refers only to the mind, as he considers the mind alone or consciousness alone to be who we are, while the body is a sort of machine.[5] Aquinas, on the other hand, thinks that the soul and the body together constitute a human being, and we will see more about why he thinks this is the case momentarily. For now, it is enough to say that according to Thomas, and to O'Connor for that matter, human beings come to know God and the world—including themselves—by interacting with God and the world, not by positing a reductive consideration of the mind itself while hyperbolically doubting the existence of God and the world.[6]

Following Aristotle, Thomas looks out to the world and recognizes a basic distinction between living and nonliving things.[7]

5. René Descartes, *Meditations on First Philosophy* §27, in *Descartes: Selected Philosophical Writings*, trans. John Cottingham, Robert Stoothoff, and Dugald Murdoch (New York: Cambridge University Press, 1988), 81–82. (See section 2.3 for review of Descartes' influence on modern thought.)

6. Cf. Aristotle, *De Anima* 3.4; *De Veritate* 10.8. We do not have any evidence that O'Connor ever read Aristotle's *De Anima*, but we do know that she would have been familiar with the work from her reading of Victor White: "St. Thomas Aquinas, assisted certainly by previous commentators, develops, synthesises, dots the i's and crosses the t's of Aristotle's *De Anima*. But not in this lay his chief contribution to the solution of the problem of man as Aristotle had left it. It was no part of St. Thomas's programme to bring Christ to Aristotle; on the contrary, as a Christian theologian, his purpose was to bring Aristotle's reasoning to the service of Christ" (Victor White, *God and the Unconscious* [London: Fontana Books, 1952], 122).

7. See Aristotle, *De Anima* 2.412a13; Thomas Aquinas, *De Anima* 2.1.219.

He writes, "To seek the nature of the soul, we must premise that the soul is defined as the first principle of life in those things in our world which live; for we call living things *animate*, and those things which have no life, *inanimate*."[8] The soul is what enables animate (living) things like plants, animals, and human beings to move themselves; inanimate (nonliving) things like rocks can be moved only by an external force. Yet although plants, animals, and human beings share this principle of life that Aristotle and Thomas call the soul, there are differences between all three forms of life, and, in fact, these three forms of life are part of a hierarchy whereby the characteristics of the lower degrees of life are contained within and exceeded by the higher.[9] This hierarchy of life is contained within a wider context known as the hierarchy of being, which stretches from the simplest inanimate things, like elements and minerals; to plants, animals, and humans; to the various ranks of angels; and ultimately to God, the source of all being.

Intellectual Life

According to Aristotle and Thomas, while humans share vegetative life with plants and animals, and have sensitive life in common with animals, they are set apart from both plants and animals by virtue of possessing *intellectual life*. Thomas states, "Now the human soul is the highest and noblest of forms. Therefore, in its power it excels corporeal matter by the fact that it has an operation and a power in which corporeal matter has no share whatever. This power is called the intellect."[10] Human beings are unique, then, because of their rationality—their ability to know and to act on what they know according to their intellect and will. We will address the operation of the will in the following

8. *ST* 1.75.1.
9. *ST* 1.78.1.
10. *ST* 1.76.1.

chapter, but for now, we turn our attention to how human beings come to know and what human beings are capable of knowing.

It may be helpful to repeat the principle that *knowledge begins in the senses.*[11] As we have stated many times, a human being is a body-soul composite, made up of both a visible and an invisible part, composed of both matter and form. Humans share with animals the ability to grasp particular things through sense knowledge, but intellectual knowledge is of a higher form, grasping not particular, visible, sensible objects but universal, invisible, spiritual ones. So here is the puzzle: How does a human being's sensible (material) knowledge lead to intellectual (spiritual) knowledge?[12] How does one come to know the universal through the particular? Thomas offers his response in the sixth article of question 84 in the first part of the *Summa*, which is included in O'Connor's Modern Library edition.

Thomas sets up his response by naming three philosophical positions represented by three philosophers: Democritus, Plato, and Aristotle. First, Democritus thinks that "all knowledge is caused by images issuing from the bodies we think of and entering into our souls."[13] Thomas notes that Democritus does not distinguish between intellect and sense; rather, he thinks that all knowledge is merely sense knowledge and that somehow all knowledge is caused by a discharge of images.[14] Gilson explains, "He imagines that little images are issuing from objects and penetrating into the matter of our soul."[15] Second, Plato thinks that "intellect differs from sense, and that it is an immaterial power not making use of a corporeal organ for its action. . . . He

---

11. See *ST* 1.84.6.
12. Thomas notes, "The intellect, according to its own mode, receives under conditions of immateriality and immobility the species of material and movable bodies; for the received is in the receiver according to the mode of the receiver" (*ST* 1.84.1).
13. *ST* 1.84.6.
14. *ST* 1.84.6.
15. Étienne Gilson, *The Christian Philosophy of St. Thomas Aquinas*, trans. L.K. Shook (Notre Dame, IN: University of Notre Dame Press, 1956), 217.

held that intellectual knowledge is not brought about by sensible things immuting the intellect, but by the participation in separate intelligible forms by the intellect."[16] According to Plato, then, the human body and sensible knowledge have no role in the act of intellectual knowledge.[17] In fact, Gilson observes, "If we accept Plato's position, we must suppose that the soul's natural operation, intellectual knowledge, meets its greatest obstacle in the natural bond uniting it to the body."[18] Third, Thomas shows that Aristotle finds the middle way between the positions of Democritus and Plato. Aristotle agrees with Democritus that sensible things that are outside the soul should produce some effect on the soul, but he does not agree that the effect is caused by a discharge of atoms because, as he notes, "nothing corporeal can make an impression on the incorporeal."[19] (Atoms are corporeal, while the soul, according to Aristotle, is incorporeal.) And Aristotle agrees with Plato that the intellect and the sense are different, but unlike Plato, Aristotle thinks that the body cooperates with the soul so that "to sense is not an act of the soul alone, but of the composite."[20] So how does Aristotle explain the process of how human beings—body-soul composites—come to intellectual knowledge? He points to an intellectual operation of the soul that the body does not share, the power of *abstraction*, which "causes the phantasms received from the senses to be actually intelligible."[21]

Let us walk through this process of abstraction using an example. When a woman stands on the brick steps of her front porch, she takes in the peacock through her senses; she sees it coming toward her, hears its feet scratching the ground, and feels its tail shake the air. Her common sense brings these

16. *ST* 1.84.6.
17. *ST* 1.84.2.
18. Gilson, *Christian Philosophy of St. Thomas Aquinas*, 213.
19. *ST* 1.84.6.
20. *ST* 1.84.6.
21. *ST* 1.84.6.

perceptions together and gives her an image or phantasm of this particular peacock. The sensitive powers of the soul perceive what is material and particular (sensible species), but they do not allow her to know the immaterial and universal (intelligible species), for that is the unique work of the intellectual powers of the soul. The agent intellect, shining its light on the phantasm, abstracts the intelligible species, and the passive intellect is then "informed" by this intelligible species to enable intellectual thinking. Subsequently, through composing and dividing, the woman can form concepts of what she has grasped by simple intelligence. In our example, the intellect "abstracts" the essence of "peacock" from the phantasm of this individual peacock. So what the woman standing on the brick steps actually comes to know is the universal species "peacock" by way of encountering this particular peacock on her front lawn. She knows the nature, the what-ness—or *quiddity*—of peacock, which is existing in this particular peacock that is standing before her, scratching the ground with its feet. And because she knows the nature of "peacock," she is able to know that this particular thing standing before her is a peacock.

It is important to note that for Thomas—and especially for O'Connor—the human knower does not know the essences of things in themselves as God does but as human beings do.[22] This approach to knowledge recognizes that the human being possesses "a light just sufficient in order to acquire the knowledge of the intelligibles to which it can raise itself by means of sensible things,"[23] meaning that the woman does not know the universal form of "peacock" in and of itself, but because she is able to abstract the intelligible species "peacock," she is able to know that this particular thing standing before her is a peacock. Human beings know by means of the intelligible species and by means of concepts abstracted from our experience of concrete

22. See *ST* 1.84.5.
23. Gilson, *Christian Philosophy of St. Thomas Aquinas*, 215; Cf. *ST* 1-2.109.1.

individual essences or natures. When the concrete peacock places us in touch with the real essence of the peacock, we are learning not from the eternal idea in the mind of God, as the angels do (through the medium, Aquinas tells us, of infused angelic species), but from one embodied expression of that idea. Human beings learn gradually of the essence of a thing by starting from its immediate accidents and then "breaking in" intellectually from the outside to get progressively more information on what it is essentially. We then move from a vague idea of the essence to a deeper and more perceptive understanding, never exhausting its nature or essence; on the contrary, the more our knowledge of an essence increases, the more its mystery is revealed, and the deepening mystery inexorably directs the knower back to the ultimate mystery of God. Human knowledge, therefore, begins in wonder and ends in wonder.[24]

PEGIS' INTRODUCTION AND ITS INFLUENCE ON O'CONNOR

Now that we have presented a general understanding of Thomas' theory of human knowledge, we turn our attention to Pegis' "Introduction" in O'Connor's personal copy of *Introduction to St. Thomas Aquinas*. Pegis' introduction is composed of four major sections, but it is only the third section—the most philosophical— that O'Connor intentionally marked up with her pen. The purpose of this section of our study is to highlight two specific aspects of Thomistic epistemology that we did not address in detail in our general overview—*the human being as knower* and *abstraction but not abstractions*—and to show that these aspects had a lingering effect on O'Connor's Hillbilly Thomism.

---

24. Thanks to Dr. Joel Johnson for this excellent insight concerning wonder as the starting and ending points of Thomistic epistemology.

The Human Being as Knower

First, we see that Pegis reminds O'Connor that the human person is not just a soul or a mind, as Plato and Descartes would suggest, but a body-soul composite:

> We are invited by St. Thomas Aquinas, therefore, to look upon
> the human composite of soul and body as being the complement
> of the intellectual nature of the soul. If the knowledge of truth
> is the aim of a spiritual substance, and if the soul, which is such
> a substance, is an incarnate spirit, then it is incarnate in order
> to do the work of a spirit; and, what is no less decisive, it must
> do a spiritual work as an incarnate spirit.[25]

Anything that a human being does, therefore, he or she does as a human being, not simply as a soul, or a mind, or a consciousness. Pegis uses the phrase "incarnate spirit" twice to emphasize the unique nature of human beings as rational beings, set apart from angelic beings. Human beings discover the spiritual within the material, not apart from it. The human body, therefore, is not an obstacle to the soul's pursuit of intellectual knowledge but the way by which and through which human beings attain intellectual knowledge, because they are, by nature, incarnate spirits. Pegis explains,

> To say that man must do a spiritual work as an incarnate spirit
> is to say that *as a knower* man is a composite being. Where the
> Platonic knower is a pure reason, and the Cartesian knower a
> pure mind, the Thomistic knower is, *as knower*, the composite of
> soul and body. Let us say this in another way. Man as a knower
> must be partly material in order to be adequately a knower. Of
> course, such a notion is bound to sound scandalous to modern

25. Pegis, *Introduction to Saint Thomas Aquinas*, xxiii.

ears. For we are the heirs of generations of philosophic specula-
tion according to which man is a *thinker* and a *mind*.[26]

Descartes opts for *thinker* rather than *knower* because he is
a rationalist and distrusts sensible knowledge, while Thomas,
on the other hand, insists the senses are the starting point for
knowledge—for knowing, not simply thinking. Minds think;
human beings know. We noted above that human beings share
with other nonrational animals the sensitive powers of the soul,
which are all involved in how human beings come to know
what-is. To understand the human being simply as thinker is to
reduce the human being to a mind alone, ignoring the human
body, reducing the person to half of his or her nature.

Pegis further explains the necessity of the human body for
the human knower:

> Man as a knower must be such that he can give existence, within
> his knowledge, not to abstract essences, but to sensible beings.
> That is why man as a knower needs a body; for, through the
> senses of his body he can give sensible existence in the order of
> knowing to that which is sensible in the order of being. The body
> as part of the knowing man answers for St. Thomas Aquinas
> the two questions which knowledge poses for him. In knowing
> sensible being, how do we know it as sensible, which it is, and
> as being, which it likewise is?[27]

We have noted that, according to Thomas, what human
beings actually come to know through the process of abstraction is the *nature* or the *quiddity* of a thing, which is spiritual,
as the agent intellect abstracts the intelligible species from the
sensible species. But the agent intellect is only able to abstract
the universal after encountering it by way of a phantasm, which

26. Pegis, xxiii.
27. Pegis, xxvi.

is particular and a product of sense knowledge, meaning that it comes by way of the human body and is therefore corporeal. The human knower, then, is able to grasp the nature "peacock" and can then identify the bird standing in front of her as *this* peacock" because of the cooperation of the body-soul composite that, by its very nature (as incarnate spirit), is able to identify the universal and spiritual in the sensible and particular.

Abstraction but Not Abstractions

O'Connor criticized modernity for its *general distrust of the concrete*, a result of modernity's attraction *to* and embrace *of* the abstract.[28] Now that we have offered a general account of Thomistic epistemology, we can see it at work in O'Connor's narrative art: Flannery O'Connor depends upon Thomistic abstraction in her epistemology in order to avoid abstract subjects in her narrative art. In other words, because O'Connor believes that there is a real world and that we can know it—and, according to Thomas, we come to know it through the process of abstraction—the world that O'Connor presents in her narrative art is real, concrete, and particular; it is anything but abstract. Pegis explains the relationship between abstraction and the sensible this way:

> To know is to be; to know sensible things is, by means of knowing, to be sensible things. To St. Thomas, knowing first presents itself in the mode of act; for it is the mode of act which is the mode of being. If we think of knowledge as intellectual abstraction, we shall never explain why we know being from the point of view of its actuality. If St. Thomas believes that abstraction is not working in a void, and that conceptualization is rooted in the actuality of things, it is because before the work

28. By "abstract" here I mean an "idealism" that results from solipsism and departs from the concrete existence of God's creation. The distinction I am making in the title of this section, therefore, is between *abstraction as the epistemological process* and *abstract ideas as subjects for literature.*

of abstraction and conceptualization by the intellect (or, rather, by man through the intellect) there is the work of giving sensible existence, within man's knowledge, to the sensible being of things. In other words, being (the being of and in sensible things) first comes to us in the way that it is, as sensible actuality, and human knowing begins by being the exercise by man of the sensible act of being in things.[29]

We have already noted the number of times that O'Connor has repeated the Thomistic principle that *knowledge begins in the senses*. This principle is important for O'Connor, not as a philosopher, but as an artist, because she thinks "fiction begins where human knowledge begins—with the senses—and every fiction writer is bound by this fundamental aspect of his medium."[30] Moreover, because art is made by humans and for humans, the best art is rooted in the natural process of human knowing, and the most effective artists have a keen grasp of the sensory. O'Connor insists upon remaining within the real—the what-is—when making her art; she does not ignore the human body or deny its role in coming to know the world. In fact, in "The Nature and Aim of Fiction," her Thomistic epistemology is on full display:

I think we have to begin thinking about stories at a much more fundamental level, so I want to talk about one quality of fiction which I think is its least common denominator—the fact that it is concrete—and about a few of the qualities that follow from this. We will be concerned in this with the reader in his fundamental human sense, because the nature of fiction is in large measure determined by the nature of our perceptive apparatus. The beginning of human knowledge is through the senses, and the fiction writer begins where human perception

29. Pegis, *Introduction to Saint Thomas Aquinas*, xxvi–xxvii.
30. *MM*, 42.

begins. He appeals through the senses, and you cannot appeal to the senses with abstractions. It is a good deal easier for most people to state an abstract idea than to describe and thus re-create some object that they actually see. But the world of the fiction writer is full of matter, and this is what the beginning fiction writers are very loath to create.[31]

And in "Writing Short Stories," she once again emphasizes the foundational role of sense knowledge in narrative art:

Fiction operates through the senses, and I think one reason that people find it so difficult to write stories is that they forget how much time and patience is required to convince through the senses. No reader who doesn't actually experience, who isn't made to feel, the story is going to believe anything the fiction writer merely tells him. The first and most obvious characteristic of fiction is that it deals with reality through what can be seen, heard, smelt, tasted, and touched.[32]

O'Connor is convinced that our access to the world always involves our human bodies, or, as Pegis notes, it is through "the being of and in sensible things,"[33] because human beings are incarnate spirits. It is because of the cooperation of our sensible powers and intellectual powers as human beings that O'Connor rightly calls her art *incarnational*, not only because of her belief in the Incarnation of God in the person of Jesus Christ, but also because of her understanding of the human person as an incarnate spirit. Bieber Lake writes, "Concrete, particular, located, contingent, absurd: fiction's method is incarnational. Its laws are of the flesh; know these laws and you will know

---

31. *MM*, 67.
32. *MM*, 91.
33. Pegis, *Introduction to Saint Thomas Aquinas*, xxvii.

the spirit that inhabits them."[34] According to O'Connor, good art will always be made according to the way the world is and the way we human beings come to experience the world, which is always through, as Pegis notes, "our sensible act of being in things."[35]

In the final paragraph of the third part of his introduction, Pegis writes the following:

> That is why abstraction as St. Thomas understands it is not a separation from existence; it is the consideration by the intellect of the essential elements within the actuality of things. In other words, given St. Thomas' view of sensible knowledge, we are bound to say that for him abstraction always takes place within the apprehended actuality of things.[36]

Pegis makes it clear that abstraction is a human act; it is the cognitive act of an incarnate spirit, and the purpose of abstraction is not to serve an abstract cerebral existence but to assist human beings in their navigation of the actual, real world. O'Connor depends upon this ability of human beings to come to know things in the world—first through the senses and then through abstraction—in order to know the real and then present the real to her readers. She makes this most interesting remark: "The type of mind that can understand good fiction is not necessarily the educated mind, but it is at all times the kind of mind that is willing to have its sense of mystery deepened by contact with reality, and its sense of reality deepened by contact with mystery."[37]

34. Christina Bieber Lake, *The Incarnational Art of Flannery O'Connor* (Macon, GA: Mercer University Press, 2005), 28.
35. Pegis, *Introduction to Saint Thomas Aquinas*, xxvii.
36. Pegis, xxvii.
37. *MM*, 79.

SEEING AND KNOWING

In the first paragraph of his *Metaphysics*, Aristotle writes:

> All men by nature desire to know. An indication of this is
> the delight we take in our senses; for even apart from their
> usefulness they are loved for themselves; and above all others
> the sense of sight. For not only with a view to action, but even
> when we are not going to do anything, we prefer seeing (one
> might say) to everything else. The reason is that this, most of all
> the senses, makes us know and brings to light many differences
> between things.[38]

Moreover, Aristotle considers sight to be "the most highly developed sense,"[39] and Thomas Aquinas agrees, noting that sight "is the most spiritual, the most perfect, and the most universal of all the senses."[40] Flannery O'Connor also gives priority to the sense of sight, particularly when it comes to her narrative art. She explains, "The novelist is required to open his eyes on the world around him and look. If what he sees is not highly edifying, he is still required to look. Then he is required to reproduce, with words, what he sees."[41] O'Connor is convinced that the more one sees, the more one knows; therefore, learning to see is a fundamental requirement of an artist, as only the one who knows what-is can reproduce what-is in one's art.

The relationship between *seeing* and *knowing* has a long and philosophically rich history. The Bible frequently links sight and knowledge, with the meaning of seeing often going beyond the mere physical notion of bodily sight to a deeper spiritual wisdom,[42] as when Jesus himself teaches, "The eye is the lamp of

38. Aristotle, *Metaphysics* 1.980a21–27.
39. Aristotle, *De Anima*, trans. R.D. Hicks (Amherst, NY: Prometheus Books, 1991), 3.3.429a2–4.
40. *ST* 1.78.3.
41. *MM*, 177.
42. Consider the Old Testament story of Tobit, who loses his vision and eventually regains it (which features O'Connor's favorite archangel, St. Raphael),

the body. So, if your eye is healthy, your whole body will be full of light; but if your eye is unhealthy, your whole body will be full of darkness."[43] In both the philosophical and the biblical tradition, then, the eye and sight and vision are all regularly associated with human cognition—with knowing and understanding.

This linguistic association between seeing and knowing is not only a matter of history; it continues to be relevant today. When English speakers want to ensure that they are being understood, they will often begin their sentence with the word *look*, as in "Look, here is what I mean . . ." And if the hearer understands what the speaker has said, the hearer will often respond with the pithy "I see." The words "look" and "see" in these examples are ultimately about human understanding. In the following sections, we will examine this relationship between seeing and knowing first as presented in the writings of O'Connor and then in a classic text by Betty Edwards.

O'Connor's Insistence on Looking and Staring

In 1959, *The Atlanta Journal and Constitution Magazine* ran an article entitled "An Afternoon with Flannery O'Connor." The essay's author, Betsy Lochridge, recognized something profound about O'Connor's vision, noting, "Her dark eyes are sharply observant—her paintings of churches and farm scenes, which line the dining room of the farmhouse, testify to how much and how well she sees."[44] We will address the relation between O'Connor's painting and writing in a moment, but for now, it is

---

or the miraculous healings of the blind by Jesus in the New Testament (e.g., Matt. 9:27–30; Mark 8:22–25; Mark 10:46–52; Luke 18:35–43; John 9:1–12), or Jesus' critique of the Pharisees (Matt. 15:14) as "the blind leading the blind." Physical seeing, biblically speaking, is often indicative of spiritual seeing. Yet, at other times, those who are blind are actually the ones who can see, because this spiritual kind of "seeing" or "knowing" is actually of a superior kind.

43. Matt. 6:22–23.

44. Betsy Lochridge, in *Conversations with Flannery O'Connor* (Jackson, MS: University Press of Mississippi, 1987), 37.

enough to emphasize the essential activity of "looking" in the epistemological life of the Hillbilly Thomist. Lochridge continues:

> When her morning's writing is done, she settles into a rocker on the front porch and just looks.
>
> The view is sweeping, the perspective wide. There is a blue haze of hills in the distance; to the right are broad pastures grazed by calves and a meditative bull. Fields gilded with goldenrod slope down to a dazzling pond. Peacocks sweep majestically through the front yard and pea fowl and Chinese geese stalk the paths among tangles of morning glories, and casual rows of zinnias and tiger lilies.[45]

O'Connor spent time every afternoon intently looking, seeing, and staring at this panoramic view. Many things she saw and came to know in the course of this daily study eventually made their way into her fiction—the bull ("Greenleaf"), the broad pastures ("A Circle in the Fire"), the pond ("Good Country People"), and the peacock ("The Displaced Person")—so that others could see what she saw and know what she knew, not as abstract ideas to be stated, but as concrete realities to be shown.

O'Connor is convinced that one of the primary responsibilities of the narrative artist is to see, which allows the artist to know, and then to show. She believed that "for the writer of fiction, everything has its testing point in the eye, an organ which eventually involves the whole personality and as much of the world as can be got into it. Msgr. Romano Guardini has written that the roots of the eye are in the heart."[46] Although O'Connor, as we have seen time and time again, credited the depth of her artistic vision to her Catholic faith, she also realized that she had great personal responsibility as an artist to look and to see with her own eyes. She explains, "Your beliefs will be the light by which

45. Lochridge, 38.
46. *MM*, 144.

you see, but they will not be what you see and they will not be a substitute for seeing."[47] According to O'Connor, the dogmas and doctrines of the Church will guide and illuminate one's vision, but the artist has to see the world herself, through her own eyes, and to report what she sees.

"The King of the Birds"

The first essay in *Mystery and Manners*, entitled "The King of the Birds,"[48] is an excellent place to begin a study of O'Connor's habit of looking and staring. O'Connor describes how she came to be interested in peacocks, recounting the "mild day in October" when she and her mother stopped by the train station to retrieve a crate of peafowl—"a peacock and hen with four seven-week-old pea-biddies"—she had ordered from Eustis, Florida.[49] Arriving home, O'Connor brings the peafowl into their new pen:

> As soon as the birds were out of the crate, I sat down on it and began to look at them. I have been looking at them ever since, from one station or another, and always with the same awe as on that first occasion; though I have always, I feel, been able to keep a balanced view and an impartial attitude. The peacock I had bought had nothing whatsoever in the way of a tail, but he carried himself as if he not only had a train behind him but a retinue to attend it. On that first occasion, my problem was so greatly what to look at first that my gaze moved constantly from the cock to the hen to the four young peachickens, while they, except that they gave me as wide a berth as possible, did nothing to indicate they knew I was in the pen.[50]

---

47. *MM*, 91.
48. "The King of the Birds" is the original title that O'Connor gave to this piece, although when *Holiday* published it in September of 1961, the title was changed to "Living with a Peacock" (*MM*, 235).
49. *MM*, 5.
50. *MM*, 6.

The first thing O'Connor reports doing once the birds have exited their crate is *to look at them*, and she reports that she has been *looking at them* ever since. Knowledge begins in the senses, according to O'Connor, so it makes perfect sense that before she begins to tell her readers about her observations of the peacock, she first reminds us of her epistemological process: that observations come *from observing*, that insights come from "seeing into" things. She does not state these principles directly, but she certainly shows them to her reader. It is also worth noting that in this short paragraph O'Connor uses the words *view, gaze, look* (twice), and *looking*. Aristotle claims that we "delight" in our senses, "particularly in the sense of sight,"[51] and his claim is manifested in O'Connor's testimony that she has continued to look at her peafowl "with the same awe as on that first occasion."[52]

After O'Connor has shown her reader her own process of coming to know the birds (i.e., by attentively looking at them), she offers a rich description of what she observes:

> For a chicken that grows up to have such exceptional good looks, the peacock starts life with an inauspicious appearance. The peabiddy is the color of those large objectionable moths that flutter about light bulbs on summer nights. Its only distinguished features are its eyes, a luminous gray, and a brown crest which begins to sprout from the back of its head when it is ten days old. This looks at first like a bug's antennae and later like the head feathers of an Indian. In six weeks green flecks appear in its neck, and in a few more weeks a cock can be distinguished from a hen by the speckles on his back. The hen's back gradually fades to an even gray and her appearance becomes shortly what it will always be.[53]

51. Aristotle, *Metaphysics* 1.1.980a23–24.
52. *MM*, 6.
53. *MM*, 7.

O'Connor's observations and insights do not happen all at once but over a period of time. She studies the peabiddies, attentively watching them develop into peacocks and peahens. Thomistically speaking, she witnesses their natural potential become actualized over time—she watches them become what they are. O'Connor recognizes small details and makes important distinctions in terms of shape, color, and other identifying marks, reminding us of Aristotle's claim that sight "makes us know and brings to light many differences between things."[54] Because O'Connor looks so carefully and attentively at the birds, she is able to receive a rich phantasm that she is then able to share with her readers, so that her readers, although not in front of the birds themselves, are able to "see" them in their imaginations, having their own phantasms from which to come to better know the nature of peafowl.

Her next step in this essay is to move from a description of the birds themselves to descriptions of other human beings observing the birds, specifically their reactions to the peacock when he spreads his tail. She notes, "With his tail spread, he inspires a range of emotions, but I have yet to hear laughter."[55] O'Connor reports that most people are silent the first time they see a peacock spread his majestic tail, although she notes that some people whistle and even that an old woman once cried "Amen! Amen!" at the sight.[56] In reporting the varying but appropriate reactions of other spectators, O'Connor shows that she is not alone in her appreciation of the strange, objective beauty of the peacock, although she is quick to note that not everyone is able to see it. She writes, "Many people, I have found, are congenitally unable to appreciate the sight of a peacock. Once or twice I have been

54. Aristotle, *Metaphysics* 1.1.980a27.
55. *MM*, 9.
56. *MM*, 10.

asked what the peacock is 'good for'—a question which gets no response from me because it deserves none."[57]

An important aspect of knowing is the ability to affirm what one knows through a judgment, which eventually results in signifying what one knows, most often through human speech. O'Connor gives an example of this process, recalling some memorable visitors to her farm—"An old man and five or six white-haired, barefooted children"[58]—and their coming-to-know *peacock*, either for the first time, or more deeply than before:

> The old man had got out of the car and was gazing at the peacock with an astounded look of recognition. "I ain't seen one of them since my grandaddy's day," he said, respectfully removing his hat. "Folks used to have' em, but they don't no more."
>
> "Whut is it?" the child asked again in the same tone he had used before.
>
> "Churren," the old man said, "that's the king of the birds!"
>
> The children received this information in silence. After a minute they climbed back into the car and continued from there to stare at the peacock, their expressions annoyed, as if they disliked catching the old man in the truth.[59]

It is worth noting two important actions of the old man in this account. First, he "got out of the car," meaning that the view from standing outside of his car was qualitatively better than the view from sitting inside his car, so he took deliberate and intentional action to position himself in such a way that he could get the best look at the bird. Second, O'Connor tells us that he was "gazing at the peacock," which is different from "*glancing* at the peacock" or "*glimpsing* the peacock," both of which are quick, nonreflective, disinterested, almost unintentional ways of looking

57. *MM*, 10.
58. *MM*, 12.
59. *MM*, 13.

at things. To *gaze*, on the other hand, is to look at something in such a way as to study it; it is to stare with the purpose of coming to know something or to know something better.

It is also worth noting that the old man had seen a peacock before—many years ago—so he did have an image of a peacock stored in his memory. However, this particular sight of this particular peacock, which he refers to as "the king of the birds" (which is likely how a peacock was described to him upon his initial encounter with a peacock as a child), gives him a deeper understanding of and a deeper wonder about the bird that is peacock. When the children ask him in wonder about this most unique bird, his answer renders them silent, yet O'Connor tells us that they "continued to stare at the peacock." Aristotle thinks that all human beings wonder and that wonder is the beginning of philosophy—the beginning of knowing reality—and the reaction of the children offers excellent evidence to support this claim.[60] *Silence* and *staring* are important to the process of knowing, according to O'Connor, and they work in tandem. Giving one's attention to what-is, to the being of another, is the way one comes to know what a thing is and how it exists, and although O'Connor is not concerned with offering a detailed account of this epistemological process, she nonetheless offers a convincing narrative account of its phenomenon.

Painting and Seeing

While Flannery O'Connor is famous for her narrative art, it is less well known that she also painted, and that she did so not as a hobby or diversion but as an intentional discipline that enhanced and supported her primary craft. O'Connor was convinced that painting helped her to see, because painting made her look and stare and gaze at reality, which is how she thinks one is able to come to know what-is. She explains, "Now learning to see is

60. Aristotle, *Metaphysics* 1.2.983a14–15.

the basis for learning all the arts except music. I know a good many fiction writers who paint, not because they're any good at painting, but because it helps their writing. It forces them to look at things. Fiction writing is very seldom a matter of saying things; it is a matter of showing things."[61] As we have noted above, O'Connor is convinced that an artist is only able to show things if an artist has first seen things, so this sort of artistic cross-training—being a writer who also paints—makes perfect sense to one who understands her epistemological approach to reality.

Seeing takes practice, just as virtue takes practice, and O'Connor took great interest in any activity that improved her artistic vision. Journalist Frank Daniel visited O'Connor at Andalusia in 1962 and reported, "Paintings by Miss O'Connor hang in several rooms of her home. Asked if painting is a relaxation, she said it isn't—that it is hard work."[62] In other words, if painting helps one to see, and if painting is hard work, then it is hard work to learn to see, and it takes time and effort to learn to see, but it is essential, according to O'Connor, that the narrative artist learn to see. She explains, "Any discipline can help your writing: logic, mathematics, theology, and of course and particularly drawing. Anything that helps you to see, anything that makes you look. The writer should never be ashamed of staring. There is nothing that doesn't require his attention."[63] We have already offered sufficient evidence that O'Connor spent a good deal of time simply staring and looking, particularly in the afternoons, from her front porch, and even from within the confines of a peafowl pen. What she took in through her eyes in the afternoons she would report in the mornings during her three hours of writing, as well as in her painting.

61. *MM*, 93. It is also true, as we have stated earlier, that O'Connor was a cartoonist.
62. Frank Daniel, "Flannery O'Connor Shapes Own Capital," *The Atlanta Journal* and *The Atlanta Constitution*, July 22, 1962, in *Conversations*, 92.
63. *MM*, 84.

Betty Edwards' Theory: Drawing Is Seeing

Betty Edwards' instructional text *Drawing on the Right Side of the Brain*[64] was first published in 1979, the same year as O'Connor's *The Habit of Being*, fifteen years after O'Connor's death. Edwards' thesis is that the art of drawing is not primarily about acquiring "drawing skills" in the usual sense but about fundamental *seeing* skills.[65] Edwards states that the true subject of her book is not "art with a capital A" or even drawing, but that its "true subject is *perception*."[66] Along with Aristotle, Aquinas, and O'Connor, Edwards recognizes an important relation between seeing and knowing.

Edwards is not a philosopher, but her thinking is very much in tune with Thomistic epistemology. Without using philosophical jargon, she argues that knowledge begins in the senses, particularly in the eyes, and that the more one sees, the more one knows. She thinks that modern culture has become too rationalistic, emphasizing the logical, conceptual, and analytic aspects of knowing (popularly symbolized as the domain of "the left brain") while too easily dismissing the important role of perception, intuition, imagination, and creativity in knowing (aspects associated with "the right brain").[67] Her solution is to recover an appreciation for the contribution of the right side of the brain in the powers of seeing and knowing. She quotes Albert Einstein: "The intuitive mind is a sacred gift, and the rational mind is a faithful servant. We have created a society that honors the servant and has forgotten the gift."[68] Thomistically speaking, we can say that what Edwards is analogously recognizing here is the cooperation of the sensitive soul and the intellective soul,

---

64. Betty Edwards, *Drawing on the Right Side of the Brain*, 4th ed. (London: Penguin Books, 2012). Special thanks to artist and friend Jeff Pasek for introducing me to this book and to these ideas.
65. Edwards, *Drawing on the Right Side of the Brain*, xv.
66. Edwards, xiv.
67. Edwards, xvii, xv.
68. Edwards, xv.

particularly his account of receiving the sensible species and forming a phantasm. Edwards' emphasis on "learning to see" is a guide to forming richer phantasms, since when one sees things properly, one sees more of what is there, more of reality. When the agent intellect is able to work on more fully formed phantasms, it can abstract more deeply from them the nature or quiddity or essence of things seen, which eventually results in better conceptual thinking, which is, as we have noted above, the key characteristic of intellectual life. Human beings need phantasms in order to know because their conceptual knowledge depends upon their sensitive knowledge, and artists especially need rich phantasms to make art because the artist is re-presenting what the eye has seen.

According to Thomas, human beings are not simply thinkers but knowers; Betty Edwards' thesis—that with the proper practice anyone can become not simply a drawer but a seer—supports this epistemological claim.

The Five Fundamental Drawing Skills

Edwards makes a comparison between *learning to draw* and *learning to read*. She claims that drawing and reading can be viewed as similar combinations of distinct skills:

Drawing Skills

- The perception of edges (seeing where one thing ends and another starts)
- The perception of spaces (seeing what lies beside and beyond)
- The perception of relationships (seeing in perspective and in proportion)
- The perception of lights and shadows (seeing things in degrees of values)
- The perception of the *gestalt* (seeing the whole *and* its parts)

Reading Skills

- Phonetic awareness (knowing that alphabet letters represent sounds)
- Phonics (recognizing letter sounds in words)
- Vocabulary (knowing the meanings of words)
- Fluency (being able to read quickly and smoothly)
- Comprehension (grasping the meaning of what is read)[69]

Edwards thinks that learning to draw and learning to read are both skills "made up of component subskills that are learned step by step,"[70] and that the first four steps require direct teaching, while the fifth one occurs as an outcome of the first four.[71] The culmination of Edwards' five drawing skills in the perception of the *gestalt* is reminiscent of O'Connor's comments regarding what Maritain calls "the habit of art." She writes, "I think this is more than just a discipline, although it is that; I think it is a way of looking at the created world and of using the senses so as to make them find as much meaning as possible in things."[72] O'Connor never uses the word *gestalt*, but she is very attentive to the artist's ability to see things in depth by paying careful attention to them. Here is the advice she offers to the college student interested in writing fiction:

> My advice is to start reading and writing and looking and listening. Pay less attention to yourself than to what is outside you and if you must write about yourself, get a good distance away and judge yourself with a stranger's eyes and a stranger's severity.
>
> Remember that reason should always go where the imagination goes. The artist uses his reason to discover an answering

69. Edwards, xxiv–xxv.
70. Edwards, xxiv.
71. Edwards, xxv.
72. *MM*, 101.

reason in everything he sees. For him, to be reasonable is to find in the object, in the situation, in the sequence, the spirit which makes it itself.

The short story writer particularly has to learn to read life in a way that includes the most possibilities—like the medieval commentators on scripture, who found three kinds of meaning in the literal level of the sacred text. If you see things in depth, you will be more liable to write them that way.[73]

Ultimately, the contribution that Edwards makes toward understanding O'Connor's Hillbilly Thomism in her *five fundamental drawing skills* is that she offers sufficient evidence to support the Thomistic claim that the senses—and the sense of sight in particular—are essential in coming to know reality. Gilson notes, "The causes of visible forms are not themselves visible. Art is there to give them visible appearance and to reveal them to us through the medium of sense perception."[74] Edwards' attention to the way in which sense perception—specifically at work in the act of drawing—is foundational to human knowing illuminates an important and explicitly stated analogy in the artistic life of Flannery O'Connor: that she viewed the craft of painting and the craft of writing stories as epistemologically parallel activities, demanding similar habits of mind.

Drawing Negative Spaces and Writing about Sin

In the previous chapter, we noted that Flannery O'Connor makes use of the grotesque to reveal reality by showing a distortion of reality or a privation of reality. There is an important relation between O'Connor's notion of the grotesque and Edwards' principle of drawing negative spaces. In both cases, by presenting the

73. Flannery O'Connor, "A Symposium on the Short Story," *Esprit* 3 (Winter 1959): 8–13, in *Conversations*, 17.
74. Étienne Gilson, *Painting and Reality: The A.W. Mellon Lectures in the Fine Arts* (New York: Pantheon Books, 1957), 187.

absence or lack of a thing (being), that thing (being) is able to be known. For example, O'Connor writes, "Often the nature of grace can be made plain only by describing its absence."[75] Edwards offers an example, not about grace and sin, but about drawing a sheep with horns. She writes:

> In drawing the sheep, a "hard" part would be drawing the horns, which are foreshortened and curve off into space in unexpected ways that make the horns difficult to see and draw. Another hard part would be the arrangement of the legs in the foreshortened view of the animal. What to do? Don't draw the horns or the legs at all. Close one eye, focus on the negative spaces of the horns and the legs, draw those and you get the horns and legs—for free! Moreover, you will get them right, because you have no names for those shapes, no pre-existing symbols to rush in, and no knowledge of why they are the way they are. They are just shapes.[76]

In both examples, O'Connor and Edwards argue that paying attention to absence is helpful in coming to know what is present, or, more Thomistically stated, recognizing nonbeing or privation of being is an important way that human beings come to know being. Edwards writes:

> Emphasis on negative spaces *unifies* your drawing and *strengthens* your composition. Emphasis on negative spaces automatically creates unity, and, conversely, ignoring negative spaces inevitably *dis-unifies* an artwork. For reasons that are hard to put into words, we just like to look at artworks with strong emphasis on negative spaces. Who knows—perhaps it is our human longing

75. *MM*, 204.
76. Edwards, *Drawing on the Right Side of the Brain*, 113.

to be unified with our world, or perhaps because in reality we *are* one with the world around us.[77]

Replacing Edwards' understanding of "negative spaces" with O'Connor's understanding of sin in this quotation would result in an argument perfectly consistent with Hillbilly Thomism: that naming sin *unifies* and *strengthens* art, and that to ignore sin *dis-unifies* art. This is the case, O'Connor would say—as we saw in the previous chapter—because to acknowledge sin is to acknowledge reality. O'Connor writes, "The novelist doesn't write about people in a vacuum; he writes about people in a world where something is obviously lacking, where there is the general mystery of incompleteness and the particular tragedy of our own times to be demonstrated, and the novelist tries to give you, within the form of the book, a total experience of human nature at any time."[78]

God, Happiness, Drawing, and Silence

Although O'Connor's *Introduction to St. Thomas Aquinas* only contains a few articles from the *Summa contra Gentiles*, the articles it does contain are important here—particularly chapters 35–37 from book III—as they attend to knowing God and finding happiness, which, according to Thomas, are ultimately one and the same. He writes,

> Nevertheless it is evident that the end of any intellectual substance, even the lowest, is to understand God. For it has been shown [in SCG 3.37] that God is the last end towards which all things tend. And the human intellect, although the lowest in the order of intelligent substances, is superior to all that are devoid of understanding. Since then a more noble substance has not a less noble end, God will be the end also of the human

77. Edwards, 118.
78. *MM*, 167.

intellect. Now every intelligent being attains to its last end by understanding it, as we have proved. Therefore, the human intellect attains to God as its end, by understanding Him.[79]

Because the human soul is intellectual—going beyond the vegetative and sensitive powers of other living things—human beings seek to know God by their nature, whether they realize it or not. And, according to Thomas, true happiness for human beings is only ever found in knowing God. He explains,

> Accordingly, if man's ultimate happiness does not consist in external things, which are called goods of fortune; nor in goods of the body; nor in goods of the soul, as regards the sensitive part; nor as regards the intellectual part, in terms of the life of moral virtue; nor in terms of the intellectual virtues which are concerned with action, namely, art and prudence:—it remains for us to conclude that man's ultimate happiness consists in the contemplation of truth.[80]

Thomas thinks that contemplating the truth is ultimately directed toward the source of all truth, which is God, and he thinks that ultimate human happiness "consists solely in the contemplation of God."[81] Thomas notes that this ultimate human happiness is not experienced in this life but in the *beatific vision*, and "it is through this vision that we become most like God, and participators of His blessedness, since God understands His substance through His essence, and this is His blessedness."[82] While in this life, human beings do not have access to the beatific vision, we do prepare to know and understand God by

79. *SCG* 3.25.
80. *SCG* 3.37.
81. *SCG* 3.37.
82. *SCG* 3.51.

knowing and understanding sensible things.[83] What this means for Thomas, and for our study of O'Connor's Hillbilly Thomism, is that even the knowledge of God begins by way of the bodily senses;[84] therefore, training the senses to focus on and be attentive to reality is a necessary aspect of coming to know reality's Cause and finding a progressive happiness in that knowledge.

Betty Edwards has nothing to say about God or the beatific vision in *Drawing on the Right Side of the Brain*, but she does offer some very salient observations about the fruits of learning to draw, which, as we have shown, is ultimately a matter of learning to see. Again, analogously speaking, Thomas thinks that when we human beings come to know the essences and natures of things—not in themselves but, as we have stated, by God's divine light, the way that "visible things are seen in the light of the sun"[85]—those divine truths will bring with them what we might call "prefigurements" or "echoes" of the beatific vision. So, when Edwards reports that many of her students say, "Life seems much richer now that I am seeing more,"[86] Thomistically speaking, we can affirm her students' experience with philosophical reasoning.

We noted that in "The King of the Birds," O'Connor recognized a relation between seeing and silence.[87] She reports that when someone first sees a peacock unfold his tail, "the usual

83. Thomas insists that human beings always come to know *as human beings*, that is, as body-soul composites. He writes, "And though this mirror, which is the human mind, reflects the likeness of God in a higher way than creatures of a lower degree, yet the knowledge of God that can be gathered from the human mind does not transcend the genus of knowledge gathered from sensible things; since even the soul knows what it itself is through understanding the natures of sensible things, as we have already stated" (*SCG* 3.47).

84. "If it is stated in Holy Scripture that some have seen God, we must understand this to have been either through an imaginary vision—or even a bodily vision, when the presence of the divine power is shown by corporeal species, whether appearing externally, or formed internally in the imagination, or by gathering some intellectual knowledge of God from His spiritual effects" (*SCG* 3.47).

85. *SCG* 3.47.

86. Edwards, *Drawing on the Right Side of the Brain*, xxxiii.

87. O'Connor makes this connection between seeing and silence four different times: Cf. *MM*, 9, 10, 12, 13.

reaction is silence."[88] Human beings regularly stop talking when they are trying to understand something, whether it is another person who is speaking to them or a magnificent sight like a sunset, a beautiful painting, or a peacock's unfurled tail. Silence helps one to focus, concentrate, and be attentive to the object at hand, enabling one to better understand what one is encountering. Guardini notes, "The greatest things are accomplished in silence—not in the clamor and display of superficial eventfulness, but in the deep clarity of inner vision; in the almost imperceptible start of decision, in quiet overcoming and hidden sacrifice."[89] Edwards thinks that one of the great benefits of learning to draw is that it fosters silence. She notes, "Silence is a rare commodity in modern classrooms, and drawing is an individual, silent, timeless task."[90] One's silence is good evidence that one is paying attention.

Returning to our analogy, in the ancient Christian hymn "Let All Mortal Flesh Keep Silence," the author of the text describes the proper human response to the presence of God:

> Let all mortal flesh keep silence,
> And with fear and trembling stand;
> Ponder nothing earthly-minded,
> For with blessing in his hand,
> Christ our God to earth descendeth,
> Our full homage to demand.[91]

According to the theology of this hymn, when one is in the presence of God, the proper response is silence. And the reason for this silence is analogous to the reason for silence in the presence of a peacock's tail and in Edwards' classroom: it characterizes the

88. *MM*, 9.
89. Romano Guardini, *The Lord*, trans. Elinor Castendyk Briefs (Chicago: Henry Regnery, 1954), 15.
90. Edwards, *Drawing on the Right Side of the Brain*, xxiv.
91. "Let All Mortal Flesh Keep Silence," in *Parish Liturgy: Mass Ordinaries and Hymns for Mass and the Sacraments* (Cincinnati, OH: World Library, 1967), 162.

offering of one's full attention to reality. In the case of this ancient hymn, the object of attention is God himself made incarnate in the person of Jesus Christ; so it stands to reason that if one is moved to silence in the presence of lower realities (e.g., a peacock's tail or a drawing class), so much more so in the presence of God himself.

According to Thomas and O'Connor, human beings are made for happiness, and their ultimate happiness is union with God. However, there are degrees of happiness to be experienced by human beings in this life prior to the beatific vision. Edwards writes, "Today we are not only testing and grading our children into the ground, but we are not teaching them how to see and understand the *deep meaning* of what they learn, or to perceive the connectedness of information about the world."[92] What Edwards calls "deep meaning" is what Thomas and O'Connor will call truth and reality, and coming to know truth and reality brings with it happiness, which is why Edwards thinks that "learning to draw is a boon to happiness,"[93] because drawing helps human beings to see and know reality.

TEILHARD DE CHARDIN: NOT FOR ANSWERS, BUT FOR DIFFERENT QUESTIONS

Exemplifying a perennial paradox in the intellectual life of the Church, O'Connor once wrote, "At the age of 11, you encounter some old priest who calls you a heretic for inquiring about evolution; at about the same time Père Pierre Teilhard de Chardin, S.J. is in China discovering Peking man."[94] An honest assessment of her epistemology requires that we account for O'Connor's well-known enthusiasm for the work of Teilhard de Chardin, who was ordained a priest in 1911, earned a doctorate in paleontology from the University of Paris in 1922, and did extensive fieldwork

92. Edwards, *Drawing on the Right Side of the Brain*, xvii.
93. Edwards, xix.
94. *HB*, 366.

from 1923 to 1946 (including the famous 1929 excavation of the *Homo erectus* specimen known as Peking Man). As his career in human paleontology intertwined with his religious vocation, Teilhard approached the search for theological, philosophical, and scientific knowledge as one pursuit. Naturally, this appealed to O'Connor, who discovered in him a recognizably disciplined yet deeply creative intellect. His well-meaning effort to synthesize the evidence as he saw it, however, has often made the French Jesuit a controversial figure for many orthodox Catholics, especially in the view—potentially concerning for our purposes—of Thomists.

Teilhard was forbidden by his superiors from publishing during his lifetime, but after his death in 1955, his books—most notably *The Divine Milieu* (1957) and *The Phenomenon of Man* (1959)—began emerging. They caused a great deal of excitement, and not a little trouble, on the Catholic intellectual scene during the last few years of O'Connor's life. In 1962, the Congregation of the Doctrine of Faith gave his writings a *monitum*[95] that remains to this day.[96] While it is beyond our scope to give a comprehensive overview of Teilhard, he is perhaps best known for hypothesizing an intelligently guided evolutionary process of "convergence" by which all of creation—first matter, then life, and finally consciousness—has been and is progressing toward a goal, an "Omega Point," which is Jesus Christ.

At a time when the Church was still establishing her parameters for dialogue with modernity and responding with caution to the *nouvelle* theologians, Teilhard came under suspicion for his association with Darwinism, his unconventional and potentially subversive interpretation of Scripture passages like the Genesis account of creation and St. Paul's description of the Body of Christ,

95. A *monitum* is an official warning by the magisterium of the Catholic Church.
96. Gerard O'Connell, "Will Pope Francis Remove the Vatican's 'Warning' from Teilhard de Chardin's Writings?" *America*, November, 21, 2017, https://www.americamagazine.org/faith/2017/11/21/will-pope-francis-remove-vaticans-warning-teilhard-de-chardins-writings.

his perceived denial of the distinction between nature and grace and perhaps between the spiritual soul and material body, and his seemingly utopian or even Pelagian vision of humanity's future, all vaguely surrounded by a penumbra of unsettling mysticism.

At worst, Teilhard's critics charged him with pantheism and even with having "invented a religion of his own," as Msgr. Leo Schumacher put it in his 1968 polemic *The Truth about Teilhard*.[97] The claim that "St. Thomas Aquinas has been toppled from his throne as the universal doctor of the Catholic Church and supplanted" by Teilhard, who "has reconciled modern science with religion and Christian life with worldly occupations and the pursuit of progress," may have been popular among certain Catholics, argued Schumacher, but was in fact "not only preposterous, but downright mystifying."[98]

What did O'Connor see in Teilhard de Chardin, and is her admiration of his thought problematic for her Hillbilly Thomism? In a 1960 review of Teilhard's *The Phenomenon of Man* and Claude Tresmontant's *Pierre Teilhard de Chardin: His Thought*, O'Connor defended Teilhard against the charge of abandoning the Catholic faith. On the contrary, she argued, he was a model of docility: "Only a man of profound Catholic piety could have sustained his love for the Church and his order [while the Church and his order were preventing him from teaching and publishing], but Teilhard was a great Christian; his vision of Christ was as real as his love for science; his mind dealt in immensities. This is a work which makes demands on the scientist, the theologian and the poet."[99] She seems to have been fascinated by the creative tension between Teilhard's intellectual honesty and his obedience. "The most important non-fiction writer," she told Fr. John McCown, "is Père Pierre Teilhard de Chardin, S.J. who died in 1955 and has so

---

97. Leo J. Schumacher, *The Truth About Teilhard* (New York: Twin Circle, 1968), 13.

98. Schumacher, *Truth About Teilhard*, 37.

99. *PG*, 86.

far escaped the Index [of Prohibited Books], although a monition has been issued on him. If [writers] are good," she added, "they are dangerous."[100]

O'Connor reviewed three books about Teilhard's life and writings for *The Bulletin* and recommended him frequently to friends (his name appears nineteen times in *The Habit of Being*).[101] In January 1960, she offered to send one of his books to Betty Hester ("It is hard to read if you don't know anything about chemistry and biology and I don't, but as you get on in it, it becomes very stimulating to the imagination").[102] In her letter insisting to Alfred Corn that education and reason pose no real barrier to Christian faith, she advises him to read Teilhard and gives this telling description:

> I might suggest that you look into some of the works of Pierre Teilhard de Chardin (*The Phenomenon of Man* et al.). He was a paleontologist—helped to discover Peking man—and also a man of God. I don't suggest you go to him for answers but for different questions, for that stretching of the imagination that you need to make you a sceptic in the face of much that you are learning, much of which is new and shocking but which when

100. *HB*, 570. (Thomas Aquinas was also seen as "dangerous" in the late thirteenth century.)

101. Monsignor Schumacher wrote his polemic against Teilhard in 1968, four years after O'Connor's death, yet we can look to O'Connor's letter to Dr. T.R. Spivey dated April 9, 1960, for a sense of how she might have responded to Schumacher's accusations: "Now about Teilhard. *The Phenomenon of Man* is not a book about animals in the first place but about development. There is nothing in it about animals except the section on the development of the primates. The man is a scientist, writing as one. From your comments on him, I can't really believe you have read the book, or if you have, it was with a very hot eye and not enough sympathy to get his vision. The place to find out about his love of nature would be his autobiography. From sections of it I have read in Tremontant, I gather him to have been able to satisfy you on that score. This is a scientific age and Teilhard's direction is to face it toward Christ. His likeness to Jung is not in gnosticism. Talk about this man after you know something about him. I know you don't want it but I am going to send you a book on Teilhard's thought by a Frenchman, C. Tremontant" (*HB*, 387–388).

102. *HB*, 368.

boiled down becomes less so and takes its place in the general scheme of things.[103]

Certainly, it was appropriate for professional theologians to examine Teilhard's doctrinal orthodoxy and to critique him where necessary. What appealed to the artist O'Connor, however, was his "stimulating" and "stretching" of her imagination—like the training of a muscle—increasing her ability to render the abstract and the mysterious into the immediate and tangible. "The discovery that we owe to Teilhard," she wrote, "is that vocation of spirit is visible, concrete, and of absorbing interest. If his method did not achieve all he thought it did, he was still making an attempt which it is necessary for scientists and theologians to take over and carry further."[104] Thus conceding here the limitations of Teilhard's inquiry, O'Connor nonetheless commends him for trying to grasp how the underlying order expressed in theological formulae also unfolds organically in the dynamic procedures of bedrock and clay, proteins and enzymes, breathing lungs, and buried fossils.

A Global and Interconnected Vision

"Cosmological and Christian conceptions of the world converge in Teilhard's thought," explained philosophical historian Frederick Copleston, SJ, in his 1981 paper "Teilhard and a Global Outlook."[105] According to Teilhard, *cosmogenesis* (the process by which the universe develops through stages of greater and greater advancement and connectedness) is in fact *Christogenesis* (a process by which the created world is increasingly manifesting the mystical Body of Christ). The risen Christ—the "cosmic Christ"—appears "at

103. *HB*, 477.
104. *HB*, 127.
105. Frederick C. Copleston, "Teilhard de Chardin and a Global Outlook," in *Teilhard and the Unity of Knowledge: The Georgetown University Centennial Symposium* (New York: Paulist, 1983), 5–18.

the center of the picture" as the *telos* toward which evolution (of all kinds) is aimed.[106] Copleston continues:

> [Teilhard] tries not so much to convince people by abstract arguments but to make them "see" the relevance of Christianity, the universal role or function of Christ in a world which manifests the creative activity of God. In other words, he provides a global vision which makes Christianity's claim to universality more credible. It can be reasonably argued that this is what people need, namely a vision, and that they are more likely to be favorably impressed by a contemporary vision which widens their mental horizons than by the stock arguments of traditional apologetics.[107]

As a Catholic, O'Connor knew and believed that Christ had redeemed the whole world and that the Church's mission is universal: go proclaim the Gospel to all nations. Teilhard's vision of the interconnectivity of the whole cosmos enfleshed that universality and resonated with O'Connor, who agreed that everything in the universe had to be measured—personally, regionally, nationally, globally, and cosmically—against the truth of Christ at the center of the picture. "The longer you look at one object," she said, "the more of the world you see in it; and it's well to remember that the serious fiction writer always writes about the whole world, no matter how limited his particular scene. For him, the bomb that was dropped on Hiroshima affects life on the Oconee River, and there's not anything he can do about it."[108] O'Connor's artistic vision widened as she assimilated insights from Teilhard into her basically Thomistic intellectual orientation: we take the world as we find it; we come to know

---

106. Copleston, 16.
107. Copleston, 16.
108. Copleston, 77. (The Oconee River is a major river in Georgia and runs right along the border of Milledgeville.)

the universal by observing the particular; and when we observe violence and war on the other side of the planet, racism in our own country, or disease in our own bodies, we realize these wounds to the Body of Christ are all part of the same story.

Passive Diminishment

From the age of twenty-five onward, O'Connor suffered from lupus, the same disease that took her father's life and would eventually take hers at the age of thirty-nine. O'Connor knew that she was slowly dying, and in her search for a way to understand her suffering, affliction, and anticipated death, she found great consolation in Teilhard's doctrine of *passive diminishment*. O'Connor writes, "Père Teilhard talks about 'passive diminishments' in *The Divine Milieu*. He means those afflictions that you can't get rid of and have to bear. Those that you can get rid of he believes you must bend every effort *to* get rid of. I think he was a very great man."[109]

O'Connor was drawn to Teilhard's notion of passive diminishment because she found it to be an adequate response to the problem of human suffering and death. She understood that suffering and death are universally part of life. Sally Fitzgerald, O'Connor's friend and editor, explains,

> From Teilhard de Chardin she eventually learned a phrase for something she already knew about: "passive diminishment"— the serene acceptance of whatever affliction or loss cannot be changed by any means—and she must have reasoned that the eventual effect of such diminishment, accompanied by a perfecting of the will, is to bring increase, which is not to say that acceptance made matters easy. So [after her diagnosis and her move back to Georgia] she set about making the most she could of both her gift and her circumstances, from day to day.[110]

109. *HB*, 509.
110. *HB*, 53.

Fitzgerald notes that O'Connor "already knew about" passive diminishment from her own life experience, but an important aspect of what made Teilhard's doctrine so attractive and convincing to O'Connor was the fact that he spoke both as a man of faith and as a modern scientist, bringing the two disciplines into dialogue in order to address the perennial questions of the meaning of suffering and death.

For Teilhard and for O'Connor, knowing always comes against the ultimate horizon or backdrop, which is God, and this includes knowledge of modern science. Teilhard's doctrine of passive diminishment offered O'Connor a greater ability to understand the meaning of generation and decomposition, specifically in the human experience, and to look upon the reality of passive suffering with hope. O'Connor explains how this reality unfolded in the young life of Mary Ann, a child with terminal cancer who lived (much longer than expected) at a Dominican cancer home in Atlanta:

> The creative action of the Christian's life is to prepare his death in Christ. It is a continuous action in which this world's goods are utilized to the fullest, both positive gifts and what Père Teilhard de Chardin calls "passive diminishments." Mary Ann's diminishment was extreme, but she was equipped by natural intelligence and by a suitable education, not simply to endure it, but to build upon it.[111]

Epistemologically speaking, Teilhard was able to solidify O'Connor's knowledge of what she already believed to be true according to her Catholic faith and her reading of Thomas Aquinas regarding life, death, and the meaning of human suffering.[112] She did not think being inspired by Teilhard necessitated any

111. *MM*, 223.
112. "Tresmontant, while admitting Teilhard was not a good metaphysician, vigorously defends his orthodoxy" (*PG*, 87).

sort of "toppling" of Aquinas. Nowhere in her many comments about Teilhard can O'Connor be construed as wholly accepting his ideas as a comprehensive worldview or a complete epistemic framework, and certainly not as being willing to follow those ideas at the expense of her orthodoxy. But she did recognize in him a fellow imaginative seeker—a theologian/scientist working in the manner of an artist, beginning by looking at what-is and proceeding to draw forth unnoticed connections. She took him to represent an aspiration toward the reconciliation of the modern scientific worldview with the classical Catholic worldview, and the reconciliation of all truth of natural reason with all truth of dogmatic faith, and for this she was willing to accept a little danger in the spirit of intellectual exploration. As Aquinas drew on Aristotle and Averroes in order to enhance, not undermine, his explication of Catholic doctrine, we can accept that O'Connor incorporated convergence and passive diminishment into her imagination without ceasing to be a Thomist. "Because Teilhard is both a man of science and a believer," she predicted, "the scientist and the theologian will perhaps require a long time to sift through his thought and accept it, but the poet, whose sight is essentially prophetic, will at once recognize in this immense vision his own."[113]

O'CONNOR'S EPISTEMOLOGY IN "PARKER'S BACK"

Flannery O'Connor started writing "Parker's Back" in December of 1960, which was "concurrent with O'Connor's reading of Teilhard's *The Divine Milieu*, his second published book in America."[114] In a letter to Betty Hester dated January 21, 1961, O'Connor writes, "'Parker's Back' is not coming along too well. It is too funny to be as serious as it ought. I have a lot of trouble

---

113. *PG*, 87–88.
114. Margaret Earley Whitt, *Understanding Flannery O'Connor* (Columbia, SC: University of South Carolina Press, 1995), 150.

with getting the right tone."[115] O'Connor would come back to the story in 1964, and it would be one of the last stories she ever wrote. It was completed, Sally Fitzgerald reports, "when she was more or less in extremis."[116] "Parker's Back" was published in the April 1965 issue of *Esquire* and then appeared in O'Connor's second collection of short stories, *Everything That Rises Must Converge*, the title of which also belongs to the first story in the collection and which was inspired by Teilhard de Chardin's concept of the "Omega Point."[117] Although significant attention has been given to Teilhard's influence on O'Connor's later stories, that influence was grafted onto her Thomistic intuitions, which remain on full display, especially in "Parker's Back."

In the first two paragraphs of "Parker's Back," the narrator reports that a man named Parker is "puzzled and ashamed of himself" and that "it was himself that he could not understand."[118] According to Aristotle, to recognize a *puzzle* or a *knot* (ἀπορία)[119] is a crucial aspect of human knowledge, for in order to solve a puzzle one has to first recognize that there is a puzzle to be solved, and in order to untie a knot, one cannot remain ignorant of the knot. So the fact that Parker is puzzled by himself and cannot understand himself reveals to the reader early on that Parker himself is the puzzle to be solved, the knot to be untied. A few pages later, we learn that "long views depressed Parker,"[120]

---

115. *HB*, 427.

116. *HB*, 559.

117. The Omega Point is part of Chardin's theory inspired by evolution, which understands the risen Christ as the end point of the universe. He writes, "Autonomy, actuality, irreversibility, and thus finally transcendence are the four attributes of Omega" (Chardin, *The Phenomenon of Man* [New York: Harper & Row, 1959], 270). According to Chardin, and as understood by O'Connor, the disorder of the universe is experiencing a process of redemption in which Jesus Christ is the main actor; hence, the Omega Point is Christ himself, the Alpha and the Omega (Chardin, 257–272).

118. *CS*, 510.

119. "For those who wish to get clear of difficulties it is advantageous to discuss the difficulties well; for the subsequent free play of thought implies the solution of the previous difficulties, and it is impossible to untie a knot of which one does not know" (Aristotle, *Metaphysics* 3.1.995a25–30).

120. *CS*, 516.

which is indicative of his inability to understand himself against the backdrop of a greater whole, the *gestalt*. As we noted above, according to Thomas, human beings are knowers, not thinkers, and this reality is on display in Parker's desire not simply to think but to understand himself—to know himself.

The first time Parker "felt the least motion of wonder in himself"[121] was at the age of fourteen when "he saw a man in a fair, tattooed from head to foot."[122] We learn in a narrative flashback how Parker's wonder was triggered by the sight of the tattooed man—by *seeing something* he had never seen before—which offers evidence for the Thomistic principle that knowledge begins in the senses. Parker first sees what seems to him to be "a single intricate design of brilliant color,"[123] then he observes the man "flexing his muscles so that the arabesque of men and beasts and flowers on his skin appeared to have a subtle motion of its own."[124] Philosophically speaking, O'Connor's details and the order of their presentation are significant, for Parker first recognizes the whole (single intricate design of brilliant color) and then recognizes the parts (the arabesque of men and beasts and flowers) that make up the whole. Moreover, Aristotle teaches that the sense of sight "makes us know and brings to light many differences in things,"[125] and this principle is on display in the way that Parker makes distinctions between the three different forms of life (human, animal, plant) yet recognizes them as participants in an order of being (arabesque). This experience of seeing the tattooed man at the fair changes Parker and sets him upon a new path of understanding:

> Until he saw the man at the fair, it did not enter his head that
> there was anything out of the ordinary about the fact that he

121. *CS*, 513. (Recall the role that "wonder" plays in Hillbilly Thomism.)
122. *CS*, 512.
123. *CS*, 512.
124. *CS*, 512–513.
125. Aristotle, *Metaphysics* 1.1.980a25–27.

existed. Even then it did not enter his head, but a peculiar unease settled in him. It was as if a blind boy had been turned so gently in a different direction that he did not know his destination had been changed.[126]

At this point in the story, Parker does not yet know what it is that he wants or what it is that has changed in him—which is why O'Connor notes that "it did not enter his head," because Parker does not yet *know* or *understand*. But the experience of seeing the tattooed man at the fair has caused Parker to start wondering about his own existence and sets him in a direction to begin solving the puzzle that is his life—and life itself.

Parker decides that getting tattoos will somehow help him to understand himself, his experience at the fair, and the meaning of his existence. (He is right, but, as we shall see, not in the way that he thinks he is.) Tattoos become a sort of addiction for Parker. We are told that "the only reason he worked at all was to pay for more tattoos."[127] Parker joins the Navy, and everywhere he goes he "pick[s] up more tattoos."[128] In a very Thomistic move, O'Connor acknowledges the hierarchy of being—from artifacts, to animals, to humans—through his tattoos: "He had stopped having lifeless ones like anchors and crossed rifles. He had a tiger and a panther on each shoulder, a cobra coiled about a torch on his chest, hawks on his thighs, Elizabeth II and Philip over where his stomach and liver were respectively."[129] Yet like any addictive behavior, receiving a tattoo only assuages him for so long:

> Parker would be satisfied with each tattoo about a month, then something about it that had attracted him would wear off. Whenever a decent-sized mirror was available, he would get in

126. *CS*, 513.
127. *CS*, 513.
128. *CS*, 514.
129. *CS*, 514.

front of it and study his overall look. The effect was not of one intricate arabesque of colors but of something haphazard and botched. A huge dissatisfaction would come over him and he would go off and find another tattooist and have another space filled up. The front of Parker was almost completely covered but there were no tattoos on his back. He had no desire for one anywhere he could not readily see it himself. As the space on the front of him for tattoos decreased, his dissatisfaction grew and became general.[130]

Thomistically speaking, these passages contain a great many points for our consideration. First, Parker looks to tattoos to satisfy some deep longing within him, although the satisfaction he receives from a new tattoo is temporary at best. Second, he likes to "study" himself and the look of his tattoos in front of a mirror whenever he has the opportunity. (We recall how important *looking* and *seeing* are to knowing and understanding.) Third, he finds the sight of himself disappointing, because unlike the man at the fair whose tattoos formed an "arabesque of men and beasts and flowers," the ink on Parker's skin produces a *gestalt* "not of one intricate arabesque of colors but of something haphazard and botched." In other words, Parker recognizes a lack or a privation of order and meaning, which is true not only on the literal level of his skin but symbolically representative of the state of his soul—hence his deep dissatisfaction. Fourth, although it will take some time for Parker to realize, the *negative space* on his back will play a most important role in solving the puzzle of himself. For he already has the whole order of creation tattooed on his body, but the empty space on his back symbolically reveals his ignorance of, and potential for relationship with, the omnipotent Author of creation. Fifth, the tattoos he sees on the man at the

130. *CS*, 514.

fair are all images of concrete realities; they are not abstractions or formless designs.

Just as tattoos fail to satisfy Parker, so do the women in his life. He has married a preacher's daughter, Sarah Ruth, who is "plain, plain,"[131] who is "against color,"[132] who prefers that he wear "his shirt when he work[s],"[133] who thinks "churches [are] idolatrous,"[134] who is a poor cook ("Sarah Ruth just threw food in the pot and let it boil"),[135] and who refers to his tattoos as "a heap of vanity."[136] Although their courtship was fairly exciting, marrying Sarah Ruth has not satisfied Parker's deep longing and, in fact, has exacerbated it. Unlike Parker, who enjoys studying himself and looking at his body in a mirror whenever the opportunity presents itself, Sarah Ruth not only shuts "her eyes tight" but "turn[s] her back as well" to avoid seeing any of Parker's tattoos. Although we will soon discover that Sarah Ruth is a kind of iconoclast heretic in O'Connor's eyes,[137] her refusal to look at Parker's tattooed body is evidence that on some level she understands the Thomistic relation of seeing to knowing, whether she admits it or not. Sarah Ruth does not want her bodily senses involved in her spiritual life, and she prefers her living to be pure and clean, which is symbolized by her broom.

Parker decides that the only way to real satisfaction is to fill the empty space on his back with a new tattoo. "He visualized having a tattoo put there that Sarah Ruth would not be able to resist—a religious subject."[138] First, he considers having "an open book with holy bible tattooed under it and an actual verse printed on the page,"[139] but he anticipates Sarah Ruth's rejection of such

131. *CS*, 510.
132. *CS*, 510.
133. *CS*, 511.
134. *CS*, 518.
135. *CS*, 519.
136. *CS*, 515.
137. O'Connor notes, "Sarah Ruth was the heretic [because she believed in] the notion that you can worship in pure spirit" (*HB*, 594).
138. *CS*, 519.
139. *CS*, 519.

an image and decides that he needs "something better even than the Bible!"[140] Parker is convinced that "as urgent as it might be for him to get a tattoo, it [is] just as urgent that he get exactly the right one to bring Sarah Ruth to heel."[141] Three days later, Parker is at work, driving a tractor, picking up hay in an old woman's field and still thinking about "a suitable design for his back,"[142] when all at once he drives the tractor right into a large tree that the old woman specifically told him to avoid. The tractor flips upside down, the tree goes up in flames, and Parker's shoes fly off of his feet. The scene is reminiscent of Moses and the burning bush,[143] and the narrator reports, "If he had known how to cross himself he would have done it."[144] Parker hurries back to his truck and drives fifty miles to the city, arriving at the tattoo parlor "a little after three in the afternoon," an important and foreshadowing detail, as it is the same time two Gospel writers report Jesus dying on the cross of Calvary.[145]

O'Connor's description of Parker's eyes at this point of the story is noteworthy. We have learned that since Parker started thinking about the new tattoo for his back, "his eyes took on a hollow preoccupied expression,"[146] and that immediately after crashing into the tree his eyes were "cavernous."[147] When he finally arrives at the tattoo parlor, the artist does "not seem to recognize Parker in the hollow-eyed creature before him."[148] Parker's cavernous and hollow eyes are as empty as his back, both longing to be filled with an image that will finally satisfy the negative

140. *CS*, 519.
141. *CS*, 520.
142. *CS*, 520.
143. See Exod. 3:1–6. It is also noteworthy that this scene is reminiscent of the covenant between God and Abraham: "So shall my covenant be in your flesh an everlasting covenant" (Gen. 17:13). Just as the flesh of Abraham is marked by circumcision as a sign of his new covenant with God, so too is the flesh of Parker about to be marked by a tattoo as a sign of his new covenant with God.
144. *CS*, 520.
145. Matt. 27:46; Luke 23:44.
146. *CS*, 520.
147. *CS*, 520.
148. *CS*, 521.

space. But only the right image will do, and so Parker asks to see the book "with all the pictures of God in it."[149] The artist starts to search through his books, but he requests more information from Parker:

"Who are you interested in?" he said, "saints, angels, Christs or what?"

"God," Parker said.

"Father, Son or Spirit?"

"Just God," Parker said impatiently. "Christ. I don't care. Just so it's God."[150]

The artist finds a book filled with images of Christ and asks Parker to look through it and choose the one that he likes, telling him that "The up-t-date ones are in the back."[151] Parker begins his search at the back of the book where the modern and more assuring images of Christ are located. "Some of them he recognized—The Good Shepherd, Forbid Them Not, The Smiling Jesus, Jesus the Physician's Friend, but he kept turning rapidly backwards and the pictures became less and less reassuring."[152] The more he searches the quicker his heart beats until he arrives at an image almost at the very front of the book:

On one of the pages a pair of eyes glanced at him swiftly. Parker sped on, then stopped. His heart too appeared to cut off; there was absolute silence. It said as plainly as if silence were a language itself, go back.

149. *CS*, 521.
150. *CS*, 521–522. It is worth noting that when characters use the Lord's name in vain in O'Connor's fiction they are also indicating the power of God's name. So in this example, Parker uses the word "Christ" as a curse-word but simultaneously reveals the divinity of Jesus.
151. *CS*, 522.
152. *CS*, 522.

Parker returned to the picture—the haloed head of a flat stern Byzantine Christ with all-demanding eyes. He sat there trembling; his heart began slowly to beat again as if it were being brought to life by a subtle power.

"You found what you want?" the artist asked.

Parker's throat was too dry to speak. He got up and thrust the book at the artist, opened at the picture.

"That'll cost you plenty," the artist said. "You don't want all those little blocks though, just the outline and some better features."

"Just like it is," Parker said, "just like it is or nothing."

"It's your funeral," the artist said, "but I don't do that kind of work for nothing."[153]

We recall O'Connor's report in "The King of the Birds" that one of the most common reactions to seeing a peacock spreading his tail is silence. (She also notes, "I have yet to hear laughter."[154]) We also recall the ancient hymn "Let All Mortal Flesh Keep Silence." There is a relation between silence and understanding, and Parker's "absolute silence" when he first sees the image of the Byzantine Christ puts that relation on display. Parker is silent because he is coming to know something new and profound and concentrates so hard that not only is he unable to speak, but this silence speaks to him. He listens to the voice and goes back and indicates to the artist the image he wants on his back—the Byzantine Christ with the all-demanding eyes. The artist attempts to convince Parker to accept a simplified version of the image, but Parker refuses—it is an all-or-nothing moment for Parker. The artist tells him, "It's your funeral," which is true. If Parker is going to become a new man and find meaning and purpose in his life—and life itself—he will have to die to his old self.

153. *CS*, 522.
154. *MM*, 9.

The artist needs two days to complete the tattoo on Parker's back, and on the first day he completes the basic outline of the face, but the eyes have not yet appeared. That night Parker sleeps on a cot at the Haven of Light Christian Mission in a dormitory lit only by "a phosphorescent cross glowing at the end of the room."[155] Lying in bed, Parker reviews his day—a rudimentary *examen*—and wishes he were back home in bed with Sarah Ruth. Then, he makes two decisions. First, he decides that once the tattoo is complete he will not look at it, and second, that "all his sensations of the day and night before were those of a crazy man and that he would return to doing things according to his own sound judgement."[156] The next day, while the artist is at work on the tattoo, Parker imagines that Sarah Ruth will be "struck speechless by the face on his back,"[157] which, if it were to happen, would indicate that Sarah Ruth understood the seriousness of the new image.

The artist finishes the tattoo around four o'clock, and upon completion he tells Parker, "You can get up and look at it now."[158] Parker refuses. He sits on the edge of the table, and the artist once again says, "Go look at it."[159] Parker starts to put his shirt on, ignoring the artist's invitation, and so the artist grabs Parker by the arm and positions him between two mirrors and angrily commands, "Now *look*."[160] Parker has tried to keep the commitment he made to himself the night before of not looking at the completed tattoo, but he decides to obey the command of the artist. "Parker looked, turned white and moved away. The eyes in the reflected face continued to look at him—still, straight, all-demanding, enclosed in silence."[161] In what is now familiar

155. *CS*, 524.
156. *CS*, 524.
157. *CS*, 525.
158. *CS*, 525.
159. *CS*, 525.
160. *CS*, 525. (*An artist who commands us to look* is an accurate way to state Flannery O'Connor's artistic mission.)
161. *CS*, 526.

silence, Parker leaves the tattoo parlor, picks up a pint of whiskey at a corner shop, and drinks the entire bottle in five minutes. He makes his way over to a pool hall, where he is greeted by an acquaintance who slaps him on his back. Parker reprimands the man, informing him of the new tattoo on his back, although when asked about the image, Parker replies, "Nothing special this time."[162] But soon, the man and his friends pull up Parker's shirt and realize immediately how special the new image actually is:

> Parker felt all the hands drop away instantly and his shirt fell again like a veil over the face. There was a silence in the pool room which seemed to Parker to grow from the circle around him until it extended to the foundations under the building and upward through the beams in the roof.
>
> Finally some one said, "Christ!" Then they all broke into noise at once.[163]

The men tease Parker, asking him if "he's gone and got religion,"[164] which Parker denies. He attempts to downplay the significance of the new image on his back. Like those seeing a peacock's tail in "The King of the Birds," the men in the pool hall "yell and whistle and curse in compliment"[165] until Parker tells them to "shut up"[166] and explains that he got the tattoo "for laughs,"[167] as if it is some kind of joke. But no one in the pool hall thinks the image is a joke, least of all Parker, and when they ask

162. *CS*, 526.
163. *CS*, 526.
164. *CS*, 526.
165. *CS*, 527. Compare the reaction of the men in the pool hall to the people O'Connor describes the first time they see a peacock spread his tail: "'Amen! Amen!' an old Negro woman once cried when this happened, and I have heard many similar remarks at this moment that show the inadequacy of human speech. Some people whistle; a few, for once, are silent. A truck driver who was driving up with a load of hay and found a peacock turning before him in the middle of the road shouted, 'Get a load of that bastard!' and braked his truck to a shattering halt" (*MM*, 10).
166. *CS*, 527.
167. *CS*, 527.

him why he isn't laughing he starts a brawl with them until they throw him out, at which point we are told that "a calm descended on the pool hall as nerve shattering as if the long barnlike room were the ship from which Jonah had been cast into the sea."[168] Like Jonah, Parker will eventually make his way back to Sarah Ruth, his Nineveh, but not before spending some time examining his soul in the alley behind the pool hall. In this moment, Parker realizes that his entire life he has obeyed whatever "instinct of this kind" has come to him, and he decides that the eyes "now forever on his back [are] eyes to be obeyed."[169]

Philosophically speaking, Parker comes to a significant realization in this part of the story, as up until now he never knew anything for certain and was living in response to instinct (cogitative sense) rather than to real human understanding. *Theologically* speaking, the eyes of Christ are the eyes of the Word, the second person of the Trinity, the Way, the Truth, and the Life. The eyes of the *Christ Pantocrator*[170] demand Parker's life, but they also give him life and give his life meaning, direction, purpose, and understanding, "and he observe[s] that his dissatisfaction [is] gone."[171] Granted, the image of Jesus Christ on Parker's back is not Jesus Christ himself, but it is through the image of the Christ Pantocrator that Parker encounters the real Christ Pantocrator, and the aptness of this progression as an illustration of O'Connor's epistemology cannot be overstated. Parker's conversion and transformation come by way of an image literally on and through his flesh—not apart from it—which is how God saves his people, according to O'Connor's Catholic faith: in the Incarnation, the Word becomes human.[172]

---

168. *CS*, 527.
169. *CS*, 527.
170. *Pantocrator*: omnipotent; all-powerful; almighty.
171. *CS*, 527.
172. Parker said that he wanted an image on his back that was "something better even than the Bible!" We find that the only thing better than the Word is the Word made flesh.

Parker looks forward to seeing Sarah Ruth again and showing her his new tattoo, and with all his confidence makes his way home only to realize that she has locked him out.[173] At first, he demands that she let him in the house and then asks her why she has locked him out. She refuses to answer his question but asks him, "Who's there?"[174] He tells her, "Me . . . O.E.," but she does not open the door. She asks him once again to identify himself when "a tree of light [bursts] over the skyline. Parker [falls] back against the door as if he had been pinned there by a lance"—an obvious allusion to Christ's side being pierced on the cross. Then Parker whispers his full Christian name, Obadiah Elihue, through the door, and, at that moment, he feels "the light pouring through him, turning his spider web soul into a perfect arabesque of colors, a garden of trees and birds and beasts."[175] This is the third time in the story O'Connor uses the word *arabesque*, and it is most significant.[176] Earlier in the story, O'Connor uses *arabesque* to describe the tattooed man at the fair, and then a page later she mentions that the look of Parker's tattooed body "was not of one intricate arabesque of colors but of something haphazard and botched." But now that Parker has spoken his full Christian name,

173. Parker's return to his Sarah Ruth is one meaning of the title of the story, and he tells Sarah Ruth, "I'm back" (*CS*, 528). Another meaning is obviously the part of Parker's body that receives the tattoo. And the deepest theological meaning is that Parker has repented, and is, therefore, "back" in union with God.

174. *CS*, 528.

175. *CS*, 528.

176. Although *arabesque* does mean "an intricate pattern or design using shapes, colors, and calligraphy," it also literally means "Arab-esque" or "in the manner or style of Arabs." In Islamic art, shapes and figures are common, including plants and animals, but images of human beings are rare, and images of Muhammad are especially forbidden and considered to be idolatrous. Catholic Christianity sets itself apart from Islam most notably in the Incarnation—the belief that God became a human being. Unlike Islam, Christianity allows for and even encourages images of human beings, including Jesus Christ, who is both God and human. It is unclear whether O'Connor intended to name this important distinction between Christians and Muslims by using the word *arabesque*, but it is most worthy of theological consideration. (O'Connor may or may not have had in mind the Pantocrator in the Deesis mosaic at the Haggia Sophia when choosing her images for "Parker's Back.")

identifying himself to his wife, he feels light pouring through him, and his soul takes on a new order.

Sarah Ruth opens the door to Parker, and he wastes no time in lighting the kerosene lamp, which confuses Sarah Ruth since there is plenty of daylight. She informs him that she is not interested in making love to him, if that is what he is looking to do. He tells her to shut her mouth and then quietly says, "Look at this and then I don't want to hear no more out of you."[177] He takes off his shirt, and she looks at the new tattoo on his back, but she is not reduced to silence as he had hoped; instead, she calls it "another picture" and "more trash."[178] He tells her two more times to look at it, hoping that by looking at the image she will come to recognize the face, but she tells him, "It ain't anybody I know."[179] Parker tells her that the image is of God, which Sarah Ruth rejects, telling him, "He's a spirit. No man shall see his face," and screaming, "Idolatry!"[180] then proceeding to beat Parker across his shoulders with her broom. "He sat there and let her beat him until she had nearly knocked him senseless and large welts had formed of the face of the tattooed Christ."[181] The final sentence of the story reads: "There he was—who called himself Obadiah Elihue—leaning against the tree, crying like a baby."[182]

From one perspective, Parker seems utterly defeated, and even pathetic, as he weeps against the pecan tree, but from another perspective, we see Teilhard's passive diminishment on full display. For Parker, who has been rejected by all the men in the pool hall and now his own wife—symbolic of the rejection of the world—finally comes to understand his true self in his most diminished state, as he has finally reached Teilhard's Omega Point: Christ himself. Parker becomes the image that is on his back, as

177. *CS*, 529.
178. *CS*, 529.
179. *CS*, 529.
180. *CS*, 529.
181. *CS*, 529.
182. *CS*, 529.

he, too, has had his side pierced, his back scourged, his shoulders beaten, and the story ends with him crying out from the wood of a tree, which is his Calvary. O'Connor's detail of Parker "crying like a baby" is indicative of the new life that is now within him, the new man he has become—Teilhard's *Christogenesis*—which was only possible through the passive diminishment of the old man.[183]

Parker has come to know himself and to solve the puzzle of himself by coming to know the One who made him and who has made all things, not in some abstract way, but beginning with his senses. Obadiah Elihue Parker—the one who did not wonder about his existence until he first saw the tattooed man at the carnival, the one who became depressed by long views, the one who was a puzzle to himself, the one who could not understand himself, the one whose soul was like a spider web—came to know a new way of living, a new way of being, and a new way of knowing in the mystery of silence. He witnessed a tree go up in flames; he was beckoned by the eyes of the Byzantine Christ in the book in the tattoo parlor; he recognized that the only light in the darkness of the Haven of Light Christian Mission came from a phosphorescent cross; he knew that the new pair of eyes on his back were forever to be obeyed; and he claimed his new identity (and his new understanding of himself) by stating his full Christian name to his wife, even though she ultimately rejected him as well as the One who changed him.

Sarah Ruth believed that God was a pure spirit and that knowing him and knowing reality was strictly a spiritual activity, whereas Parker shows that human knowing—even knowing God—always involves the body, because human beings are

---

183. It seems likely that Teilhard's notion of passive diminishment may have inspired these words of O'Connor: "I don't think of conversion as being once and for all and that's that. I think once the process is begun and continues that you are continually turning inward toward God and away from your own egocentricity and that you have to see this selfish side of yourself in order to turn away from it. I measure God by everything that I am not" (*HB*, 430).

not simply minds but body-soul composites. Parker comes to knowledge, and to an understanding of himself, not by escaping his body and looking to abstractions, but by coming to know the spiritual through the material, like he comes to know Christ through an image of Christ. In "Parker's Back," O'Connor shows that the way one comes to knowledge is not symbolized in the puritanical broom of Sarah Ruth but in the arabesque of colors that is Parker's flesh.

CHAPTER FOUR

The Ethics of Flannery O'Connor

In the previous two chapters, we outlined Flannery O'Connor's metaphysical vision, in which all creation comes from God and is made to return to God, as well as her epistemological conviction that human beings are composite creatures who come to know God, the world, and themselves through a natural cooperation of the senses and the intellect. We now turn to O'Connor's ethics, which, like her metaphysics and epistemology, is deeply grounded in the Thomistic philosophical tradition.[1] In this final chapter, we will examine the role of the good; virtue; happiness and blessedness; the relationship between intellect and will; friendship; and the place of natural law in human living. We will then show how these general themes are at work in O'Connor's art and her life, with a specific focus on her understanding of human sexuality. Finally, we will demonstrate how these philosophical themes are on display in O'Connor's "The Displaced Person."

---

1. O'Connor's Modern Library copy of *Introduction to St. Thomas Aquinas* contains lengthy excepts from *Summa contra Gentiles* and *Summa theologiae* on the following topics: The End of Man (Ch. 4), Human Acts (Ch. 5), Habits and Virtues (Ch. 6), and Law (Ch. 7). These four chapters will serve as the grounding philosophical texts for this fourth chapter, as it is likely—if we take O'Connor at her word—that she was familiar with these philosophical ideas from her personal study of them.

AN OVERVIEW OF THOMISTIC ETHICAL THEORY

It is important for us at this juncture to review some basic Thomistic doctrine about the world in general so that we can gain the proper context in which to understand human beings and their actions in particular. First, Thomas and O'Connor hold that God exists, that God is good, and that God created the world and everything in it, both visible and invisible. Second, human beings are rational beings composed of matter (body) and form (soul), and that like all living things they are endowed with natural powers directing them toward a final end, which is God. Third, the way a human being achieves that end is by living according to his or her human nature, not against it—that is, by living a life proper to a human being, which both Thomas and O'Connor think is rational, possible, and ultimately enjoyable, albeit not apart from God's grace. Since this is primarily a philosophical and not a theological book, we will leave the intricacies of redemption and salvation to the theologians; suffice it to say that according to Aquinas and O'Connor, ultimate happiness can only be found in God. Moreover, Davies explains, "[Thomas] never thinks of people without thinking of them as creatures loved by God and destined for union with him by virtue of Christ. But he has things to say about human action which do not, in his view, stand or fall by virtue of the truth of Christianity."[2] It is those things to which we now turn.

The Good and God

Thomas Aquinas shares Aristotle's teleological view of human action, which he famously presented in the opening line of the *Nicomachean Ethics*: "Every art and every inquiry, and similarly every action and pursuit, is thought to aim at some good; and for this reason the good has rightly been declared to be that at

2. Brian Davies, *The Thought of Thomas Aquinas* (New York: Oxford University Press, 1992), 227.

which all things aim."[3] That human beings naturally desire some good and pursue it in their actions may not seem *prima facie* to be philosophically significant or surprising, yet such a premise reveals a most important philosophical truth: even when a man or woman is pursuing some evil or is acting maliciously, according to Aquinas, that person does so in light of the good, whether he or she knows it or not. For example, the Bible salesman who steals the prosthetic leg of a woman and leaves her helpless in the loft of a barn has certainly not committed a morally good act, but Thomas would say that the Bible salesman both stole the wooden leg and abandoned the woman in the loft because on some level he thought these were good things to do, whether because the theft brought him pleasure, made him feel powerful, or seemed to improve his collection of stolen goods from past lovers—or perhaps a combination of all three motivations. Regardless of the specific reasons, Thomas thinks we can be certain that the Bible salesman acted with an aim at some good, even if his action turned out to be an evil one. Aquinas notes, "There is no problem from the fact that some men desire evil. For they desire evil only under the aspect of good, that is, insofar as they think it good. Hence, their intention primarily aims at the good and only incidentally touches on the evil."[4] Therefore, according to the Thomistic perspective, when someone commits a bad or evil act, on some level he or she is always in pursuit of some good, and, in a roundabout way, it reveals an important truth about human nature and human beings: we are made for good, whether we know it or not.

Aristotle thinks that we human beings desire good and aim for good on account of our human nature, and Aquinas agrees but goes even further in explaining that this human nature is all

---

3. Aristotle, *Nicomachean Ethics*, trans. W.D. Ross (London: Oxford University Press, 1925),1094a1–3.

4. Thomas Aquinas, *Commentary on Aristotle's Nicomachean Ethics*, trans. C.I. Litzinger (Notre Dame, IN: Dumb Ox Books, 1993), 1.1.10.

part of God's creative plan for men and women.[5] We pause here to consider a most fundamental Thomistic claim: human nature is neither chosen nor culturally constructed, but rather *given*. As we noted in chapter 2, Aquinas holds that human beings are made for a purpose—to be with God, who is goodness itself—and this built-in orientation toward supernatural goodness explains why we pursue natural goods along the way. Whether or not one believes himself or herself to be made for God and the good does not change that fact, according to Thomas. He demonstrates that if all human action is directed toward some understanding of the good, then there must be a *source* of good toward which all things strive, an ultimate good. He offers a Platonic kind of argument: "Because nothing is good except for insofar as it is a likeness and participation in the highest good, the highest good itself is in some way desired in every particular good. Thus it can be said that the true good is what all desire."[6] And this true good, according to Thomas, is God, who is the final end for human beings and for all created things. This conception of God is, not surprisingly, shared by O'Connor: "I see God as all perfect, all complete, all powerful. God is Love and I would not believe love efficacious if I believed there were negative stages or imperfections in it."[7] And again, "I measure God by everything I am not."[8]

So according to Aristotle and Aquinas, the fact that human beings are always pursuing some good, albeit imperfectly, reveals something fundamental about the human person. For Aristotle, it means that human beings find their end, their rest, not in what he calls *apparent goods* (e.g., pleasure, wealth, honor, etc.) but in the *genuine good* of living well and doing well.[9] Aquinas agrees

5. "*Now the intellect's end and good are the true,* and its last end is the first truth. Therefore the last end of the whole man, and of all his deeds and desires, is to know the first truth, namely, God" (*SCG* 3.25).

6. Thomas Aquinas, *Commentary on NE* 1.1.11.

7. *HB*, 102.

8. *HB*, 430.

9. *NE* 1095a14–1095b12. "A real good is something I pursue as perfective or fulfilling of me and that really would perfect or fulfill me if I had it. An apparent

but goes further: the genuine good is found beyond living well and doing well; it is found in God himself, the source of all good.[10] Thomas writes,

> From the fact that they acquire the divine goodness, creatures are made like unto God. Therefore, if all things tend to God as their last end, so as to acquire His goodness, it follows that the last end of things is to become like unto God.
>
> Moreover, the agent is said to be the end of the effect in so far as the effect tends to be like the agent; and hence it is that the form of the generator is the end of the act of generation. Now God is the end of things in such wise as to be also their first producing cause. Therefore all things tend to a likeness to God, as their last end.[11]

According to Thomas, *all* created things, not just human beings, tend to God as their last end. But, as we noted in chapter 3, human beings are a particular type of creature, sharing in the vegetative attributes of plants and the sensitive attributes of animals, yet also transcending these in having a rational soul and therefore the ability to know their end and pursue their end.[12] This rational soul likens human beings to angels in that both have intelligence, but human intelligence is markedly different from angelic intelligence, as we have seen, in that human beings, because they are composite substances, come to knowledge discursively and not immediately as angels do.[13] So in tending toward their end as creatures, human beings act not as plants,

good, by contrast, is an end pursued as perfective or fulfilling of me that, if had, really would not perfect or fulfill me" (Ralph McInerny, *Ethica Thomistica: The Moral Philosophy of Thomas Aquinas* [Washington, DC: The Catholic University of America Press, 1997], 2).

10. *SCG* 3.25.

11. *SCG* 3.19.

12. "Therefore man naturally desires, as his last end, to know the first cause. But God is the first cause of all things. Therefore man's last end is to know God" (*SCG* 3.25).

13. *ST* 1.58; see section 3.2.3.

animals, or angels but uniquely as human beings, meaning that in coming to their end (or moving away from their end), human beings employ not simply an act of the intellect (as do angelic beings) nor simply a natural tendency (like a plant or animal) but, as rational animals, both.

Happiness and Beatitude

According to both Aristotle and Thomas, human beings have a final cause (the good or God), and in finding that final cause they find rest. Resting in their natural or supernatural end is what Aristotle calls *happiness* and what Thomas calls *beatitude*.[14] Happiness is found in this life by acting well and living well and in *natural beatitude*, consisting in natural contemplation of God.[15] Acting well, living well, and the natural contemplation of God are all important to Thomas; he does believe that natural happiness is the natural end for humans, but he does not think that ultimate happiness can be found in this life; it can only be experienced after death in seeing God face-to-face, in what he calls *the beatific vision*.[16] It is important to note that Thomas' notion of beatitude does not cancel or denigrate Aristotle's notion of happiness in this life but builds on it and completes it. Flannery O'Connor would have learned of this distinction from her reading of Victor White's *God and the Unconscious*:

---

14. *SCG* 3.38.

15. See Thomas Joseph White, "Imperfect Happiness and the Final End of Man: Thomas Aquinas and the Paradigm of Nature-Grace Orthodoxy," *The Thomist: A Speculative Quarterly Review* 78, no. 2 (April 2014): 247–289.

16. "Therefore man's ultimate happiness will consist in that knowledge of God which the human mind possesses after this life, a knowledge similar to that by which separate substances know him. Hence, our Lord promises us a *reward . . . in heaven* (*Matt.* v. 12) and states (*Matt.* xxii. 30) that the saints *shall be as the angels*, who always see God in heaven (*Matt.* xviii. 10)" (*SCG* 3.38). Victor White explains, "It was no part of St. Thomas's programme to bring Christ to Aristotle; on the contrary, as a Christian theologian, his purpose was to bring Aristotle's reasoning to the service of Christ" (Victor White, *God and the Unconscious* [London: Fontana Books, 1952], 122.).

So the *Summa* of St. Thomas begins by affirming what at the beginning of his *Ethics* Aristotle had been compelled to deny: the attainability of man's true and last end and bliss and completion. It was true that man could not reach the Absolute Good, but God in Christ showed that the Absolute Good not only could, but did, reach out to man and communicate to man its own eternal life.[17]

THE WILL

Now we turn to another aspect of the rational soul that distinguishes human beings from other sensitive animals: *the will*. For, according to Thomas, knowing the good is one thing, but choosing the good is another.

Voluntary and Involuntary Acts

What makes human beings unique in regard to their action is what Thomas calls *the will*, which "is the name of the rational appetite, and consequently it cannot be in beings devoid of reason."[18] He thinks that only human beings are perfectly voluntary on account of the will, which allows them to consider the consequences of their actions and freely act in ways that are impossible for nonrational animals. O'Connor agrees:

> My view of free will follows the traditional Catholic teaching. I don't think any genuine novelist is interested in writing about a world of people who are strictly determined. Even if he writes about characters who are mostly unfree, it is the sudden free action, the open possibility, which he knows is the only thing capable of illuminating the picture and giving it life. So that while predictable, predetermined actions have a comic interest for me, it is the free act, the acceptance of grace particularly,

17. White, *God and the Unconscious*, 123.
18. *ST* 1-2.6.2.

that I always have my eye on as the thing which will make a story work.[19]

According to Thomas, because human beings can think, they can also act in ways that are different from other animals. He notes, "Praise and blame attach to the voluntary act according to the perfect notion of the voluntary, which is not to be found in irrational animals."[20] For example, a human being who kills another human being or even a nonrational animal can be taken to court and tried for murder, manslaughter, or animal cruelty. But an animal that kills a human being or another animal cannot be held criminally responsible because animals lack intelligence and will (although the owner of said animal could face charges as the one responsible for allowing it to act destructively). This example displays a fundamental Thomistic distinction between rational animals and nonrational animals: "The fact that man is master of his actions is due to his being able to deliberate about them; for since the deliberating reason is indifferently disposed to opposites, the will can proceed to either. But it is not thus that voluntariness is in irrational animals."[21] According to Thomas, among animals, only human beings, because they are rational animals, must have "free choice, or otherwise counsels, exhortations, commands, prohibitions, rewards and punishments would be in vain. . . . In that man is rational, it is necessary that he have free choice."[22] So the fact that human beings can think about their actions (before, during, and after they act) and engage in such actions voluntarily makes them unique. An example of O'Connor's understanding of this principle is found in the author's note to the second edition of *Wise Blood*, where she writes:

19. *MM*, 115. Thomas does think that violence, fear, concupiscence, and ignorance can place constraints around the will, resulting in what O'Connor has in mind when she describes her characters as "mostly unfree" (see *ST* 1-2.6.4–8).
20. *ST* 1-2.6.2.
21. *ST* 1-2.6.2.
22. *ST* 1-2.83.1.

"Does one's integrity ever lie in what he is not able to do? I think that usually it does, for free will does not mean one will, but many wills conflicting in one man."[23] The good man, then, will be the one who uses his will well, as we will see below.

The Operation of the Will

According to Thomas, "the good in general, which has the nature of an end, is the object of the will."[24] Moreover, Thomas thinks that "the will can tend to nothing except under the aspect of good,"[25] which explains why he thinks that human beings are always in pursuit of some good, whether they know it or not. In this sense, we can say that the will cannot help itself; it is bent toward good.

By their nature, human beings are drawn to things that they think will fulfill them, things that they think will make them happy, so they choose to move toward such things because they consider them to be good. Not all goods are the same, as we have shown in the distinction we made between apparent and genuine goods above.[26] So how does a human being go about determining what is actually fulfilling and what will actually allow one's humanity to flourish? How does a human being avoid the lure of apparent goods in order to live the kind of life that will actually result in happiness? Aquinas thinks that the answer is found in the cooperation of the will and the intellect, which, if they cooperate well, results in the life of virtue.

We recall that the object of the intellect is the true and the object of the will is the good. But which is the higher power, the intellect or the will? Thomas thinks if we compare the intellect and will according to the universality of their objects, "the intellect

---

23. *WB*, 5.
24. *ST* 1-2.9.1.
25. *ST* 1.82.2.
26. O'Connor notes, "I don't assume that renunciation goes with submission, or even that renunciation is good in itself. Always you renounce a lesser good for a greater; the opposite is what sin is" (*HB*, 126).

is absolutely higher and nobler than the will."[27] This is because it is the intellect that understands the will and understands the good. However, Thomas also thinks that in the sense that the will can move the intellect, the will is higher.[28] According to Thomas, "The intellect moves the will in one sense, and the will moves the intellect in another."[29] His basic idea is that "these powers include one another in their acts, because the intellect understands that the will wills, and the will wills the intellect to understand. In the same way, the good is contained under the true, inasmuch as it is an understood truth, and the true under the good, inasmuch as it is a desired good."[30] In other words, it is not the will that understands how the intellect and will cooperate, but the intellect that understands; however, since these concepts can be difficult to understand, the will has to will the intellect to understand them. In this way, we see the cooperation of the will and intellect and how each power needs the other in order to allow human beings to act according to their nature as rational animals.

Flannery O'Connor puts this cooperation of intellect and will on display in her prayer journal when she writes, "Please help me to know the will of my Father—not a scrupulous nervousness nor yet a lax presumption but a clear, reasonable knowledge; and after this give me a strong Will to be able to bend it to the Will of the Father."[31] She first asks God to help her to know—with "a clear, reasonable knowledge"—and then she asks God to give her "a strong Will" to be able to act upon what she knows. O'Connor understands that the intellect and will must cooperate with each other in order to move toward the good.

---

27. *ST* 1.82.4.
28. *ST* 1.82.4.
29. *ST* 1.82.4.
30. *ST* 1.82.4.
31. *PJ*, 5.

Natural Law

Although we have shown that human beings naturally desire the good and want to be happy, it remains to be seen how it is that human beings actually go about *knowing* what is good, *choosing* to act in a way that is good, and then actually acting in a way that is good so that their lives can be good and fulfilling. Thomas thinks that human beings are naturally constituted in such a way that they can figure out some foundational and universal principles to human life, and he calls this universal set of principles the *natural law*, which is part of God's divine providence.[32] Although natural law theory was not invented by Thomas, the philosophical tradition is readily associated with Catholicism, as O'Connor notes: "The Catholic has the natural law and the teachings of the church to guide him."[33]

Thomas begins his treatment of natural law by reminding us that the first thing that humans can know is *being*, that being is good, and that "good is that which all things seek after."[34] Hence, the first precept of natural law is: "Good is to be done and promoted, and evil is to be avoided,"[35] because not doing or promoting good would keep us from the end to which we are naturally drawn. (According to Thomas, this is a most basic truth and it is true for all human beings, although he does admit that it is not equally known by all human beings.[36]) It is implied in this first precept—*do good and avoid evil*—that one has to consider

32. Thomas explains, "The light of natural reason, whereby we discern what is good and what is evil, which is the function of the natural law, is nothing else than an imprint on us of the divine light. It is therefore evident that the natural law is nothing else than the rational creature's participation of the eternal law" (*ST* 1-2.91.2).

33. *MM*, 202.

34. *ST* 1-2.94.2.

35. *ST* 1-2.94.2.

36. See *ST* 1-2.94.4. Sokolowski thinks there are four types of rational animals who cannot grasp natural law: "the impulsive, the obtuse, the immature, and the vicious" (Sokolowski, "What is Natural Law?," in Robert Sokolowski, *Christian Faith and Human Understanding: Studies on the Eucharist, Trinity, and the Human Person* [Washington, DC: The Catholic University of America Press, 2006], 221.).

what is *truly* good, making a distinction between apparent and genuine goods, because only the truly good can fulfill, complete, or perfect a human being.[37] In other words, according to Thomas, failure to think about what will truly make us happy and what will truly be good for us is a common human pitfall.

Having established the first precept of natural law—*do good and avoid evil*—Thomas thinks that three other precepts naturally flow from it.[38] First, he thinks that, like all living substances, human beings seek to preserve their own being, so *preserving human life* belongs to the natural law.[39] Second, he thinks that, like all animals, human beings are made to perpetuate their species and raise their offspring, so *procreation and child-rearing* belong to the natural law.[40] Third, because human beings are naturally endowed with reason, Thomas thinks men and women alone have a natural inclination to *know the truth about God and to live in society*, which includes shunning ignorance and avoiding offending those with whom they live.[41]

These, then, are the basic precepts of natural law according to Thomas, and so to act against these precepts of natural law would be to act against one's nature, which would be to act against what is good and therefore against what makes one happy. Thomas thinks that reasonable people should be able to recognize and appreciate natural law and live according to it, because their happiness and flourishing—not to mention the right ordering of society—depend upon it.

---

37. See McInerny, *Ethica Thomistica*, 37.
38. "All other precepts of the natural law are based upon this; so that all the things which the practical reason naturally apprehends as a man's good belong to the natural law under the form of things to be done or avoided" (*ST* 1-2.94.2).
39. *ST* 1-2.94.2.
40. *ST* 1-2.94.2.
41. *ST* 1-2.94.2.

VIRTUE

To act according to the natural law is to act virtuously, since "all virtuous acts belong to the natural law."[42] But what is virtue according to Thomas, and what does it mean to live virtuously? Thomas thinks that "virtue denotes a certain perfection of a power"[43] and that there are different kinds of human virtues (intellectual, moral, cardinal, social, and theological), but for our purposes we will focus mainly on the virtue of prudence—the queen of the virtues. Then, we will show how one acquires virtue, explain the role of the mean in understanding virtue, present the four basic Aristotelian character types in regard to virtue, note the important place of friendship in the life of virtue, and, finally, show how a life of virtue is a life of freedom.

Art and Prudence

Thomas makes an important distinction between art (*right reason of things to be made*) and prudence (*right reason of things to be done*).[44] For example, a person might write, paint, or sculpt so well as to achieve aesthetic excellence, even perfection, but excellence at being an artist does not necessarily translate into excellence in human living, which is the object of the virtue of prudence. According to the Thomistic way of thinking, an artist can be an excellent writer, painter, or sculptor, yet struggle with all sorts of vices in the moral life. Caravaggio serves as a good example. According to art historian Elizabeth Lev, Caravaggio was "unreliable both personally and professionally" and "murdered a man in 1606,"[45] yet his moral flaws did nothing to diminish the quality of his art. Thomistically speaking, Caravaggio was

---

42. *ST* 1-2.94.3.
43. *ST* 1-2.55.1.
44. *ST* 1-2.57.4.
45. Elizabeth Lev, *How Catholic Art Saved the Faith: The Triumph of Beauty and Truth in Counter-Reformation Art* (Manchester, NH: Sophia Institute, 2018), 287.

a virtuous (skilled and intuitive) artist but was far from being a morally virtuous (prudent) man. Thomas explains the distinction:

> Prudence is of good counsel about matters regarding man's entire life, and the last end of human life. But in some arts there is counsel about matters concerning the ends proper to those arts. Hence some men, in so far as they are good counsellors in matters of warfare, or seamanship, are said to be prudent officers or pilots, but not prudent absolutely; for only those are prudent absolutely who give good counsel about what concerns man's entire life.[46]

If one wants to become a good painter, Thomas would suggest that one study under someone like Caravaggio, because Caravaggio was an excellent painter; he knew how to make art according to right reason and indeed did so. However, Thomas would not hold someone like Caravaggio up as an exemplar for human living (the moral life), because although Caravaggio was an excellent artist, he was not known to be an excellent man. Rather, Thomas would point to a prudent person as a model to show one how to be a good human being, as "prudence, which deals with his action, is said to be concerned with the goods of man."[47]

Throughout his *Nicomachean Ethics*, Aristotle refers to the prudent person as "the excellent man" (σπουδαῖος) who does the right thing, at the right time, for the right reason, in the right way, with the right people; he is the "norm and measure"[48] for human living. This excellent human being is a model of prudence, as he "judges each class of things rightly, and in each the truth appears to him."[49] A prudent person does not simply know the good in a general way but is able to apply the universal good to

46. *ST* 1-2.57.4.
47. Thomas Aquinas, *Commentary on NE* 6.4.1162.
48. *NE* 3.5.1113a31–33.
49. *NE* 3.5.1113a30.

particular situations, as prudence is "a true and reasoned state of capacity to act with regard to the things that are good or bad for man."[50] In other words, the prudent or excellent person is one who knows what is good and does what is good because it is good. Aristotle and Thomas both agree that human beings cannot be good without prudence and cannot be prudent without being (morally) good or having (moral) virtue.[51] O'Connor also agrees, warmly noting, "I was reading that St. Thomas said Prudence was the highest of the virtues (those beyond Faith Hope & Charity, I presume) because it articulated all the others. Anyway, the older I get the more respect I have for old Prudence."[52]

Acquiring Virtue

But acting in a way that is good or virtuous is not the kind of thing that develops naturally in human beings. Thomas explains,

> Virtue is natural to man inchoately. It is natural to man according to the specific nature, in so far as in man's reason there are to be found naturally present certain naturally known principles of both knowledge and action, which are the seeds of intellectual and moral virtues, and in so far as there is in the will a natural appetite for the good which is in accord with reason.[53]

When Thomas states that virtue is natural to human beings "inchoately," he means that although human beings have a natural aptitude for virtue, virtue does not naturally develop in them the way that sight or hearing does. Thomas thinks virtue develops like language, as no one is born knowing how to read and write and speak, but we are born with the capacity to learn language. Virtue is in human beings potentially, but that potential needs

50. *NE* 6.5.1140b4–6.
51. *NE* 6.13.1144b31; Thomas Aquinas, *Commentary on NE* 6.9.1285.
52. *HB*, 247.
53. *ST* 1-2.63.1.

to be actualized to be perfected, and Thomas thinks this actu-
alization happens over time by habituation of acts. Just as the
more one hears, speaks, and writes in a particular language, the
more fluent one becomes, so Thomas thinks that the more one
acts in a way that is virtuous, the more virtuous one becomes.[54]
As O'Connor writes in her prayer journal, "Every virtue must be
vigorous. Virtue must be the only vigorous thing in our lives."[55]

The Golden Mean

Thomas thinks that human beings discover each natural moral
virtue as the mean between two extremes, an idea he borrows
directly from Aristotle:

> Virtue, then, is a state of character concerned with choice, lying
> in a mean, i.e., the mean relative to us, this being determined by
> a rational principle, and by that principle by which the man of
> practical wisdom would determine it. Now it is a mean between
> two vices, that which depends on excess and that which depends
> on defect; and again it is a mean because the vices respectively
> fall short of or exceed what is right in both passions and actions,
> while virtue both finds and chooses that which is intermediate.[56]

An example will help clarify this principle. Just as an excellent
athlete habitually eats the right amount of food (not too little,
not too much), achieves the right amount of sleep (not too few
hours, not too many hours), and spends the right amount of time
training (as undertraining will result in weakness and overtrain-
ing will result in exhaustion) in order to excel at her sport, so too
does the virtuous human being habitually act in a way that is

---

54. Thomas explains, "Human virtue, directed to the good which is defined
according to the rule of human reason, can be caused by human acts; for such acts
proceed from reason, by whose power and rule the good in question is established"
(*ST* 1-2.63.2).

55. *PJ*, 22.

56. *NE* 2.6.1106b35–1107a5; Cf. *ST* 1-2.64.1–4.

courageous (not cowardly or overconfident), temperate (avoiding too little pleasure and too much pleasure), just (giving others their due: not too little, not too much), and prudent (finding the mean between the deficiency and excess in all activities and choosing it) in order to excel at human living. Victor White notes, "Man is a body as well as a soul; hungry, sexual, emotional. The aim of ethics must include the integration of all these physical or partly physical factors into 'the foursquare man without shame.'"[57] (The "foursquare man" is the one who practices the four cardinal virtues mentioned above.) Both Aristotle and Thomas think that it is "difficult to be good or virtuous because we see that in every case it is difficult to discover the mean but easy to deviate from the mean,"[58] but they insist that living the virtuous life is possible and that it is the end to which we should aim.

To help one become vigorously virtuous by finding the golden mean and living according to it, Aristotle offers three guiding principles, which Thomas refers to as *admonitions*. First, he thinks that one who aims at the mean "must strive to avoid the extreme more opposed to the virtue."[59] For example, it is better to be sober than drunk, so in finding the mean for the consumption of alcoholic beverages it is better to avoid the extreme of drunkenness than that of sobriety. Second, one should cultivate well the awareness of one's own weakness so as to move intentionally in the opposite direction of that weakness.[60] For example, the person who tends naturally to sloth must drag himself toward the opposite extreme of "workaholism" in order to achieve the mean of industriousness, just as the person who tends naturally toward workaholism must drag herself toward the opposite extreme of sloth to achieve the mean of industriousness. Third, Aristotle thinks that because all human beings are naturally

57. White, *God and the Unconscious*, 121.
58. Thomas Aquinas, *Commentary on NE* 2.11.370.
59. Thomas Aquinas, *Commentary on NE* 2.11.371.
60. *Commentary on NE* 2.11.375.

inclined toward pleasure, anyone who is striving to live a life of virtue ought to beware of pleasurable things because they can easily distract us from the life of virtue.[61] Odysseus filling his sailors' ears with wax so that they would not be distracted by the pleasurable song of the Sirens in *The Odyssey* is a good literary example of this final admonition. Aristotle thinks that those who follow this advice "will be quite able to acquire the mean of virtue."[62]

The Four Types of Character

In Book VII of the *Nicomachean Ethics*, Aristotle explains that there are four basic types of human beings: *virtuous, continent, incontinent*, and *vicious*.[63] The difference between these types of people is determined by the relationship between one's reason, the inclination of one's will, and one's action in regard to the golden mean.[64]

The virtuous person is one who knows what is good, desires what is good, and acts in a way that is good habitually.[65] For example, a virtuous writer is one who knows that it is good to write every day, one who desires to write every day, and one who actually writes every day. For the virtuous writer, the daily discipline of writing is second nature to her, and she enjoys her habit of being a writer, experiencing no inner conflict regarding

61. *Commentary on NE* 2.11.376.
62. *Commentary on NE* 2.11.378.
63. *NE* 7.1.1145a15–20. In fact, Aristotle lists six types of character, but the "godlike" and the "bestial" are far extremes and therefore not central to his argument or worth exploring in this book. Although we have no evidence that O'Connor knew these four character types from reading Aristotle herself, she would have been familiar with them from Victor White in *God and the Unconscious* (pp. 174–176). J.O. Urmson also offers a helpful treatment of Aristotle's four types of character in *Aristotle's Ethics* (Oxford: Blackwell, 1988), 31–32.
64. See Robert Sokolowski, *The God of Faith and Reason: Foundations of Christian Theology* (Washington, DC: The Catholic University of America Press, 1995), 53–68.
65. We could easily substitute the words "the golden mean" for "good" in order to show the relevance of the previous section to Aristotle and Thomas' understanding of the four types of character and their relationship to the golden mean.

this activity.[66] In fact, she would only feel conflicted if she were not able to write every day.

The continent person is one who knows what is good, desires what is bad, but acts in a way that is good, habitually. So, to keep with our example, although the continent writer knows that it is good to write every day, she does not always feel like getting out of bed or sitting at her computer to write for three hours on most days, but even though she experiences this conflict between what she knows and what she wants, she acts in a way that is good and writes for three hours each day, regardless of the inner conflict she experiences.

The incontinent person is one who knows what is good, desires what is bad, and acts in a way that is bad, habitually. So the incontinent writer is one who knows that it is good to write every day, but has no real desire to get out of bed and sit at her desk and write for three hours; in fact, she regularly sleeps in and engages in all sorts of other activities besides writing on most days.

The vicious person is the one who thinks that what is bad is good, desires what is bad, and acts in a way that is bad, habitually. So, the vicious writer is one who thinks that it is bad to write every day, has no desire to write every day, and, in fact, does very little writing at all.

We have used the example of a writer to help illustrate the distinctions between Aristotle's four types of human character, and these types are to be understood in the broader scope of human living.

In O'Connor's fiction and in Thomistic theology, God's grace can and does accomplish exceptional moral change from one type to another; but on the level of nature alone, and philosophically

66. Betsy Lochridge reports the following: "Unlike many writers, Miss O'Connor enjoys the actual writing. She works on a typewriter, turns out about three pages a day" (Lochridge, "An Afternoon with Flannery O'Connor," in *Conversations with Flannery O'Connor* [Jackson, MS: University Press of Mississippi, 1987], 39).

speaking, human character is stable and predictable.[67] According to Aristotle, most people find themselves either continent or incontinent, struggling with knowing what is right and good and actually doing it,[68] and this is mostly true for O'Connor's fictional characters as well.

The Virtue of Friendship

According to both Aristotle and Thomas, friendship is most necessary for human living in that "no one in his right mind would choose to live in the possession of great external goods without friends."[69] Aristotle notes that in good times we need friends with whom we can enjoy our blessings and prosperity, and that in bad times friends are said to be "our only refuge."[70] He goes on to say

67. In terms of Flannery O'Connor's own life, we could say that O'Connor was virtuous in some ways, continent in others, and incontinent in others. For example, as a writer she was virtuous, and the same could be said of her practice of religion, her devotion to study, and her high regard for human friendship. In terms of her carnal appetites, we do have evidence that she was mostly continent and that she was growing in the virtues of temperance and chastity throughout her life, as we will see in subsequent sections of this chapter. But O'Connor did struggle with the sin of racism. She was raised in the segregated South and was actively working through this struggle up until her time of death, creating in "Revelation," one of the last stories she wrote, a protagonist recognized by many critics as a presentation of O'Connor herself. When O'Connor took the time and made the effort to allow her intellect to direct her will and appetites, as she did in her writing of fiction, she wrote some of the most important anti-racist literature of the twentieth century. However, when she allowed her passions—specifically those that had been formed by the racist elements of Southern culture—to overrule her reason, she found herself writing the kinds of things that were actually beneath her and contrary to what she knew to be true. In this sense we can understand O'Connor as a sinner who struggled with the particular sin of racism, while also remembering that people do not change overnight, even (in most cases) with the help of divine grace. Aristotle and Thomas both think that bad habits take time to break and, as O'Connor herself notes, conversion is a process: "I don't think of conversion as being once and for all and that's that. I think once the process is begun and continues that you are continually turning inward toward God and away from your own egocentricity and that you have to see this selfish side of yourself in order to turn away from it" (*HB*, 430). For more on this subject, see Angela Alaimo O'Donnell's book *Radical Ambivalence: Race in Flannery O'Connor* (New York: Fordham University Press, 2020), and her essay "The 'Canceling' of Flannery O'Connor? It Never Should Have Happened," *Commonweal*, August 3, 2020, https://www.commonwealmagazine.org/cancelling-flannery-oconnor.

68. *NE* 7.7.1150a15–16.

69. Thomas Aquinas, *Commentary on NE* 8.1.1539.

70. *NE* 8.1.1155a7–12; Thomas Aquinas, *Commentary on NE* 8.1.1539–40.

that young people need friends to keep them from error, that old people need friends to care for them and support them, and that those in the prime of their life need friends to do fine actions, "for with friends men are more able to both think and act."[71] Aristotle is convinced that friendship is such an important component of human living, and so very necessary to human happiness, that he devotes two entire books to the topic in his ethical treatise. Sokolowski explains,

> Traditionally, friendship is not listed among the moral virtues. The classical "cardinal virtues" are courage, temperance, prudence, and justice. However . . . in Aristotle's *Nicomachean Ethics* friendship plays a much more central role in the discussion of the moral virtues. Several virtues, including courage and temperance, are treated in books 3 and 4, and justice is discussed in book 5, but friendship is treated in two books, 8 and 9, toward the end of the work. I think that friendship, and specifically noble friendship, is the culmination of moral virtue; the ability to be a friend in the highest and best way is the moral perfection of human nature, according to Aristotle.[72]

Sokolowski mentions that *noble* friendship is one of three kinds of friendship that Aristotle presents in his *Nicomachean Ethics*.[73] The other two are friendships of *utility* and friendships of *pleasure*. What distinguishes these three types of friendship from each other is their object. In a friendship of utility, one engages in the friendship because one can gain something useful from it.[74] Similarly, in a friendship of pleasure, one engages in the friendship because one gains something pleasurable from it; pleasure is the object. However, perfect friendship (also known as

71. *NE* 8.1.1155a8–15; Thomas Aquinas, *Commentary on NE* 8.1.1540.
72. Sokolowski, *Christian Faith*, 206.
73. See *NE* 8.3.1156a6–1156b33; Thomas Aquinas, *Commentary on NE* 8.3.1563.
74. *NE* 8.3.1156a10; Thomas Aquinas, *Commentary on NE* 8.3.1566.

complete, noble, real, true, or virtuous friendship, or friendship of character) has as its object not utility or pleasure but the other person, which is why perfect friendship endures in a way that friendships of utility and pleasure do not. Aristotle writes,

> Perfect friendship is the friendship of men who are good, and alike in virtue; for these wish well alike to each other *qua* good, and they are good in themselves. Now those who wish well to their friends for their sake are most truly friends; for they do this by reason of their own nature and not incidentally; therefore, their friendship lasts as long as they are good—and goodness is an enduring thing.[75]

For Aristotle and for Thomas, perfect friendship is what human beings are made for, as perfect friendship does not see the useful or the pleasant as its end, but the good of the other person. In fact, for Thomas Aquinas, the highest form of friendship is not with another human being but with God himself, who first loved us. The true friend, therefore, wants what is best for the other person, just as she wants what is best for herself. True friendship includes benefits and pleasures, but it remains even in the absence of such benefits or pleasures, for true friendship is concerned with what is actually good and not what may be momentarily pleasurable or useful.

In the Thomistic tradition, one's friends reveal one's character.[76] If one is friends with God, who loves perfectly, we will see the love of God on display in the life of the one who is truly friends with him. And if one has good, real, true friendships with other people, these friendships offer evidence that one is a good, real, and true person himself or herself. Aristotle explains, "Only good men can be friends; for bad men do not delight in each other unless

---

75. *NE* 8.3.1156b6–12; Thomas Aquinas, *Commentary on NE* 8.3.1574–1577.
76. See Thomas Aquinas, *Commentary on NE* 9.11.1909.

some advantage come of the relation."[77] This is what Sokolowski means when he says that friendship is the culmination of moral virtue, hence Aristotle's climactic placement of friendship in the *Nicomachean Ethics* as seen above. For if one is truly living a life of virtue, striving for the good in knowing, desiring, and acting, one's life will not be lived in a solitary manner but in a community of similarly striving people called friends.[78] This is why Aristotle says that friendship "is a virtue or implies virtue"[79] and why Thomas says that "friendship is a virtue in that it is a habit of free choice . . . or at least it accompanies virtue insofar as virtue is the cause of true friendship."[80]

Concrete reality matters in the Thomistic tradition, as it is through the visible that we come to know the invisible—through matter that we come to know form—and this is no less true in regard to human character and virtue. One's character is revealed in one's life and particularly in one's friends.

HUMAN FREEDOM

Flannery O'Connor presents a Thomistic understanding of human freedom when she writes, "The Catholic novelist believes that you destroy your freedom by sin; the modern reader believes, I think, that you gain it in that way. There is not much possibility of understanding between the two."[81] In other words, we have seen that, according to Aquinas, human beings are teleological creatures who are made for the true and the good (God) and that they find their happiness—their rest, their flourishing—only when they live according to their nature, which as we have seen means living virtuously, according to the natural law, and with

---

77. *NE* 8.4.1157a19; Thomas Aquinas, *Commentary on NE* 8.4.1591.
78. Even the religious monk who lives a solitary life does so in communion with God and other monks, as in the final days of Hazel Motes at the conclusion of *Wise Blood*.
79. *NE* 8.1.1155a.
80. Thomas Aquinas, *Commentary on NE* 8.1.1538.
81. *MM*, 116.

good friends. To live in this way is to be free, according to the Thomistic tradition. One is free *not* when one does whatever one wants to do, in whatever way one wants to do it, for whatever reason one wants to do it, whenever one wants to do it, and with whomever one wants to do it. Rather, one is free when one does the right thing, in the right way, for the right reason, at the right time, with the right people. Human freedom, according to Thomas, does not emerge simply from one's own will but from the cooperation of one's intellect and will in human action.[82] There is in the Thomistic tradition an objectivity to human freedom, in that freedom comes as a result of living according to one's nature, in contrast to the modern and postmodern notion that freedom is arbitrary, exercised when will is given absolute power.

For example, a superior basketball player like LeBron James habitually makes the most difficult blocks, passes, and shots look easy and effortless. He is so good at playing the game of basketball that, beyond merely knowing and following the rules of the game and executing its fundamental skills, he no longer needs to think about these things; we can say he has made them part of his second nature as a basketball player. While the actions of lesser players are to one degree or another constrained by their own need to think and make choices during gameplay, James' mastery gives him real freedom to achieve surpassing excellence. In the same way, the morally virtuous person is the most free at human living, according to the Thomistic view, because the virtuous person lives according to his or her nature in an effortless sort of way. Unlike the continent person, who acts well but whose inner conflict points to some defect in freedom, the virtuous person experiences no inner conflict but real freedom to achieve human excellence. This is why O'Connor, as Hillbilly Thomist, thinks that a person destroys his or her freedom by sinning: to

82. See Eleonore Stump, *Aquinas* (London: Routledge, 2003), 278.

sin is to act against God and one's nature, and, from the Thomistic perspective, it is contrary to a life of happiness and human flourishing.[83]

O'CONNOR ON NATURAL LAW, HUMAN SEXUALITY, AND FRIENDSHIP

Having presented a general overview of Thomas' ethical system, we turn now to Flannery O'Connor in order to explore how these themes permeate her life and her art. We will direct our attention specifically to O'Connor's understanding of human sexuality because it is within this realm that the Thomistic influence is clearest.

The Meaning of Sex According to O'Connor

By now, it should come as no surprise that Flannery O'Connor holds a traditional Catholic and Thomistic understanding of human sexuality. She thinks that sex is only morally permissible between a married man and woman in a way that is procreative[84]—keeping in mind that "morally permissible" should always be understood in light of what is good for men and women according to their natural end, which is happiness. This position is grounded in Church teaching and Scripture, but also in natural law.[85] Sexual acts that do not have a tendency to result in pro-

83. Victor White offers a helpful summary of the teleological theory of virtue we have been discussing, a summary that O'Connor would have read: "Aristotle said that ethical inquiry and teaching cannot be undertaken without a knowledge of the human *psyche*; and rightly so, for what is ethics but the pattern of habit and conduct with a view to the *telos*, the end and fulfilment, the balance of health, of the whole human soul and all its parts? This standpoint, which is that of St. Thomas, not to speak of the Fathers of the Church, seems to be virtually ignored in the kind of teaching which presents morality solely as an extrinsically imposed code of arbitrary regulations rather than as a *life of virtue*, of a 'second nature' which responds to and integrates the innate needs and tendencies of the whole man" (White, *God and the Unconscious*, 173–174).

84. "Procreative" here does not mean that every time a husband and wife come together in the marital act, they do so with the specific intent of creating a new life, but it does mean that they remain open to the possibility of life and that they refrain from any actions against nature that would prevent a child from being conceived.

85. "There is in man an inclination to things that pertain to him more specially [than does the universal inclination to self-preservation], according to

creation are acts against nature and therefore against happiness (e.g., masturbation, contraceptive sex, same-sex sex, etc.). In her prayer journal, she notes, "The Sex [sic] act is a religious act & when it occurs without God it is a mock act or at best an empty act."[86] O'Connor's understanding of the meaning of sex may strike the postmodern reader as strange, antiquated, even shocking, but it is important to remember that less than a century ago this teaching was shared by all the major Christian traditions—as it had been for almost two millennia—and remains the teaching of the Catholic Church to this very day.[87]

The Virtue of Purity and Its Foil

It would be a grave mistake to suggest that O'Connor thinks the Thomistic teaching on human sexuality is easily put into practice; nonetheless, she does think that it is good, true, and attainable.[88] In the Catholic Thomistic tradition, human sexuality has its own special virtue, known as *chastity*, which O'Connor most often refers to as *purity*.[89] From a young age, she would have been familiar with the virtue of purity through her study of the

that nature which he has in common with other animals; and in virtue of this inclination, those things are said to belong to the natural law *which nature has taught to all animals*, such as sexual intercourse, the education of offspring and so forth" (*ST* 1-2.94.2).

86. *PJ*, 31.

87. See Paul VI's *Humanae Vitae* and John Paul II's *Theology of the Body*. (It is interesting to wonder how O'Connor would have responded to the *Theology of the Body*, considering her lack of appreciation for the bridegroom analogy: "I've never spent much time over the bride-bridegroom analogy," and "In some pious writers there is a lot about the Church being the bride of Christ. This kind of metaphor may have helped that age to get a picture of a certain reality; it fails to help most of us. The metaphor can be dispensed with" [*HB*, 136, 369].)

88. Because this is a philosophical investigation and not a theological one, I have intentionally avoided examining the role of grace and the infused virtues in Thomas' system, but it should be noted here that chastity deals with spiritual union with God rather than with "unlawful things" and that the full meaning of purity is only understood in light of Thomas' theology (see *ST* 2-2.151.2).

89. Thomas considers chastity a virtue but makes a distinction between chastity and purity that O'Connor does not make—"purity is directed at chastity, not as a virtue distinct therefrom, but as expressing a circumstance of chastity"— perhaps because her *Introduction to St. Thomas* did not contain the pertinent articles (see *ST* 2-2.151.1, 4).

Baltimore Catechism and its presentation of the sixth and ninth commandments, which warn against any and all behaviors and thoughts violating sexual purity.[90] At times, Catholics receive harsh criticism for their views on human sexuality, but it should be clear by now that these views are illuminated by a robust Thomistic metaphysics, which insists that human beings are composite beings made for the good, and therefore, what human beings do and do not do, specifically in the realm of sexuality, is of great consequence to their happiness. This is to say that if sexuality is part of our human nature, then there must be a virtuous way to be a sexual being, and according to O'Connor, this way of being/acting is what she calls the virtue of purity. Yet while she believes in the virtue, she never claims to be an expert in understanding or practicing it. She writes, "Purity strikes me as the most mysterious of the virtues and the more I think about it the less I know about it."[91] Like all the virtues, purity is difficult; it takes time, effort, good teachers/exemplars, the support of friends, and lots of practice to acquire; as O'Connor famously wrote, "In us the good is something under construction."[92]

According to O'Connor—and consistent with Aristotle and Thomas—if purity is a virtue, then it can be defined by comparison to its excesses: "a mock state of innocence" and "the obscene," both of which, she thinks, are forms of sentimentalism. O'Connor explains,

> Sentimentality is an excess, a distortion of sentiment usually in the direction of an overemphasis on innocence, [and] innocence, whenever it is overemphasized in the ordinary human condition, tends by some natural law to become its opposite. We lost our innocence in the Fall, and our return to it is through the Redemption which was brought about by Christ's death and by

90. See *Baltimore Catechism*, lessons 19–20, a. 254–258, 272–278.
91. *HB*, 117.
92. *MM*, 226.

our slow participation in it. Sentimentality is a skipping of this process in its concrete reality and an early arrival at a mock state of innocence, which strongly suggests its opposite. Pornography, on the other hand, is essentially sentimental, for it leaves out the connection of sex with its hard purpose, and so far disconnects it from its meaning in life as to make it simply an experience for its own sake.[93]

O'Connor refers to "the hard purpose," what Thomas calls "the natural end" or "the final cause," of sex, which, as we have seen, is procreation. Sex is serious metaphysical and moral business, according to O'Connor, but because of the fall, human beings tend to want to diminish that seriousness and reduce human sexuality to the sentimental: mock innocence or obscenity.

These two vices were present in the culture of O'Connor's day but are even more prevalent in the twenty-first century. By way of example, in cinema, mock innocence is a standard feature of what is known as the "romantic comedy,"[94] a genre of film in which almost every romantic relationship—as brief or as shallow as it may be—leads to some sexual activity, but only in the rarest of depictions is that activity marital or procreative. On the other extreme, in pornography, the sexual act is reduced to a co-mingling of body parts between strangers. Both kinds of film intentionally avoid, ignore, or reject what O'Connor calls "the hard purpose" of sex for the sake of an inferior pleasure— emotional in the case of romantic comedies and physical in the case of pornography—thereby denying the sexual act its natural end. This is not to say that O'Connor is against bodily pleasure *per se*, but that pleasure apart from what is actually good and virtuous is a kind of pleasure that will not last or satisfy the

---

93. *MM*, 147–148.
94. A Hillbilly Thomist might call this sort of film a "sentimental comedy."

human person, so in the end, it ought to be avoided.[95] Purity, she thinks, is the virtue that protects the human person from veering off into these extremes of sexual activity that jeopardize human flourishing and real happiness.

Flannery O'Connor does not offer a systematic account of the virtue of purity, but she says enough that we know it was an important component in her understanding of reality, specifically to her understanding of the human person as he or she relates to God and other human persons. Her understanding of purity is rooted in her understanding of human nature, but she also thinks that the fullest meaning of purity is only understood in light of her Catholic faith, specifically in the Resurrection. She writes,

> I am always astonished at the emphasis the Church puts on the body. It is not the soul she says that will rise but the body, glorified. I have always thought that purity was the most mysterious of the virtues, but it occurs to me that it would never have entered the human consciousness to conceive of purity if we were not to look forward to a resurrection of the body, which will be flesh and spirit united in peace, in the way they were in Christ. The resurrection of Christ seems the high point in the law of nature."[96]

According to O'Connor, the body never acts without the soul; when the body acts, the whole human person acts. Sexual acts are always working either with nature toward a life of happiness, or against nature toward a life of unhappiness. O'Connor thinks that the human person—composed of both body and soul—is by nature meant for purity, a virtue which she consistently endorses with confidence, intelligence, and humility:

95. Recall Aristotle's third admonition: "Now in everything the pleasant or pleasure is most to be guarded against; for we do not judge it impartially" (*NE* 2.9.1109b8).
96. *HB*, 100.

I think the phrase "naive purity" is a contradiction in terms. I don't think purity is mere innocence; I don't think babies and idiots possess it. I take it to be something that comes either with experience or with Grace so that it can never be naive. On the matter of purity we can never judge ourselves, much less anybody else. Anyone who thinks he's pure is surely not.[97]

We noted in chapter 2 that O'Connor's metaphysical foil is Nietzsche, and so it should come as no surprise that Nietzsche continues to play the role of foil in regard to O'Connor's ethics as well, particularly in the sexual arena. Edmondson explains,

In her view, modern sexuality is the edge of the nihilistic blade, cutting its swath through traditional morality. O'Connor's judgment is confirmed by Nietzsche's teaching on the Dionysian dimension of the human personality, best elaborated in his first book *The Birth of Tragedy*, a study in the philosophical elements of the tragic art form. The book argues that the ancient Greeks' aesthetic life rested on the foundation of two pillars, the Apollonian and the Dionysian. The influence of Apollo in ancient Greek life is evident with the preoccupation with order, harmony, and discipline, and emblematic of this interest is Greek classical sculpture. The Dionysian impulse among the Greeks gave birth to the tragic art form; and, whereas the Apollonian is associated with the rational side of human nature, the Dionysian emanates from a different source, that part of the human being given to nonrational expressiveness, to abandon, and even to excess. Nietzsche further argues that the Dionysian influence is under appreciated by a world that gives undue attention to the Apollonian, [an] obsession with order and reason promulgated by the fame of the Greek philosopher, Socrates.[98]

97. *HB*, 126.
98. Henry Edmondson, *Return to Good and Evil: Flannery O'Connor's Response to Nihilism* (New York: Lexington Books, 2002), 27–28.

O'Connor champions the golden mean of the virtue of purity, while Nietzsche champions what he takes to be sexual liberation from constraint. For O'Connor, the virtue of purity protects the human person from the inherent dangers of vicious behavior, while for Nietzsche, "the traditional restraints upon excessive sexual expression are a denial of life itself."[99] We will see below how these contradicting views show up in O'Connor's narrative art, but for now we will turn to a few more examples of Thomistic ethical principles at work in O'Connor's canon.

Contraception and Reproductive Technologies

According to Flannery O'Connor, Thomas Aquinas, and the teaching of the Catholic Church, sexual acts are proper only to a husband and wife and only in a way that is *procreative*. This is not to diminish the value of what is known as the *unitive* aspect of married life and love, but it is to say that the ends of marriage and of each marital act are to be *both procreative and unitive* at the same time.[100] Flannery O'Connor died before the great debate over the birth control pill in the 1960s that resulted in the eventual publication of Pope Paul VI's controversial encyclical *Humanae Vitae* in 1968, but the fact that Paul VI maintained the Church's traditional teaching based in natural law would not have surprised her. In a letter to Betty Hester dated June 27, 1959, she wrote,

> The Church's stand on birth control is the most absolutely spiritual of all her stands and with all of us being materialists at heart, there is little wonder that it causes unease. I wish various fathers would quit trying to defend it by saying that the world can support 40 billion. I will rejoice in the day when they say: This is right, whether we all rot on top of each other or not,

99. Edmondson, 27.
100. See *Humanae Vitae* 11.

dear children, as we certainly may. Either practice restraint or be prepared for crowding.[101]

In referring to "all of us being materialists at heart," O'Connor is acknowledging a culture-wide philosophical rejection of what we have shown to be the "natures" of things. As we noted earlier, a materialist worldview is one that rejects formal and final cause, granting that only material and efficient causes are accessible, let alone knowable. In the absence of formal and final causality, materialists think that human beings themselves determine what things are and what they are for, rather than looking to nature for answers. So, for the materialist, there is no natural law and no human nature to serve as guides for human action, specifically in the sexual arena, and this lack of direction is an affront to O'Connor's far more robust metaphysical view of reality, the human person, and human sexuality.

In a lengthy letter to her friend Cecil Dawkins, O'Connor, firmly grounded in the principles of natural law, once again defends the Church's prohibition against birth control:

> The Church has always been mindful of the relation between spirit and flesh; this has shown up in her definitions of the double nature of Christ, as well as in her care for what may seem to us to have nothing to do with religion—such as contraception. The Church is all of a piece. . . . The Catholic can't think of birth control in relation to expediency but in relation to the nature of man under God.[102]

O'Connor is not a philosopher, nor is she formally trained in natural law theory, so she is not able to generate the kind of arguments for the Church's teaching against birth control that one would expect from a moral philosopher or a moral theologian,

101. *HB*, 338.
102. *HB*, 365–366.

but she does point to the proper source, "the nature of man under God," to ground her claims. She seems to have been familiar with the section on law in her Modern Library copy of the *Summa*, wherein Thomas explains the relationship between natural law and eternal law:

> The light of natural reason, whereby we discern what is good and what is evil, which is the function of the natural law, is nothing else than an imprint on us of the divine light. It is therefore evident that the natural law is nothing else than the rational creature's participation of the eternal law.[103]

When O'Connor writes that the Catholic teaching on birth control cannot be understood "in relation to expediency but in relation to the nature of man under God," she is making a philosophical statement. It is natural law theory—not pragmatism, utilitarianism, naturalism, or positivism—that guides her thinking and the thinking of the Church. O'Connor's understanding of the human person and of human sexuality in particular is metaphysically robust, and although she is not always able to make philosophically refined arguments, it is abundantly clear that she understands that there are refined philosophical arguments to be made.[104]

To conclude this section, we turn to two recondite sentences from a letter O'Connor wrote to Betty Hester on May 19, 1956, making a very important Thomistic philosophical distinction between rational and nonrational animals in regard to sex. She writes, "I agree with you about the bulls. Nothing wrong with

103. *ST* 1-2.91.2.
104. In her review of Kenneth Walker's *Life's Long Journey*, O'Connor chides, "This may be explained for the author's obvious distaste for the Church's stand on birth control which Dr. Walker believes should be one of the chief factors in our effort to direct evolution. No attempt is made [by Walker] to do justice to or even to understand the Catholic position on this subject. It is dismissed as superstition and the fatuous observation is made that the Church sanctions death control but not birth control" (*PG*, 117–118).

artificial insemination as long as it's animals."[105] In an age where in vitro fertilization is widely practiced and considered by many to be morally acceptable, O'Connor's words may seem insensitive and jarring, but in light of all we have presented thus far in this chapter, her logic should be clear. Sexual union for humans is reserved to a married man and woman and in a way that is both procreative and unitive at the same time. Birth control denies the procreative end of the sexual act, as we have seen above, but something like artificial insemination separates the unitive aspect from the procreative aspect, which is why O'Connor thinks that such a practice is permissible for nonrational animals but not for rational animals.

Flannery O'Connor did not live to see the first child born through in vitro fertilization (IVF), but the same principles that informed her position against artificial insemination (AI) in humans would hold in a Thomistic critique of IVF for humans. The difference between the two is that in AI, sperm is harvested from the male and delivered directly into the female in hopes of fertilization, while in IVF the sperm is harvested from the male and eggs are harvested from the female and conception takes place in a laboratory and then embryos are implanted within the female. The similarity, philosophically speaking, is that in both AI and IVF, the procreative act is separated from the unitive act. In the Thomistic tradition, it is morally justifiable to use technologies that correct, maintain, and sustain procreative potential, but not in ways that separate the procreative and unitive ends of the marital act.

Human beings, because they are rational animals, are able to make distinctions between an act of marital intercourse and an act of marital infidelity; between a procreative act and a contraceptive act; between a nocturnal emission and an act of masturbation; between an act of marital lovemaking and an act

105. *HB*, 158.

of rape; between a man and a woman procreating and animals reproducing. Because animals lack reason, they are not responsible for the ways in which they reproduce, but O'Connor thinks that human beings are responsible for their sexual activity because they are endowed with intellect and will. This distinction is also why she thinks that artificial insemination is morally permissible for animals but not for humans, because such an act knowingly and deliberately violates the natural law. Such actions, O'Connor thinks, are not good for human beings or for society at large because they go against nature and the natural order of things.

THE MEANING OF SEX IN O'CONNOR'S ART

There are no "sex scenes" per se in Flannery O'Connor's fiction, but, as we have already seen in "Good Country People," *Wise Blood*, *The Violent Bear It Away*, "A Temple of the Holy Ghost," and "The River," O'Connor is not naïve about sex. Her treatment of sex in her narrative art is to make it present, though not explicit, in a manner faithful to her Thomistic understanding of the human person. As we have shown above, rather than show what something is, O'Connor prefers to show what something is not through her employment of the grotesque. O'Connor thinks that encountering distortions forces her readers to think about what has been distorted, in order to come to an understanding of how things ought to be in an undistorted state, and this is no less true in her treatment of human sexuality. She rarely shows models of virtue, purity, and procreative marital love; rather, she shows anti-heroes of vice, lust, contraception, and even rape.

Two short stories are of great interest in this regard, as both reveal O'Connor's Thomistic understanding of the meaning of sex by way of the grotesque.

"A Stroke of Good Fortune"

O'Connor tried to prevent "A Stroke of Good Fortune" from being included in her first collection of short stories, but her editor

Robert Giroux acted against her wishes.[106] The story is about Ruby Hill, the thirty-four-year-old wife of Bill Hill, who thinks she is sick with some mysterious condition, but by the story's end discovers that she is pregnant, which comes as a shock to her because, unlike her mother, who had eight children, Ruby has intentionally had none. We learn that "she would have had five children right now if she hadn't been careful."[107] The story is filled with subtle references to sexuality: the staircase where most of the story takes place has "twenty-eight steps in each flight—twenty-eight," a reference to what in O'Connor's time was thought to be the number of days in a normal menstrual cycle; six-year-old Hartley Gilfeet's toy gun, which Ruby accidentally sits on, is described as "nine inches of treacherous tin"; and we are told that Hartley's late father was named "Rodman."[108]

Ruby discovers she is pregnant after explaining her symptoms to her neighbor Laverne Watts. Laverne has no doubt that Ruby is with child and even teases her about her condition with some comic song and dance culminating in the words "MOTHER! MOTHER!"[109]

> Ruby's mouth opened wordlessly and her fierce expression vanished. For a half-second she was motionless; then she sprang from the chair. "Not me!" she shouted. "Not me!"
>
> Laverne stopped and only watched her with the wise look.
>
> "Not me!" Ruby shouted. "Oh no not me! Bill Hill takes care of that! Bill Hill takes care of that! Bill Hill's been taking care of that for five years! That ain't going to happen to me!"
>
> "Well old Bill Hill just slipped up about four or five months ago, my friend," Laverne said. "Just slipped up . . ."

106. *HB*, 75.
107. *CS*, 98.
108. *CS*, 98.
109. *CS*, 104.

"I don't reckon you know anything about it, you ain't even married, you ain't even . . ."

"I bet it's not one, I bet it's two," Laverne said. "You better go on to the doctor and find out how many it is."[110]

Although Flannery O'Connor embraces a Catholic and Thomistic understanding of human sexuality, she is fully aware that many people do not share that understanding, and she reflects this view in some of her fictional characters. Bill Hill,[111] to whom Ruby defers responsibility for their contraception, was either practicing coitus interruptus or using condoms as birth control, and he failed in his execution of it (an argument can be made that his failure was intentional, as "he was maybe more happy lately").[112] Either way, O'Connor uses a distortion of the natural law to reveal the natural law. In a letter to Sally and Robert Fitzgerald, she wrote that this story "is, in a way, Catholic, being about the rejection of life at the source, but too much of a farce to bear the weight."[113]

"The Comforts of Home"

No Flannery O'Connor story is a more direct tribute to St. Thomas Aquinas than "The Comforts of Home," although—in typical O'Connor fashion—this tribute is not sentimental but comically grotesque and violent. To the average reader, the tribute is easily overlooked, but to the Thomist, O'Connor's intentions are indisputably clear. O'Connor was very familiar with the famous story in which St. Thomas' family—attempting to change his

---

110. *CS*, 104.
111. Bill Hill, whose name is a clever play on hillbilly, seemingly comes to embrace the natural law after five years of rejecting it.
112. *CS*, 99.
113. *HB*, 85.

mind about his commitment to consecrated religious life with the Dominicans—locked him in a room with a prostitute.[114]

A few things worth noting from this story are pertinent to our study. First, that St. Thomas at the time of this incident was a novice in the Dominican order.[115] As a Christian, St. Thomas would have already been expected to practice chastity, but as a consecrated religious, his commitment to purity would have been even more formalized because it was a commitment to celibacy. (In Catholic Christianity, every Christian is called to chastity, which for those who are not married means abstaining from sexual relations; for those who are married, it means engaging in sexual relations according to the natural law; and for a consecrated religious like Aquinas, it means celibacy, which is a lifelong commitment to sexual abstinence.) It is most important to note here that the celibate life renounces sex and marriage not because conjugal love is bad but because it is good; more precisely, it is imperfectly good and can thus be forsworn for the sake of a plenary devotion of one's self to God. As we have seen, according to the Thomistic way of thinking, the love of God is a higher good than even the intimate conjugal love shared between a husband and wife; celibacy is thus a profound expression of that deep, intimate, loving friendship with God.

Second, after this episode, St. Thomas went on to pursue his philosophical studies and his contemplative life. This may make the medieval monk seem like a great bore from a modern and postmodern perspective, but to O'Connor's way of thinking, it is a perfect expression of virtuous living, the kind of living that brings about real freedom and true happiness.[116] A virtuous person

114. "His brothers didn't want him to waste himself being a Dominican and so locked him up in a tower and introduced a prostitute into his apartment; her he ran out with a red-hot poker" (*HB*, 94).

115. Jean-Pierre Torrell, *Saint Thomas Aquinas*, vol. 1, *The Person and His Work*, trans. Robert Royal (Washington, DC: The Catholic University of America Press, 1996), 10.

116. Pieper notes the underappreciated relation between purity and the intellectual life: "Since we nowadays think that all a man needs for acquisition of

is able to discern between that which brings momentary sensual pleasure and that which brings real human flourishing and lasting happiness—even if at times it means renouncing bodily pleasures—and then acts accordingly. O'Connor understood that the actions of St. Thomas were taken in order to promote virtue:

> The more I read St. Thomas the more flexible he appears to me. Incidentally, St. John [of the Cross] would have been able to sit down with the prostitute and said, "Daughter, let us consider this," but St. Thomas doubtless knew his own nature and knew that he had to get rid of her with a poker or she would overcome him. I am not only for St. Thomas here but am in accord with his use of the poker. I call this being tolerantly realistic, not being a fascist.[117]

O'Connor makes an important distinction here between St. John of the Cross and St. Thomas Aquinas, claiming that St. John would have been able to sit down and reason with the prostitute, while St. Thomas knew himself ("his own nature") well enough that the best action for him was to chase her out of the room with the hot poker. Both saints would have acted virtuously (and in a way that was good not only for themselves but for the prostitute as well) but not identically. O'Connor thinks that St. John would have been able to bring the woman to conversion through conversation but that the same tack would not have been good for St. Thomas; therefore, in chasing her away, he chose the best means of protecting and encouraging not only his purity

truth is to exert his brain more or less vigorously, and since we consider an *ascetic* approach to knowledge hardly sensible, we have lost the awareness of the close bond that links the knowing of truth to the condition of purity. St. Thomas says that unchastity's first-born daughter is blindness of the spirit. Only he who wants nothing for himself, who is not subjectively 'interested,' can know the truth. On the other hand, an impure, selfishly corrupted will-to-pleasure destroys both resoluteness of spirit and the ability of the psyche to listen in silent attention to the language of reality." Josef Pieper, *The Silence of St. Thomas*, trans. John Murray and Daniel O'Connor (New York: Pantheon Books, 1957), 19–20.

117. *HB*, 97.

but hers as well. We recall Aristotle's second admonition when it comes to striving for the golden mean: know your weakness and drag yourself in the opposite direction.[118] O'Connor seems to think that this is exactly the sort of thing that St. Thomas was doing in his interaction with the prostitute: "It would be fashionable today to be in sympathy with the woman, but I am in sympathy with St. Thomas."[119]

In addition to the story of St. Thomas and the prostitute, O'Connor was also familiar with an extraordinary grace given to the Dominican friar by God, perhaps as a reward for his courage in the aforementioned incident: "Apparently after a while in his life, St. Thomas was relieved of all temptations of the flesh and certainly this was necessary if he was to write a *Summa*."[120]

O'Connor's knowledge of St. Thomas' biography is essential to understanding "The Comforts of Home," specifically in seeing the protagonist, Thomas, as a grotesque presentation of St. Thomas Aquinas. The Thomas in "The Comforts of Home" is a thirty-five-year-old intellectual who, like St. Thomas Aquinas, has "a large frame," "need[s] his books," and spends most of his days alone in his room studying.[121] We learn that "at his desk, pen in hand, none was more articulate than Thomas."[122] He lives with his mother, who takes care of him and recognizes that he is a "brilliant smart person."[123] It is Thomas' mother who invites a nineteen-year-old, delinquent, suicidal, nymphomaniac woman into their home, an act of kindness that Thomas describes as "a mockery of virtue."[124]

The young woman, who calls herself Star Drake—her real name is Sarah Ham, though the narrator (reflecting the

118. *NE* 2.9.1109b1–5.
119. *HB*, 94.
120. *HB*, 258.
121. *CS*, 383.
122. *CS*, 391.
123. *CS*, 385.
124. *CS*, 384.

perspective of Thomas) frequently refers to her as "the slut"—sneaks into Thomas' room one night, completely naked:

> She had invaded his room. He had waked to find his door open and her in it. There was enough light from the hall to make her visible as she turned toward him. The face was like a comedienne's in a musical comedy—a pointed chin, wide apple cheeks and feline empty eyes. He had sprung out of his bed and snatched a straight chair and then he backed her out the door, holding the chair in front of him like an animal trainer driving out a dangerous cat. He had driven her silently down the hall, pausing when he reached it to beat on his mother's door. The girl, with a gasp, turned and fled into the guest room.[125]

It is difficult not to see the parallel between the story of St. Thomas and the prostitute and the encounter between this Thomas and Star Drake, but this scene is also where the similarities end. After St. Thomas Aquinas fended off the prostitute—for his sake and for hers—he reportedly was relieved of all temptations of the flesh for the remainder of his life. Such is not the case for the fictional Thomas, whose temptations only increase after this incident. At a crucial point in the story, Thomas decides to hide his pistol—which Star had taken from his room earlier as part of a suicidal threat but then returned—in Star's red pocketbook in order to entrap her. Thomas' pistol and Star's red pocketbook take on some Freudian symbolism:

> He grabbed the red pocketbook. It had a skin-like feel to his touch and as it opened, he caught an unmistakable odor of the girl. Wincing, he thrust in the gun and then drew back. His face burned an ugly dull red.

125. *CS*, 384.

"What is Tomsee putting in my purse?" she called and her
pleased laugh bounced down the staircase. . . .

"Tomsee is being naughty," she said in a throaty voice. . . .

"Tomsee put his pistol in my bag!" the girl shrieked.[126]

This Thomas is the antithesis, the counter-exemplar, the foil
of St. Thomas Aquinas, for rather than growing in the virtue of
purity and standing as a heroic model of chastity, this Thomas
is filled with a lust that not only brings him great shame and
embarrassment but soon results in his accidentally killing the
one he loved,[127] the one who gave him life and provided for his
comfort, leaving him home alone with "the slut" who symbolically
stands as the antithesis of comfort, life, and love.

In "The Comforts of Home," Flannery O'Connor presents her
reader with a vicious version of Thomas Aquinas—an anti-saint—
showing through his character how human beings are deprived
when they lack the virtue of purity. In this way, her use of the
grotesque is effective: "If you have the values of your time, you
can usually write without having to shock anyone to attention;
but if you want to show something that the majority don't believe
in or wish to see, then you have to get and hold their attention
usually by extreme means."[128] According to O'Connor's way of
thinking, the virtue of purity leads to happiness and life, while
its privation leads to misery and to death, as seen clearly here in
the contrasting witnesses of the two Thomases.

O'CONNOR'S CELIBATE VOCATION

Flannery O'Connor never married. This biographical information could be taken by twenty-first-century readers to mean
that O'Connor's life was unsatisfying and loveless, but such was
simply not the case. We recall that, according to O'Connor's way

---

126. *CS*, 402–403.
127. "Thomas loved his mother" (*CS*, 385).
128. O'Connor, *Conversations*, 43.

of thinking, God is personal and relational: God is love, and he created human beings for love, so the deepest longing of the human heart—the final end of the human person—is God, and resting in God is the way one finds happiness, meaningful and lasting friendship, and love.[129] So, as real and as important as romantic love can be, romantic love is not the highest love, nor the most satisfying. O'Connor explains,

> Man's desire for God is bedded in his unconscious & seeks to satisfy itself in physical possession of another human. This necessarily is a passing, fading attachment in its sensuous aspects since it is a poor substitute for what the unconscious is after. The more conscious the desire for God becomes, the more successful union with another becomes because the intelligence realizes the relation in its relation to a greater desire & if this intelligence is in both parties, the motive power in the desire for God becomes double & gains in becoming God-like. The modern man isolated from faith, from raising his desire for God into a conscious desire, is sunk into the position of seeing physical love as an end in itself.[130]

It is important to recognize in this quotation that O'Connor sees the final end of all human desire to be God, which means that, even in the most romantic of relationships, the romantic love itself is not the final end, but God, who is love, is. So according to O'Connor, the truly miserable and lonely person is not the one without romance but the one without God, whether she is romantically involved or not.

Like her hero St. Thomas Aquinas, Flannery O'Connor lived celibately, which, as we recall, is a renunciation of the goodness

129. See chapter 2.
130. *PJ*, 30–31.

of conjugal love for the sake of the love that grounds all love.[131] In fact, she understood that her particular vocation as a writer included a call to celibate living: "There is a great deal that has to either be given up or be taken away from you if you are going to succeed in writing a body of work. There seem to be other conditions in life that demand celibacy besides the priesthood."[132] Like many people—including married people—O'Connor did experience loneliness, suffering, and loss, yet her life was not a miserable one, for it was filled with deep love, meaningful friendships, and happiness.

O'Connor was a faithful Catholic and took the teachings of the Church seriously. This meant that for her—as an unmarried woman—sex was off-limits, although she was not naïve and knew full well that the exercise of the virtue of chastity separated her from many of her peers. In a letter to Cecil Dawkins dated December 23, 1959, O'Connor describes her experience at Yaddo, living as a Catholic among fellow artists who did not share her moral philosophy:

> Liquor was not served by the management but of course you could get your own and in any collection of so-called artists you will find a good percentage alcoholic in one degree or another. There were a good many parties at which everybody contributed something for the liquor. I went to one or two of these but always left before they began to break things. In such a place you have to expect them all to sleep around. This is not sin but Experience, and if you do not sleep with the opposite sex, it is assumed that you sleep with your own. This was in pre-beatnik days but I presume it is all about the same. At the

131. The Catholic understanding of the vocation of celibacy is grounded in Jesus' teaching in Matt. 19:12: " For there are eunuchs who have been so from birth, and there are eunuchs who have been made eunuchs by others, and there are eunuchs who have made themselves eunuchs for the sake of the kingdom of heaven." See also *ST* 2-2.152.4.

132. *HB*, 176.

breakfast table they talked about Seconal and barbiturates and now maybe it's marujana [sic]. You survive in this atmosphere by minding your own business and by having plenty of your own business to mind; and by not being afraid to be different from the rest of them.[133]

Philosophically speaking, O'Connor was putting Aristotle's admonitions to find the golden mean into practice.[134] She was not prudish in the pejorative sense of the word but in the etymological sense, insofar as she practiced the virtue of prudence in the company of her fellow artists. She kept her focus on her ends (knowing, loving, and serving God and writing good fiction) and avoided activities (excessive drinking, drugs, and promiscuity) that would keep her from flourishing as an artist and a human being. We see in O'Connor's own life the embodiment of her moral philosophy.

This is not to say that O'Connor was without moral struggles in the area of purity. On November 11, 1946, she reported in her prayer journal an experience that sounds similar to that of Thomas Aquinas: "The desires of the flesh—excluding the stomach—have been taken from me. For how long I don't know but I hope forever."[135] This period of purity would not last forever, as ten months later, O'Connor wrote in the same journal, "Today I have proved myself a glutton—for Scotch oatmeal cookies and erotic thought. There is nothing left to say of me."[136] As with all virtues, to develop purity is to develop a habit, so even if O'Connor failed to hit the golden mean from time to time, purity remained a virtue that she highly esteemed and constantly strove to attain. O'Connor also realized that although she desired to live a virtuous life like St. Thomas, the virtue of purity would look different in

133. *HB*, 364.
134. A recapitulation of Aristotle's admonitions: 1. steer clear of contrary extremes; 2. know your weakness; 3. beware of pleasure (*NE* 2.9.1109a30–1109b12).
135. *PJ*, 23.
136. *PJ*, 40.

her life than it would in his: "I believe there are as many types of saints as there are souls to be saved. I am quite interested in saving my soul but I see this as a long developmental evolutionary process, extending into Purgatory, and the only moment of it that concerns me in the least is the instant I am living in."[137]

Finally, it is important to note that although O'Connor lived a celibate life and practiced the virtue of purity, she did experience romantic love. The most famous instance is O'Connor's relationship with a book salesman named Erik Langkjaer:

> Flannery and Erik quickly discovered they had much in common. Both were intelligent, sophisticated and well read—qualities that marked them as outsiders in the community they were living in. Both felt a sense of homelessness, of not belonging to their respective worlds. Though Erik was not a believer, he was fascinated by theological questions and readily engaged in conversation with Flannery. Over the course of the next few months, he would return to Andalusia regularly—sometimes going as much as one hundred miles out of his way—for a total of ten or twelve visits, during which they would take long walks, go for car rides, or go out to lunch. O'Connor entered into a rare intimacy with Langkjaer. She discussed her disease—a deeply personal and private subject—in part to offer explanation for her swollen features and thinning hair, the results of steroids she had to take. She also shared with him the painful fact of her father's premature death from lupus. Langkjaer, too, confided in Flannery, sharing an account of his troubled childhood in Denmark during the war and his father's death.[138]

O'Connor may have had other experiences with romantic love that remain secret; as she writes, "That my stories scream to you

---

137. *HB*, 361.
138. Angela Alaimo O'Donnell, *Flannery O'Connor: Fiction Fired by Faith* (Collegeville, MN: Liturgical, 2015), 85–86.

that I have never consented to be in love with anybody is merely to prove that they are screaming an historical inaccuracy."[139] However one interprets these biographical hints, it remains the case that O'Connor evidently embraced the life of a writer and that she was committed to the virtue of purity within that vocation.

O'CONNOR'S FRIENDSHIPS

Aristotle and Thomas think that friendship is a virtue, or a kind of virtue, and Sokolowski sees friendship as the culmination of moral virtue, as we have seen above. We now turn our attention briefly to some of O'Connor's deep and abiding friendships—not only with God, but with angels, saints, and with other human beings—in order to demonstrate how her life serves as an embodiment of Thomistic philosophy.

Friendship with God, Angels, Saints, and Humans

We have shown above that O'Connor believes in a God who is personal and relational and that she thinks that this belief is rationally justified. O'Connor's prayer journal alone is sufficient evidence that she shared friendship with God; she addresses most entries to him as one would begin a letter to a friend.[140] We have also shown that O'Connor believes in the existence of pure intellectual beings—angels, including the devil—and that she thinks this position is also reasonable.

In a letter to Janet McKane a month before she died, O'Connor wrote,

> Do you know anything about St. Raphael besides his being an archangel? He leads you to the people you are supposed to meet and in the prayer to him composed I think by Ernest Hello, the

---

139. *HB*, 170.
140. William Sessions writes, "But to whom did she write these letters, these entries? Who was this lover she identified as such? In the journal, she generally named this presence God" (*PJ*, ix).

words Light & Joy are found. It's a prayer I've said every day for many years. Will send you a copy if you don't know it.[141]

Philosophically speaking, we have here a key to understanding the robust metaphysical framework that grounds O'Connor's friendships. She thinks that the deepest, most meaningful, and necessary friendship for human beings is with God, but she also thinks that God created angels partly for the purpose of befriending humans, and that St. Raphael—"popularly considered a patron saint of friendship and marriage"[142]—specifically helps humans befriend other humans, seen here in O'Connor's friendship with McKane. According to O'Connor, all these friendships are related and are necessary for human flourishing.

In addition to angels like St. Raphael, O'Connor also believed in friendship with the saints, meaning those men and women who have died and are now in union with God in heaven. One of her closest friends, judging by the numerous times O'Connor mentions her in her prayer journal, is "my dear Mother whom I do love, Our Lady of Perpetual Help,"[143] whom she also affectionately calls "My Lady of Perpetual Help."[144] This "Lady" is obviously the Blessed Virgin Mary, the Mother of God.[145] Flannery O'Connor

141. *HB*, 590. Here is the St. Raphael Prayer in its entirety:
O Raphael, lead us toward those we are waiting for, those who are waiting for us: Raphael, Angel of happy meeting, lead us by the hand toward those we are looking for. May all our movements be guided by your Light and transfigured with your joy.

Angel, guide of Tobias, lay the request we now address to you at the feet of Him on whose unveiled Face you are privileged to gaze. Lonely and tired, crushed by the separations and sorrows of life, we feel the need of calling you and of pleading for the protection of your wings, so that we may not be as strangers in the province of joy, all ignorant of the concerns of our country. Remember the weak, you who are strong, you whose home lies beyond the region of thunder, in a land that is always peaceful, always serene and bright with the resplendent glory of God. (O'Donnell, *Fiction Fired by Faith*, 91)

142. Gooch, *Flannery*, 245.
143. *PJ*, 12.
144. *PJ*, 35.
145. In a letter to Janet McKane dated June 5, 1963, O'Connor describes her favorite statue in New York City: "I went to the Cloisters twice and I particularly remember one statue that I saw there. As I remember it was about four feet high and on a pedestal. It was the Virgin holding the Christ child and both were laughing;

believed that this woman who once lived on earth was now living with God for eternity and that she could share a friendship with her. The thought that one can befriend a saint in heaven may strike the nonbeliever and even the non-Catholic Christian as superstitious or even absurd, but for O'Connor the Hillbilly Thomist, it is a perfectly reasonable position. In fact, Flannery O'Connor not only enjoyed reading St. Thomas Aquinas but actually considered herself to be friends with him, even giving him a nickname—"St. T."—as friends often do.[146] O'Connor's belief that it is possible to befriend God and the friends of God (angels and saints) is an essential component of O'Connor's understanding of the human person and the life of virtue, for, as we have seen, if friendship is the culmination of moral virtue, and if the final end of human beings is happiness and eternal life with God, then it matters who one's friends are, and it is reasonable that one would strive to make friends with those who have already achieved that end and the One who is that end. O'Connor explains, "This action by which charity grows invisibly among us, entwining the living and the dead, is called by the Church the Communion of Saints. It is a communion created upon human imperfection, created from what we make of our grotesque state."[147]

We have already cited numerous letters written by Flannery O'Connor to a wide variety of people whom O'Connor would consider to be her friends, albeit at different levels of intimacy. These many letters offer evidence that although O'Connor never married, and although she did suffer loneliness from time to time (as most people do), friendship played an essential role in her life, and specifically in her quest to live a life of virtue.

Not surprisingly, O'Connor's closest friends were people like Robert and Sally Fitzgerald, with whom she would "mix a

not smiling, laughing. I've never seen any models of it anywhere but I was greatly taken with it and should I ever get back to the Cloisters, which is unlikely, I mean to see if it is there" (*HB*, 523).

146. *HB*, 110, 368, 370.
147. *MM*, 228.

pitcher of martinis, share an evening meal, and talk late into the night about their common passions—literature and religion."[148] O'Connor lived with the Fitzgeralds after her time at Yaddo and developed "a deep and abiding friendship with the Fitzgerald family that would last the rest of her life."[149] O'Connor had many lay Catholic friends, but she also made friends with priests and religious men and women, many of whom would visit her regularly at Andalusia, including the Hawthorne Dominican sisters who ran Our Lady of Perpetual Help Home for terminal cancer patients in Atlanta and the Trappist monks of the Monastery of the Holy Spirit in Conyers.[150]

Many of O'Connor's friends did not share her Catholic faith or her love for St. Thomas Aquinas, but most were well-read and would readily engage O'Connor in conversation and correspondence that was anything but superficial. For example, Louise Abbot reports, "My relationship with Flannery was fine friendship, which lasted about eight years, eight good years for me. And we both loved to read, of course."[151] O'Connor's friendship with Maryat Lee was unique, and that uniqueness is on full display in their correspondence with one another. A sign of the friendship between O'Connor and Lee is found in the nicknames they gave each other:

> The two women adopted pet names . . . and, along with them, alternate personalities: Flannery dubbed Maryat "Raybutter," "Raybalm," and "Rayfish"—all variations on Rayber, Maryat's favorite character in *The Violent Bear It Away*—and Maryat invented nicknames for Flannery based on the boy prophet she

148. O'Donnell, *Fiction Fired by Faith*, 59.
149. O'Donnell, 58.
150. The Dominicans and Trappists inherited O'Connor's peacocks upon her death.
151. Louise Abbot, in *At Home with Flannery O'Connor: An Oral History*, ed. Bruce Gentry and Craig Amason (Milledgeville, GA: The Flannery O'Connor-Andalusia Foundation, 2012), 7.

so identified with, including "Tarbabe," "Tarsoul," "Tarsquawk," and "Tarfunk."[152]

Regardless of the level of intimacy of the friendship, the benefits of O'Connor's friendships were never one-sided; those who claimed to have been friends with O'Connor consistently reported that her friendship was also beneficial to them.[153]

Friendship with Betty Hester

Of all O'Connor's friendships, the most interesting, the most controversial, and the most significant with respect to O'Connor's Hillbilly Thomism is her friendship with Hazel Elizabeth (Betty) Hester, a file clerk from Atlanta, identified in *The Habit of Being* simply as "A."[154]

O'Connor's friendship with Hester began with a letter. We do not have the original letter that Hester wrote to O'Connor, but we do know that 274 letters were written between the two women over nine years,[155] one of which is O'Connor's response to Hester's original letter. In it, we see the seeds of their friendship:

> I am very pleased to have your letter. Perhaps it is even more star-tling to me to find someone who recognizes my work for what I try to make it than it is for you to find a God-conscious writer near at hand. The distance is 87 miles but I feel the spiritual distance is shorter.[156]

After offering some responsive commentary on matters of faith and literature raised by Hester, O'Connor signs off:

---

152. Angela Alaimo O'Donnell, *Radical Ambivalence: Race in Flannery O'Connor* (New York: Fordham University Press, 2020), 53.
153. *At Home with Flannery O'Connor: An Oral History* offers 116 pages of evidence to this claim.
154. *HB*, 89–90.
155. Lorraine Murray, *The Abbess of Andalusia: Flannery O'Connor's Spiritual Journey* (Charlotte, NC: Saint Benedict, 2009), 53.
156. *HB*, 90.

You were very kind to write me and the measure of my appreciation must be to ask you to write me again. I would like to know who this is who understands my stories.[157]

The timing of Hester's initial letter to O'Connor was providential, as "Flannery was in need of a dear friend. Betty's perceptive letter came just three months after the news from Erik of his engagement, and the same month as his marriage."[158] O'Connor may well have believed that it was the intercession of St. Raphael—patron of friendship—that brought her and Hester together. On January 17, 1956, she reported that "a couple of years ago the Catholic Worker sent me a card on which was printed the prayer of St. Raphael,"[159] and, as noted above, O'Connor acknowledged that she had been praying this prayer "every day for many years."[160] Since O'Connor first wrote to Hester on July 20, 1955, this timeline suggests that it is most likely that O'Connor had been praying the St. Raphael prayer prior to receiving Hester's first letter, and so it could be argued that her prayer was answered.

O'Connor and Hester shared a great deal in common. They were both single, living with relatives, similar in stature, shy, highly intelligent, well-read; they both enjoyed writing; and they both cherished meaningful conversation. The two women also had their differences. O'Connor was a faithful Catholic who staunchly defended her orthodox faith, while Hester was suspicious of organized religion, reminding O'Connor of Simone Weil.[161] Not unlike her friendship with the Fitzgeralds, O'Connor's friendship with Hester was nourished by books and religion. Scholars have frequently noted that the most philosophically and

157. *HB*, 90.
158. Gooch, *Flannery*, 269.
159. *HB*, 132.
160. *HB*, 590.
161. "Simone Weil's life is the most comical life I have ever read about and the most truly tragic and terrible" (*HB*, 105. Cf. Paul Elie, *The Life You Save May Be Your Own: An American Pilgrimage* [New York: Farrar, Straus and Giroux, 2003], 271).

theologically profound, carefully composed letters in *The Habit of Being* are those written by O'Connor to Hester.

About a year into their correspondence, Hester decided to become Catholic. O'Connor was overjoyed, as she understood this decision to be good not only for Hester's soul but also for their friendship. O'Connor writes,

> I want to do something celebrative when you come into the Church, which desire brings me sharply up against the idiocy of all human gestures. You can imagine me holding some kind of figurative candle and croaking the proper responses. But what I will do is go to Communion for you and your intention Easter morning, and since we will then share the same actual food, you will know that your being where you are increases me and the other way around.[162]

Hester was baptized on March 31, 1956, taking the baptismal name Magdalen, and a little over a year later was confirmed with O'Connor as her sponsor,[163] taking Gertrude as her Confirmation name.[164] It was a few months after her Confirmation that Hester decided to share with O'Connor some embarrassing and painful personal information, what she called her "history of horror."[165] Gooch explains,

162. *HB*, 149–150.

163. O'Connor was honored by the invitation: "I'll be real pleased to be your sponsor for Confirmation—that is, if I read that right and am not just inviting myself. Once I was godmother for a child in California by proxy and I had to send a statement saying I was willing. I don't know if that's necessary for sponsors but if it is, drop me a card and I will send it on. I never have been anybody's sponsor before. What's it mean? I am supposed to come and ask you what the fruits of the Holy Ghost are once a year or something?" (*HB*, 154).

164. George Kilcourse, *Flannery O'Connor's Religious Imagination: A World with Everything Off Balance* (New York: Paulist, 2001), 8.

165. Hester hinted at this history earlier as she was preparing for her Confirmation, as O'Connor mentions in her letter dated May 5, 1956: "I am highly pleased to be asked to do it [be a Confirmation sponsor] and as for your horrible history, that has nothing to do with it. I'm interested in the history because it's you but not for this or any other occasion" (*HB*, 154).

Hester had endured a particularly difficult childhood, as her father abandoned the family when she was young. At age thirteen,
she watched her mother commit suicide while neighbors, believing her mother to be playacting, refused to call the police. . . .

The decisive event that she related to Flannery, though,
occurred in Germany, where she was dishonorably discharged
from the military for sexual indiscretion, having been intimately
involved with another woman. . . . In her coming-out letter to
Flannery, Betty spoke of feeling "unbearably guilty" for her part
in the incident, and offered to end their friendship to prevent
scandal from being visited on the author.[166]

O'Connor immediately responded, "I can't write you fast
enough and tell you that it doesn't make the slightest bit of difference in my opinion of you, which is the same as it was, and that
is: based solidly on complete respect."[167] Then O'Connor reminds
Hester, "I am your confirmation sponsor, self-appointed from the
time you first wrote to me and appointed by you afterwards, which
means I have the right to stay where I have been put."[168] Finally,
O'Connor makes a very important distinction for her friend
between who she is and what she has done: "Where you are wrong
is in saying that you *are* a history of horror. The meaning of the
Redemption is precisely that we do not have to *be* our history."[169]
Hester struggled to understand O'Connor's distinction, and so
O'Connor wrote her back with further clarification: "Perhaps
what I should have said is that you are more than your history. I
don't believe the fundamental nature changes, but that it's put to

166. Gooch, *Flannery*, 281.
167. Flannery O'Connor, "Letter to Betty Hester," October 31, 1956,
Manuscript, Archives, and Rare Book Library, Emory University.
168. O'Connor, "Letter to Betty Hester."
169. Flannery O'Connor. "Letter to Betty Hester," November 18, 1956, in
Collected Works, ed. Sally Fitzgerald (New York: Library of America, 1988), 1007.

a different use when a conversion occurs and of course it requires vigilance to put it to the proper use."[170]

O'Connor's response is grounded in her philosophical understanding of the human person and the virtue of chastity, and she makes an important distinction between what she calls "fundamental nature" and "proper use." What O'Connor means by "fundamental nature" is Hester's sexual orientation or attraction. Although she confuses Thomistic terms here—one's fundamental nature, according to Thomas, is one's human nature, regardless of one's sexual orientation—her distinction remains sound: her point is to distinguish between one's desire and acting upon one's desire. What O'Connor means by "proper use" is essentially the virtue of purity, which, as we have seen, may be arduous to acquire but is well worth the effort.

It is important to note that O'Connor does not attempt to change Hester's sexual orientation or attraction, but encourages her friend to live virtuously—chastely—which she thinks is possible through the help of conversion (turning toward Christ) and can be maintained by vigilance.[171] Moreover, O'Connor's testimony for chastity is not only presented by argument in her letters to Hester but more importantly and more convincingly in and through O'Connor's own life as one practicing the virtue of chastity. Never once does O'Connor tell Hester that chastity, or the life of virtue, or the life of a Catholic Christian will be easy, but she does encourage Hester to live it because she believes that this way of living is good and true. And she offers her a living, breathing example through her own celibate witness that such a life is possible for her too.

O'Connor embodies not only the virtue of purity but the virtue of friendship, and she shows how a true friend is always about the business of the well-being of her friends, encouraging them

170. *HB*, 184.
171. For further argumentation, see Damian Ference, "Flannery O'Connor, Pope Francis, Gays and Lesbians," *Chicago Studies* 55, no. 1 (Winter 2016), 101–111.

and supporting them in striving for a life of virtue. Even after Hester eventually left the Church, O'Connor—deeply saddened by the news—remained friends with her. O'Connor respected Hester's free will, but she would not support choices that compromised Hester's virtue, and she remained deeply concerned for her well-being.[172] In a letter dated June 22, 1963, O'Connor wrote, "Your views on morality are for never-never land. We don't live in it."[173] Yet O'Connor never abandoned her friend and continued to write to her regularly. One of the last letters O'Connor ever wrote was to Hester—a letter in which she shared with her some good news about her new short story, "Revelation." She informed Hester that she had received "a letter from the O. Henry prize people & it got first."[174] When O'Connor died, about a week after writing Hester this final letter, Gooch reports that Hester attended O'Connor's funeral Mass and sobbed uncontrollably throughout the entire liturgy at the loss of her dear and faithful friend.[175]

O'CONNOR'S ETHICS IN "THE DISPLACED PERSON"

The longest short story in Flannery O'Connor's canon is about Mrs. McIntyre, a widow, twice divorced, who struggles to maintain her farm with the hired help of Mr. Shortley (who lives on

172. "[Hester] is now against all intellectualism. She thinks she's at last discovered how to be herself and has at last accepted herself. She says she's always tried to be somebody else because she hated herself, but now she can be herself. It's as plain as the nose on her face that now she's being Iris Murdoch, but it is only plain to me, not her. What I am afraid of is that the reaction is going to set in in a couple of months, or maybe not that soon, but sometime, and when it does bang. Everything runs to extremes with her as you can see. . . . All I'm praying is that she'll come back to earth gradually so she won't realize the drop so much" (HB, 460). Sadly, O'Connor's prediction was accurate: "In 1998, on the day after Christmas, Hester died at age seventy-six from a self-inflicted gunshot wound" (Murray, Abbess of Andalusia, 52). The following letters offer testimony to O'Connor's fidelity toward Hester after Hester decided to leave the Church: October 28, 1961 (HB, 451–453); November 11, 1961 (HB, 453–454); and November 25, 1961 (HB, 454–455).

173. HB, 526.

174. HB, 594. The O. Henry Prize is an annual American award given to writers of exceptional short stories.

175. Gooch, Flannery, 369.

the farm with his wife and their two children) and two black employees, Astor and Sulk. Although not Catholic herself, Mrs. McIntyre arranges with Fr. Flynn, the local parish priest, to bring the Guizac family—recent immigrants from Poland—to her farm and immediately adds Mr. Guizac to her workforce. On a literal level, Mr. Guizac is the displaced person, but O'Connor's real concern in this story, as we shall see, is not so much a physical or geographical displacement as it is a metaphysical, epistemological, and ethical one.

The two words O'Connor chooses to begin this narrative—"The peacock"[176]—carry great significance.[177] As we saw above, O'Connor had an affinity for birds, peafowl in particular. In the Christian tradition, peacocks symbolize the Transfiguration of Christ and eternal life, but in "The Displaced Person," the peacock serves as a symbol of the Incarnation and of the possibility of friendship with God. Evidence for this interpretation is found in O'Connor's beautiful and detailed descriptions of the bird and in the relation of the bird with Fr. Flynn. The second paragraph of the story offers the first detailed account of the majestic bird's appearance:

> His tail—glittering green-gold and blue in the sunlight—lifted just enough so that it would not touch the ground. It flowed out on either side like a floating train and his head on the long blue reed-like neck was drawn back as if his attention were fixed in the distance on something no one else could see.[178]

176. *CS*, 194–235.
177. O'Connor gives her own interpretation of the peacock's role in the story: "As to the peacock, he was there because peacocks might be found properly on such a [farm] but you can't have a peacock anywhere without having a map of the universe. The priest sees the peacock as standing for the Transfiguration, for which it certainly is a most beautiful symbol. It also stands in medieval symbology for the Church—the eyes are the eyes of the Church" (*HB*, 118).
178. *CS*, 194.

In O'Connor's narrative art, the sun and the horizon line are always indicative of God and his transcendent mystery, which, philosophically speaking, is tied up in what is good, true, and beautiful. A few lines before this paragraph begins, we hear that Mrs. Shortley "ignored the white afternoon sun," but in the peacock, we find a participation in the sun both in the way his body reflects its light and also in the mysterious object of his vision. The peacock symbolizes God's presence on earth, but Fr. Flynn is the only character in the story to fully recognize this presence and thus perceive the bird's beauty; he does attempt to share his vision and understanding with Mrs. McIntyre and Mrs. Shortley, but to no avail.

Fr. Flynn is enamored by the beauty of the peacock, a response symbolic of his friendship with and love for God, as O'Connor unmistakably associates the peacock—"as if he had just come down from some sun-drenched height"—with the radiant face of Moses after encountering God on Mount Sinai.[179] Moreover, while the priest enjoys the peacock as an end in himself, Mrs. McIntyre and Mrs. Shortley view the bird pragmatically. Fr. Flynn's mouth "drop[s] open" in awe at the beauty of the bird and his face is "glowing with pleasure," while the two women, blind to the reality before them, see no real value in the peacock's being—Mrs. McIntyre reducing him to "another mouth to feed," followed by Mrs. Shortley's dismissive appraisal: "Nothing but a peachicken." The two women take Fr. Flynn's way of relating to the peacock as indicating a naïve "second childhood," but their pejorative judgment doubles as a theological reference to Baptism and the childlike nature that rightly characterizes a mature Christian,[180] yet another sign of Fr. Flynn's friendship with God.

---

179. See Exod. 34:27–35 (which also foreshadows Christ's Transfiguration, the revelation of his divinity to three Apostles in the presence of Elijah and Moses on Mount Tabor; see Matt. 17:1–8).
180. Cf. John 3:3, Matt. 18:3.

The most virtuous and therefore the most free character in "The Displaced Person" is Fr. Flynn, and the source of his virtue and freedom is his friendship with God, symbolized by the peacock. Although O'Connor often writes critically of clergy (and religious women) in her letters,[181] in her fiction celibate priests and nuns symbolize virtue, truth, goodness, happiness, purity, the presence of God, and friendship with God.[182] Unlike Mrs. Shortley and Mrs. McIntyre, who are constantly annoyed, suspicious, angry, and resentful, familiar only with friendships of utility, Fr. Flynn is calm, kind, friendly, contemplative, and truly interested in other people as people (not for pleasure or utility); he is a model not only of human virtue but of noble friendship, which Fr. Flynn extends to the Guizac family and to Mr. Guizac in particular.

After bringing the Guizac family to the farm and introducing them to Mrs. McIntyre, Fr. Flynn visits the farm regularly, not only to check in on the Guizac family, but to spend time in conversation with Mrs. McIntyre and to admire the peacock.[183] This triadic dynamic between the peacock, the residents of the farm, and the priest discloses Fr. Flynn's mission, which is to mediate the noble friendship that he shares with God to everyone he meets, treating them not as black or white, landowner or hired help, man or woman, American or Polish, but as human beings made in the image and likeness of God, who will only find their true happiness through friendship with God. Fr. Flynn has

---

181. Examples: "It is just like them to get some dumb Sister to review her book" (*HB*, 270); "Apparently she has met nothing but idiot priests all her life, also idiot nuns" (*HB*, 309); "It takes a very tough Catholic to stand the good nuns—that is the average run of them. I have come across a few who are educated women of a high scholastic achievement, but for the most part they know nothing of the world and have a kind of hot-house innocence which is of very little help to anyone who has to be thrown into the problems of the modern world" (*HB*, 330); "Most of the priests I know are not neurotic but most are unimaginative and overworked. Also the education they get at the seminaries leaves much to be desired" (*HB*, 347).

182. The priest in "The Enduring Chill" and the nun in "A Temple of the Holy Ghost" are but two examples of models of celibate virtue in O'Connor's stories.

183. *CS*, 209.

nothing to gain from these friendships with the people on the farm, just as God has nothing to gain in befriending humanity. In other words, God's friendship with humanity comes without strings attached; it is unconditional, and so too is the friendship that Fr. Flynn wishes to extend to all those on the farm, as it is an extension of that unconditional friendship of God.

There are four sets of people living on Mrs. McIntyre's farm—Mrs. McIntyre, the Shortleys, Astor and Sulk, and the Guizacs—and their names all offer the reader clues about their respective identities. The Guizacs are the only group who are already friends with God, and the first indication of this reality is found in the name Mrs. Shortley gives them: "All of them's last name was something that only they themselves and the priest could pronounce. All she could make out of it was Gobblehook."[184] To "gobble a hook" is how a fish is caught by a fisherman, and if we understand Fr. Flynn to be the virtuous "fisher of men" working for God, we can take the Guizac family as those who have gobbled the hook of the Gospel.[185]

Mr. Guizac's virtuous character is symbolized by his equally virtuous craftsmanship: "He was an expert mechanic, a carpenter, and a mason. He was thrifty and energetic."[186] Third, Mrs. McIntyre says of Mr. Guizac, "That man is my salvation!"[187] Mrs. McIntyre recognizes something good and right and true in Mr. Guizac that sets him apart from all the other help that she has had on her farm and who currently staff her farm, and although she cannot see beyond his practical use to her, she does note a relation between Mr. Guizac and Jesus Christ, whom she claims was "just another D.P."[188]

Mrs. McIntyre's name reveals that her "entire" vision of reality is limited to the confines of her farm. And although she has been

184. *CS*, 196.
185. Cf. Matt. 4:18–19.
186. *CS*, 201.
187. *CS*, 203.
188. *CS*, 229.

married three times, she identifies most as the widow of her first husband, "the Judge," understanding herself to be the one and only judge of her farm, passing judgment on the living and the dead who work and have worked for her. As judge, Mrs. McIntyre is committed to her legal obligation but not to her moral one, since a consideration of her moral obligation would force her to acknowledge a source of morality beyond the perimeter of her farm.[189] Rather than seeing herself as dependent upon God and as a potential friend of God, Mrs. McIntyre sees herself as a kind of god, and she sees the farm as her creation, stating, "I'm the one around here who holds all the strings together. If you don't work, I don't make any money and I can't pay you. You're all dependent on me but you each and every one act like the shoe is on the other foot."[190]

Because of this perspective, Mrs. McIntyre is, at best, only capable of what Aristotle called "friendships of utility." She eventually understands Fr. Flynn and the Guizacs as a threat to her little kingdom, and she thinks of the Shortleys, Astor, and Sulk primarily as workers, not as fellow human beings. People are only worth something to Mrs. McIntyre as long as they can work for her and help her maintain her position as the one who holds all the strings; all her friendships have strings attached. Mrs. McIntyre sees other human beings as "extras" and as potential competitors who threaten to "upset the balance" of her farm.[191] At one point she complains, "People are selfish. . . . They have too many children,"[192] a common critique of Catholic families in O'Connor's time and in our own. Mrs. McIntyre proclaims, "I'm not theological. I'm practical!"[193] which explains why she lacks happiness; knowing only practical friendships renders her life unfulfilled.

189. *CS*, 228.
190. *CS*, 217.
191. *CS*, 231.
192. *CS*, 216.
193. *CS*, 225.

Although they profess Christian faith, the Shortleys' understanding of reality is short-sighted. In particular, Mrs. Shortley sees according to her own imagination and inner visions, but not according to reality. When the Guizac family first arrives on the farm, she is surprised that they look "like other people. Every time she had seen them in her imagination, the image she had got was of the three bears, walking single file, with wooden shoes on like Dutchmen and sailor hats and bright coats with a lot of buttons."[194] On another occasion, Mrs. Shortley is standing directly before the peacock (symbolizing friendship with God) but misses him entirely: "She might have been looking at a map of the universe but she didn't notice it any more than she did the spots of sky that cracked the dull green of the tree. She was having an inner vision instead."[195] She and Mr. Shortley, who is half the worker Mr. Guizac is, are highly suspicious of the priest who (she thinks) has "come to destroy,"[196] and they see the Guizac family as a great threat to their livelihood on the farm.

The black laborers, Astor and Sulk, although not yet in communion with Fr. Flynn and the Guizacs, are closer to the life of virtue than Mrs. McIntyre or Mr. and Mrs. Shortley. The name Astor is one letter short of the word Pastor, indicating that with some direction from the priest, Astor would be well on his way toward a fuller, more meaningful life of friendship with God and others as part of a Christian flock or congregation. The name Sulk describes what a person does who is not happy. As long as he remains on the farm, Sulk remains unhappy, but by the end of the story, we learn that he is "taken with a sudden desire to see more of the world,"[197] indicating that his truncated vision has been expanded, and so too his understanding of the meaning of life.

194. *CS*, 195.
195. *CS*, 200.
196. *CS*, 210.
197. *CS*, 235.

We noted above that Flannery O'Connor had a great devotion to St. Raphael the archangel and that she prayed a prayer to St. Raphael daily, believing that St. Raphael assisted people in finding the friends they needed for the journey through this life to their "true country," which is eternal life and friendship with God.[198] O'Connor explains that she intentionally worked elements of the St. Raphael prayer into "The Displaced Person":

> It was some time before it dawned on me Raphael was an archangel, the guide of Tobias. The prayer had some imagery in it that I took over and put in "The Displaced Person"—the business about Mrs. Shortley looking on the frontiers of her true country. The prayer asks St. Raphael to guide us to the province of joy so that we may not be ignorant of the concerns of our true country.[199]

Fr. Flynn and the Guizacs are aware that their true country is friendship with God, which extends far beyond the confines of the farm, but Mrs. McIntyre and her other employees are not yet convinced; they limit their vision of reality to their immediate worldly surroundings—the farm itself—and so they are in need of being *displaced*. And, indeed, that displacement eventually comes to all of them through Mr. Guizac, the displaced person.

After overhearing Mrs. McIntyre tell Fr. Flynn that she is planning to fire Mr. Shortley so as to give Mr. Guizac a raise, Mrs. Shortley runs back to her house and insists that her family pack up their belongings and leave the farm, informing her husband,

---

198. Recall the relation of seeing and knowing from chapter 3—*knowledge begins in the senses*. If one's sight is limited, so is one's knowledge. In the book of Tobit, St. Raphael is the guide of Tobias, the protagonist. By the end of the story, Raphael is the one who helps Tobias cure the blindness of his father, Tobit. One can read this physical blindness as symbolizing the blindness of sin, which keeps one from seeing reality clearly. It is this spiritual blindness that Mrs. McIntyre, the Shortleys, Astor, and Sulk all suffer, albeit to differing degrees. God is the only one—symbolized in the peacock and mediated by Fr. Flynn—who is able to cure this spiritual blindness.

199. *HB*, 132.

"You ain't waiting to be fired!"[200] On the way out of town—with rocking chairs, beds, and chickens on top of their car, and the entire family and the rest of their belongings inside it[201]—Mrs. Shortley suffers a violent stroke resulting in her death, although none of her kin realize what has happened. Her daughters ask, "Where we goin, Ma?" while Mrs. Shortley, her body "rolled back still against the seat and her eyes like blue-painted glass, seemed to contemplate for the first time the tremendous frontiers of her true country."[202]

Near the end of the story, Mrs. McIntyre grows tired of Mr. Guizac and is most upset with his attempt to arrange for his sixteen-year-old cousin from Poland to marry Sulk. She has already informed Fr. Flynn that she plans to eventually let go of Mr. Guizac, stating, "He doesn't fit in. I have to have somebody who fits in."[203] In this section of the story, what is said about Mr. Guizac is also meant to be said about God, specifically Christ—the exemplar of true friendship with God—symbolized by the peacock, who is walking in their midst during this conversation. Mrs. McIntyre wants to uninvite Mr. Guizac from her farm, while Fr. Flynn tells her, "Give him time. . . . He'll learn to fit in."[204] Once again, Fr. Flynn is taken by the majestic beauty of the peacock, who has decided to spread his tail before them; he murmurs, "The Transfiguration."[205] O'Connor writes:

> She had no idea what he was talking about. "Mr. Guizac didn't have to come here in the first place," she said, giving him a hard look.
> The cock lowered his tail and began to pick grass.

---

200. *CS*, 212.
201. The image of the Shortleys' overloaded car is an indication of the priority they give to material possessions and their lack of attention to spiritual ones.
202. *CS*, 214.
203. *CS*, 225.
204. *CS*, 225.
205. *CS*, 226.

"He didn't have to come in the first place," she repeated, emphasizing each word.

The old man smiled absently. "He came to redeem us," he said and blandly reached for her hand and shook it and said he must go.[206]

A few weeks later, Mr. Shortley returns to the farm, and Mrs. McIntyre, saddened to learn of the death of Mrs. Shortley, rehires him and continues to look for a way to rid herself and the farm of Mr. Guizac and his family. "One night she dreamed that Mr. Guizac and his family were moving into her house and that she was moving in with Mr. Shortley."[207] This dream, along with another in which the figure of the priest gives voice to her conscience, induces a powerful desire to fire Mr. Guizac at once, but she is unable to gather enough courage to actually let him go, as we learn that she has never "discharged anyone before; they had all left her."[208]

On a cold Saturday morning, Mrs. McIntyre finally decides to fire Mr. Guizac. "She began to understand that she had a moral obligation to fire the Pole and that she was shirking it because she found it hard to do."[209] Wearing a black coat and a black hat "to keep the glare out of her eyes," Mrs. McIntyre walks out to where Mr. Guizac is working, lying on the frosty ground and repairing a small tractor in the "silver" sun.[210] Like Mrs. Shortley, Mrs. McIntyre is presented in stark contrast to the brightness of the sun. As all her workers are gathered around, a second, larger tractor (left idling on the hill by Mr. Shortley) slips its brake and begins to roll toward Mr. Guizac, who is still on his back, unaware of the danger. No one speaks a word of warning or does anything to stop the progress of the big tractor.

206. *CS*, 226.
207. *CS*, 231.
208. *CS*, 231.
209. *CS*, 233.
210. *CS*, 234.

She had felt her eyes and Mr. Shortley's eyes and the Negro's eyes come together in one look that froze them in collusion forever, and she had heard the little noise the Pole made as the tractor wheel broke his backbone. The two men ran forward to help and she fainted.[211]

When Mrs. McIntyre comes to, a crowd has gathered around the dying Mr. Guizac. Fr. Flynn is there, giving him last rites ("murmuring words she didn't understand"[212]) and Viaticum ("slipping something into the crushed man's mouth"[213]). Mrs. McIntyre cannot understand what is happening and feels as if she is "in some foreign country," which she is: the death of the displaced person has finally displaced her, pushing her—along with Mr. Shortley, Astor, and Sulk—in a new direction, toward their true country.

The story ends with Mrs. McIntyre back on her farm, but alone, with severe Parkinson-like symptoms, confined to her bed "with only a colored woman to wait on her."[214] Her only regular visitor now is Fr. Flynn: "He came regularly once a week with a bag of breadcrumbs and, after he had fed these to the peacock, he would come in and sit by the side of her bed and explain the doctrines of the Church."[215] O'Connor's own interpretation of the end of this story is that Mrs. McIntyre is in a kind of purgatory, "entirely helpless to herself,"[216] where God—present in the person of Fr. Flynn—is finally able to take up his proper role as a true friend in her life, assisting her toward her final end.

In the "Displaced Person," we see O'Connor's ethical vision on full display. According to O'Connor, human beings are made for happiness, which is synonymous with a friendship with God.

211. *CS*, 234.
212. *CS*, 234.
213. *CS*, 235.
214. *CS*, 235.
215. *CS*, 235.
216. *HB*, 118.

The celibate Fr. Flynn serves as a model of the virtuous life; he is the most free character in the story and also the happiest, and although he may appear somewhat aloof to the pragmatic Mrs. McIntyre, the Catholic priest is an embodiment of the contemplative, philosophical, and virtuous life. Fr. Flynn knows that human beings are made for God and only find their end—their rest, their happiness—in God, and his interactions with the peacock symbolize his own intimate friendship with God, a friendship without conditions, as God befriends humanity out of love, not because he wants or needs something. So too, then, does Fr. Flynn attempt to extend this unconditional, noble friendship with God to everyone on the farm. For most of the story, Mrs. McIntyre, the Shortleys, Astor, and Sulk are reluctant to accept God's unconditional friendship, as they are all stifled by truncated metaphysical vision and friendships of utility. But the tragic death of Mr. Guizac—the displaced person—serves to displace them in such a way that their lives open to the possibility of being reoriented toward a life of virtue, happiness, and true freedom through friendship with God.

A Thomist Three Times Removed

Writing a book on Flannery O'Connor is a daunting task for many reasons. Knowing she never pulled punches when reviewing a book she disliked makes it hard for me not to wonder about what Flannery might say about this work. And although some of the best books in O'Connor scholarship over the last two decades started out as dissertations,[1] I cannot help but think of O'Connor's appraisal of Sister Bernetta Quinn's book on modern poetry: "Only the well-informed reader . . . will be interested in these essays . . . in which lurks the not very well laid ghost of a doctoral dissertation."[2] If there is a ghost of a dissertation present in this book, I pray that at least it will be a friendly and interesting one.

We began by considering two quotations from Flannery O'Connor, written six years apart, regarding her Thomistic influence: "Everyone who has read *Wise Blood* thinks I'm a hillbilly nihilist, whereas I would like to create the impression over the television that I'm a hillbilly Thomist,"[3] and "I am a Thomist three times removed and live amongst many distinctions. (A Thomist three times removed is one who doesn't read Latin or St. Thomas but gets it by osmosis.)"[4] Because so much of Flannery

---

1. E.g., Bruner, O'Donnell, Srigley, Wilson.
2. *PG*, 31.
3. *HB*, 81.
4. *HB*, 439.

O'Connor's philosophical formation came to her by way of a preconciliar Catholicism shaped by the Thomistic revival of the early twentieth century, it is a difficult task to tease O'Connor's specific Thomistic influence from her general Catholic milieu, despite the fact that she claimed to have read from the *Summa* for twenty minutes every night. The fact that she calls herself both "a hillbilly Thomist" and "a Thomist three times removed" offers evidence to this complicated intermingling. Yet if we had to choose one philosopher who influenced O'Connor (and Catholicism in general before the Second Vatican Council) more than any other, we would be hard-pressed to name anyone but St. Thomas Aquinas. This observation is not meant to denigrate the *nouvelle théologie*, for O'Connor was starting to read many of the theologians whose work helped form the documents of the council (all of whom were aware of, and in dialogue with, St. Thomas), but the fact is that O'Connor's fundamental understanding of reality comes by way of the Catholic Thomistic tradition. Amidst the diversity of theological perspectives she was encountering, she clearly did claim Thomism as something that resonated with her, and she affirmed it by name.

It is true that Flannery O'Connor is not a professional Thomistic philosopher in the academic sense, but it is also true that she makes an important contribution to the Thomistic tradition. O'Connor's artistic brand of Thomism—what we have been calling Hillbilly Thomism—is not a philosophical school or system, but rather a general collection of Thomistic inclinations, indications, intuitions, presumptions, and themes that ground her narrative art. Her Thomistic art does not concern itself with subtle metaphysical, epistemological, or ethical distinctions the way that the work of a professional philosopher does; rather, it offers a general account of reality and its meaning in the modern world: *Things have an end. Things have meaning. Things are connected.*[5]

My basic task in this book has been to systematize what has not been systematized—that is, to offer a thorough account of how the philosophy that O'Connor read influenced her thought and became foundational to her narrative art. Brian Barbour has observed that "O'Connor's Thomism is so pervasive, so deftly assimilated into the action and idiom of her work, as to be nearly invisible to many of her readers."[6] The purpose of this work, then, has been to help make O'Connor's Thomistic influence indubitably visible for literary O'Connor scholars, for philosophers (especially the Thomistic kind), and for the everyday reader of Flannery O'Connor interested in better understanding her narrative art. Allow me to be more specific.

I hope that this book will make a welcome contribution to Flannery O'Connor studies, specifically in offering a systematic presentation of the philosophy that grounds the art of the one who called herself a Hillbilly Thomist. As I have argued throughout this book, there are many lenses through which one can study O'Connor and her narrative art—literary, spiritual, historical, sociological, psychological, feminist, etc.—but I also think that, without a proper account of her primarily Thomistic philosophical foundations, access to the deepest meaning of her narrative art is next to impossible to discover. What often happens when students first read fiction by Flannery O'Connor is that they don't understand what they just read, and they are confused about whether or not they like it, but most of them want to know more and talk about the story. They want to know if all the violence

5. Anthony Esolen, introduction to Dante's *Inferno* (New York: Modern Library, 2005), xvii.
6. Brian Barbour, "'His Trees Stood Rising Above Him': Philosophical Thomism in Flannery O'Connor," *Renascence* 70, no. 4 (Fall 2018): 245. Regarding Flannery O'Connor's philosophical Thomism, Barbour writes, "Without a lively awareness of how and why she was using it, any response to her work is unnecessarily compromised" (p. 266).

is a sign of nihilism or if something more is going on that they have not yet been able to grasp. They want to know what kind of person writes about the drowning of children, a man completely covered in tattoos, or a worker left to be crushed by a rolling tractor. Students want a context or a backdrop against which to understand all these bizarre and intriguing dramatic actions, and I have written this book to offer that context and backdrop.

To my mind, trying to understand Flannery O'Connor and her narrative art apart from her Hillbilly Thomism is like trying to understand the New Testament apart from the Old Testament, or like trying to understand Jesus apart from his Jewishness. Both can be done, but the outcome will leave something wanting. In fact, to keep with our Thomistic theme, I do not think it is an exaggeration to argue that the soul of O'Connor's fiction is her Thomism. If a student desires to understand what gives O'Connor's narrative art life, he or she must study O'Connor's Hillbilly Thomism.

Flannery O'Connor claimed to be a Thomist three times removed. My hope for you in having read this book is that you can say at least the same about yourself. If you are not a professional philosopher or theologian, chances are that you do not have the time or the desire to become a bona fide Thomist, but this book contains enough of the essential components of Thomism to help you understand Flannery O'Connor and the philosophical foundations of her narrative art by familiarizing you with a Hillbilly Thomism or a Thomism three times removed.

I also hope that this book has helped you see how fiction may be a starting point for philosophy, especially the O'Connor kind. It is true that philosophy attempts to answer life's most important questions, but it is also true that good art and specifically good literature are often the means by which people first start asking such questions. I have taught philosophy at our little college seminary in Cleveland for a while now, and before students begin my ethics course, I always assign them a short story ("For the Relief of

Unbearable Urges" by Nathan Englander). They love it and come to class eager and interested from day one. As we read Aristotle, Mill, Kant, Wojtyła, Anscombe, Singer, and MacIntyre throughout the semester, we apply insightful philosophical commentary and analysis to that story and other stories we read along the way. Good fiction gives flesh to important philosophical ideas.

When I teach contemporary philosophy, I conclude my section on Nietzsche by reading O'Connor's "Good Country People" with my seminarians. As much as my students enjoy my little reenactment of Nietzsche's Madman and his lantern, they really come to understand the consequences of Nietzsche's vision when they encounter Hulga/Joy and sympathize with her after she is duped by a guy who calls himself Manley Pointer. They see what "beyond good and evil" looks like and get a stark but clear view of the *Übermensch* in all his glory. O'Connor's short story embodies Nietzsche's philosophy in a manner that is both helpful and enjoyable for students of philosophy. According to Étienne Gilson, "Philosophers start from art in the hope that its study will open new vistas on philosophical problems to them, whereas artists, when they philosophize, do so in the hope of clearing up for themselves difficulties inherent in their art."[7] If you have not yet attempted to work some fiction into your philosophy courses, perhaps this book has given you the encouragement to do so.

Finally, I want to say a word about my use of Betty Edwards' *Drawing on the Right Side of the Brain* in chapter 3. When I returned from CUA with my licentiate in philosophy back in 2009, I had anticipated teaching ethics and philosophy of the human person, but had not anticipated teaching epistemology, so, needless to say, my first time teaching that course was rough. However, as the years passed, I became a better teacher and eventually redesigned the course. My thought was that this course should not simply teach my students what Plato, Augustine, Aquinas, Descartes,

7. Étienne Gilson, *Painting and Reality: The A.W. Mellon Lectures in the Fine Arts* (New York: Pantheon Books, 1957), x.

Hume, Kant, and Sokolowski thought about how one could know or what one could know, but also help them actually come to better know the world in which they live. I remember coming across an article that encouraged its readers to put down their phones, stop taking pictures, and learn to draw.

I forwarded that article to an artist friend, who recommended that I read Betty Edwards' classic text, which I did. I liked it so much and found it so helpful that I incorporated drawing into my epistemology course. On the very first day of class, after making our way through the syllabus, I took all my students up to our seminary chapel and asked them each to find one item—a window, a statue, some piece of liturgical furniture, etc.—look at it, and then write one paragraph about it. The very next class, we made our way back to the chapel, each of us with pencil, eraser, and sketchbook in tow. This time, however, rather than simply glancing at an object for a minute, each student had an hour to study it and to draw it. I encouraged them to "draw what you see" as Edwards does in her text and as O'Connor does in her fiction—present what-is. Then I assigned my students a three-page paper contrasting what they saw in their initial glance at their objects on the first day of class to what they came to know about those objects after looking at them and drawing them for an hour in silence. The difference noted by my students between a short glance and a long, intentional look at an object was obvious and edifying. Although it is true that on the second day of the course, my students had not yet learned about Thomistic abstraction, they were already learning to see and coming to understand that looking, drawing, and silence play an important role in coming to know the world around them. This activity helped my students come to know the world in the way of the Hillbilly Thomist, and that is my motivation for including the Edwards section in this book. We live in a time in which our students are trained to take quick looks at screens, and reading assignments, and even each other, but O'Connor and Edwards both remind us of the necessity of long, loving looks at reality for human beings. So perhaps for those of you who teach an epistemology course, you might add a pencil, eraser, and sketchbook to your list of course materials in the future. And maybe even add "Parker's Back" to your required reading while you're at it.

Finally, I hope that this book has been both a challenge and a comfort to you in coming to better understand Flannery O'Connor's fiction and the influence of her friend "St. T." on her narrative art. As I mentioned in the introduction, I was introduced to Flannery O'Connor in college, and when I first started reading her stories, I knew they were good and enjoyed them, but I didn't quite know what I was reading. It took years of study and research and rereading her novels and stories and letters and essays (not to mention reading biographies and commentaries and attending many conferences) to come to adequately understand O'Connor's artistic vision, which, I have argued here, is firmly grounded in her Hillbilly Thomism. It would please me to no end to know that after reading this book, you were able to go back and reread some of your favorite O'Connor stories—on your own, in your book club, or in the classroom—and come away with a deeper insight into the dramatic action presented on each page and a better understanding of what is on the line in O'Connor's fiction.

I should also say that as much as I hope this book assisted your understanding of Flannery O'Connor's narrative art and the influence of Thomism upon it, I also hope this work introduced you to two new friends. Or, if you were already friends with St. Thomas and Flannery, I hope reading this book has helped deepen your friendship with them. I can say without exaggeration that my life would be poorer, and my priesthood would be less meaningful, apart from my friendship with Flannery. Moreover, my three years studying St. Thomas Aquinas at the Angelicum strengthened my friendship with St. T., and reading his work and studying his life deepened my faith and helped me to love God and others more. May you be able to say something similar after reading this book.

Bibliography

PRIMARY WORKS OF FLANNERY O'CONNOR

O'Connor, Flannery. *The Cartoons of Flannery O'Connor at Georgia College*. Edited by Marshall Bruce Gentry. Milledgeville, GA: Georgia College, 2010.

———. *Collected Works*. Edited by Sally Fitzgerald. New York: Library of America, 1988.

———. *The Complete Stories*. New York: Farrar, Straus and Giroux, 1971.

———. *Conversations with Flannery O'Connor*. Edited by Rosemary Magee. Jackson, MS: University Press of Mississippi, 1987.

———. *Everything That Rises Must Converge*. New York: Farrar, Straus and Giroux, 1965.

———. *Flannery O'Connor: The Cartoons*. Edited by Kelly Gerald. Seattle, WA: Fantagraphic Books, 2012.

———. *A Good Man Is Hard to Find and Other Stories*. San Diego: Harcourt, 1955.

———. *Good Things Out of Nazareth: The Uncollected Letters of Flannery O'Connor and Friends*. Edited by Benjamin B. Alexander. New York: Convergent Books, 2019.

———. *The Habit of Being: Letters of Flannery O'Connor*. Edited by Sally Fitzgerald. New York: Farrar, Straus and Giroux, 1979.

———. "Higher Mathematics: Flannery O'Connor's College Journal." *Image*, no. 94 (Fall 2017): 67–77.

———. *The Letters of Flannery O'Connor and Caroline Gordon.* Edited by Christine Flanagan. Athens, GA: The University of Georgia Press, 2018.

———. *Mystery and Manners: Occasional Prose.* Edited by Sally and Robert Fitzgerald. New York: Farrar, Straus and Giroux, 1969.

———. *A Prayer Journal.* Edited by W.A. Sessions. New York: Farrar, Straus and Giroux, 2013.

———. *The Presence of Grace and Other Book Reviews by Flannery O'Connor.* Edited by Carter W. Martin. Athens, GA: The University of Georgia Press, 1983.

———. *Three by Flannery O'Connor: Wise Blood; A Good Man Is Hard To Find; The Violent Bear It Away.* New York: Signet Books, 1962.

———. *The Violent Bear It Away.* New York: Farrar, Straus and Giroux, 1996.

———. *Wise Blood.* New York: Farrar, Straus and Giroux, 1998.

FLANNERY O'CONNOR'S SOURCES (PERSONAL LIBRARY AND REVIEWED BOOKS)

Gilson, Étienne. *Painting and Reality: The A.W. Mellon Lectures in the Fine Arts.* New York: Pantheon Books, 1957.

———. *The Unity of Philosophical Experience.* New York: Charles Scribner's Sons, 1937. (Reprint—San Francisco: Ignatius, 1999.)

Guardini, Romano. *The Lord.* Translated by Elinor Castendyk Briefs. Chicago: Henry Regnery, 1954.

Lynch, William. *The Image Industries.* New York: Sheed & Ward, 1959

Maritain, Jacques. *Art and Scholasticism with Other Essays*. Translated by J.F. Scanlan. New York: Charles Scribner's Sons, 1930. (Reprint—Minneapolis, MN: Filiquarian, 2007.)

Teilhard de Chardin, Pierre. *The Divine Milieu*. New York: Harper & Row, 1965.

———. *The Phenomenon of Man*. New York: Harper & Row, 1959.

Thomas Aquinas. *Introduction to Saint Thomas Aquinas*. Edited with Introduction by Anton C. Pegis. New York: Modern Library, 1948.

Voegelin, Eric. *Order and History*, vol. 3, *Plato and Aristotle*. Baton Rouge, LA: Louisiana State University Press, 1957.

White, Victor. *God and the Unconscious*. Foreword by C.G. Jung. London: Collins, Fontana Books, 1952.

SECONDARY SOURCES

Aristotle. *De Anima*. Translated by R.D. Hicks. Amherst, NY: Prometheus Books, 1991.

———. *Metaphysics*. Translated by W.D. Ross. Oxford: Clarendon, 1930.

———. *Nicomachean Ethics*. Translated by W.D. Ross. London: Oxford University Press, 1925.

———. *Physics*. Translated by R.P. Hardie and R.K. Gaye. Oxford: Clarendon, 1930.

———. *Selections*. Translated by Terence Irwin and Gail Fine. Indianapolis, IN: Hackett, 1995.

Augustine. *The Confessions of Saint Augustine*. Translated by John K. Ryan. New York: Image Books, 1960.

Barbour, Brian. "'His Trees Stood Rising Above Him': Philosophical Thomism in Flannery O'Connor." *Renascence* 70, no. 4 (Fall 2018): 245–271.

Bennet, Eric. "O'Connor and the Dogma of Creative Writing." In *Reconsidering Flannery O'Connor*, ed. Alison Arant and Jordan Cofer, 217–233. Jackson, MS: University Press of Mississippi, 2020.

Bieber Lake, Christina. *The Incarnational Art of Flannery O'Connor*. Macon, GA: Mercer University Press, 2005.

Campbell, Charles L. "Ministry with a Laugh." *Interpretation: A Journal of Bible and Theology* 69, no. 2 (2015): 196–208.

Carroll, Noël. *Humour: A Very Short Introduction*. Oxford: Oxford University Press, 2014.

Chesterton, G.K. *Saint Thomas Aquinas: The Dumb Ox*. New York: Image Books, 1956.

Copleston, Frederick C. "Teilhard de Chardin and a Global Outlook." In *Teilhard and the Unity of Knowledge: The Georgetown University Centennial Symposium*. New York: Paulist, 1983.

Davies, Brian. *The Thought of Thomas Aquinas*. Oxford: Oxford University Press, 1992.

Descartes, René. *Meditations on First Philosophy*. In *Descartes: Selected Philosophical Writings*, trans. John Cottingham, Robert Stoothoff, and Dugald Murdoch, 73–122. New York: Cambridge University Press, 1988.

Doering, E. Jane and Ruthann Knechel Johansen. *When Fiction and Philosophy Meet: A Conversation with Flannery O'Connor and Simone Weil*. Macon, GA: Mercer University Press, 2019.

Edmondson, Henry. *Return to Good and Evil: Flannery O'Connor's Response to Nihilism*. New York: Lexington Books, 2002.

Edwards, Betty. *Drawing on the Right Side of the Brain*, 4th ed. London: Penguin Books, 2012.

Elie, Paul. *The Life You Save May Be Your Own: An American Pilgrimage*. New York: Farrar, Straus and Giroux, 2003.

Esolen, Anthony. Introduction to Dante's *Inferno*. New York: Modern Library, 2005.

Ference, Damian. "Flannery O'Connor, Pope Francis, Gays and Lesbians." *Chicago Studies* 55, no. 1 (Winter 2016): 101–111.

———. "Springsteen's Catechist: Flannery O'Connor's Influence on Bruce Springsteen." *Flannery O'Connor Review* 17 (2019): 129–146.

Feser, Edward. *Aquinas: A Beginner's Guide*. London: Oneworld, 2009.

Gentry, Marshall Bruce. *Flannery O'Connor's Religion of the Grotesque*. Jackson, MS: University Press of Mississippi, 1986.

Gilson, Étienne. *The Christian Philosophy of St. Thomas Aquinas*. Translated by L.K. Shook. Notre Dame, IN: University of Notre Dame Press, 1994.

Gooch, Brad. *Flannery: A Life of Flannery O'Connor*. New York: Little, Brown and Company, 2009.

Israel, Jonathan I. *Radical Enlightenment: Philosophy and the Making of Modernity 1650–1750*. Oxford: Oxford University Press, 2001.

John Paul II. *Letter to Artists*. Boston: Pauline Books and Media, 1999.

———. *Man and Woman He Created Them: A Theology of the Body*. Boston: Pauline Books and Media, 2006.

Kilcourse, George. *Flannery O'Connor's Religious Imagination: A World with Everything Off Balance*. New York: Paulist, 2001.

Kinney, Arthur. *Flannery O'Connor's Library: Resources of Being.* Athens, GA: The University of Georgia Press, 1985.

Lev, Elizabeth. *How Catholic Art Saved the Faith: The Triumph of Beauty and Truth in Counter-Reformation Art.* Manchester, NH: Sophia Institute, 2018.

Madden, James D. *Mind, Matter, and Nature: A Thomistic Proposal for the Philosophy of Mind.* Washington, DC: The Catholic University of America Press, 2013.

Maritain, Jacques. *St. Thomas and the Problem of Evil.* Translated by Gordon Andison. Milwaukee, WI: Marquette University Press, 1942.

McInerny, Ralph. *Ethica Thomistica: The Moral Philosophy of Thomas Aquinas.* Washington, DC: The Catholic University of America Press, 1997.

Montgomery, Marion. *Hillbilly Thomist: Flannery O'Connor, St. Thomas and the Limits of Art.* Volume 1. Jefferson, NC: McFarland and Company, 2006.

———. *Hillbilly Thomist: Flannery O'Connor, St. Thomas and the Limits of Art.* Volume 2. Jefferson, NC: McFarland and Company, 2006.

———. *Why Flannery O'Connor Stayed Home.* La Salle, IL: Sherwood Sugden and Company, 1981.

Murray, Lorraine. *The Abbess of Andalusia: Flannery O'Connor's Spiritual Journey.* Charlotte, NC: Saint Benedict, 2009.

Murray, William. "Friedrich Nietzsche, Flannery O'Connor, and the Limiting Power of Certainty." In *Reconsidering Flannery O'Connor,* ed. Alison Arant and Jordan Cofer, 127–139. Jackson, MS: University Press of Mississippi, 2020.

Nietzsche, Friedrich. *The Anti-Christ.* Translated by H.L. Mencken. Tucson, AZ: See Sharp, 1999.

O'Connell, Gerard. "Will Pope Francis Remove the Vatican's 'Warning' from Teilhard de Chardin's Writings?" *America*. November 21, 2017. americamagazine.org/faith/2017/11/21/will-pope-francis-remove-vaticans-warning-teilhard-de-chardins-writings.

O'Donnell, Angela Alaimo. *Flannery O'Connor: Fiction Fired by Faith*. Collegeville, MN: Liturgical, 2015.

———. *Radical Ambivalence: Race in Flannery O'Connor*. New York: Fordham University Press, 2020.

Paul VI. *Humanae Vitae*. Encyclical letter. July 25, 1968. Vatican.va.

Percy, Walker. *Signposts in a Strange Land*. New York: Farrar, Straus and Giroux, 1991.

Pieper, Josef. *The Silence of St. Thomas*. Translated by John Murray and Daniel O'Connor. New York: Pantheon Books, 1957.

Schumacher, Leo S. *The Truth About Teilhard*. New York: Twin Circle, 1968.

Sill, Gertrude Grace. *A Handbook of Symbols in Christian Art*. New York: Collier Books, 1975.

Sokolowski, Robert. *Christian Faith and Human Understanding: Studies on the Eucharist, Trinity, and the Human Person*. Washington, DC: The Catholic University of America Press, 2006.

———. *The God of Faith and Reason: Foundations of Christian Theology*. Washington, DC: The Catholic University of America Press, 1995.

———. "The Role of Philosophy in Priestly Formation." Keynote address. Mount St. Mary's Seminary, Emmitsburg, MD. May 24, 2010.

Srigley, Susan. *Flannery O'Connor's Sacramental Art*. Notre Dame, IN: University of Notre Dame Press, 2004.

Stump, Eleonore. *Aquinas*. London: Routledge, 2003.

Taylor, Charles. *A Secular Age*. Cambridge, MA: The Belknap Press of Harvard University Press, 2007.

Thomas Aquinas. *Commentaria in octo libros Physicorum Aristotleis*. Romae: S.C. de Propaganda Fide, 1889.

———. *Commentary on the Metaphysics of Aristotle*. Translated by John P. Rowan. Chicago: Henry Regnery, 1961.

———. *Commentary on Aristotle's Nicomachean Ethics*. Translated by C.I. Litzinger. Notre Dame, IN: Dumb Ox Books, 1993.

———. *De Veritate: The Disputed Questions on Truth*. Translated by Robert Mulligan. Chicago: Henry Regnery, 1952.

———. *On the Principles of Nature in Opuscula I Treatises*. Translated by Cyril Vollert, Robert T. Miller, R.A. Kocourek, Francis J. Lescoe, and Gerald B. Phelan. Green Bay, WI: Aquinas Institute, 2018.

———. *The Soul: A Translation of St. Thomas Aquinas' De Anima*. Translated by John Patrick Rowan. St. Louis, MO: Herder, 1949.

———. *Summa theologiae*. Translated by Fathers of the English Dominican Province. Notre Dame, IN: Christian Classics, 1948.

Torrell, Jean-Pierre. *Saint Thomas Aquinas*, vol. 1, *The Person and His Work*. Translated by Robert Royal. Washington, DC: The Catholic University of America Press, 1996.

———. *Saint Thomas Aquinas*, vol. 2, *Spiritual Master*. Translated by Robert Royal. Washington, DC: The Catholic University of America Press, 1996.

Urmson, J.O. *Aristotle's Ethics*. Oxford: Blackwell, 1988.

Watts, Alan. *Myth and Ritual in Christianity.* Boston: Beacon, 1968.

White, Thomas Joseph. "Imperfect Happiness and the Final End of Man: Thomas Aquinas and the Paradigm of Nature-Grace Orthodoxy." *The Thomist : A Speculative Quarterly Review* 78 (2014): 247–289.

Whitt, Margaret Earley. *Understanding Flannery O'Connor.* Columbia, SC: University of South Carolina Press, 1995.

Wilson, Jessica Hooten. *Giving the Devil His Due: Demonic Authority in the Fiction of Flannery O'Connor and Fyodor Dostoevsky.* Eugene, OR: Cascade Books, 2017.

Wippel, John F. *The Metaphysical Thought of Thomas Aquinas: From Finite Being to Uncreated Being.* Washington, DC: The Catholic University of America Press, 2000.

COLLECTIONS

At Home with Flannery O'Connor: An Oral History. Edited by Bruce Gentry and Craig Amason. Milledgeville, GA: The Flannery O'Connor-Andalusia Foundation, 2012.

Parish Liturgy: Mass Ordinaries and Hymns for Mass and the Sacraments. Cincinnati, OH: World Library, 1967.

A Political Companion to Flannery O'Connor. Edited by Henry T. Edmondson. Lexington, KY: University Press of Kentucky, 2017.

Reconsidering Flannery O'Connor. Edited by Alison Arant and Jordan Cofer. Jackson, MS: University Press of Mississippi, 2020.

The Roman Missal. New Jersey: Catholic Book Publishing Co., 2010.

Saint Joseph Baltimore Catechism: The Truths of Our Catholic Faith Clearly Explained and Illustrated. New York: Catholic Book Publishing Co., 1969.

Index